Dear Victim, It's Time for Us To Break Up Now!

A Story of Empowerment Through Forgiveness, Strength and Love

Tammy S. Loftis

AUTHOR'S NOTE

First I want to say thank you from the bottom of my heart for choosing my book to add to your collection of inspiration. I am truly honored you chose Me! Before you dive into the deepest parts of my heart and life as you read this book, I want you to know there will be places you come to that may be hard to read or sound harsh. That's because my life in that moment was harsh and hard to live for me. There were places in the book where the editor(s) wanted to take out and/or polish the things I went through, and I changed them back to my original words because they were a true depiction of my life in those moments. They were true feelings and real conversations that were raw and unfiltered. I was vulnerable in sharing the deepest parts of my life in order to show people that you can have shitty things that happen in your life and turn them into Extra-Ordinary Experiences if and when you choose to do so, just as I have done. There are places in here that are not "grammatically correct." I chose not to change them because my Life, in those moments, was not grammatically correct.

So Please, excuse my mess, as I am still a work in progress!

Forward

By Jen Kazmierczak
Owner and Founder
BestLife Creation Society

When Tammy came to BestLife wanting to become a life coach, the first thing I recognized about her was her tenacity, determination and eagerness to experience life to the fullest. Quickly she developed into a leader, I was always amazed by her high energy and enthusiasm about life, and I am even more amazed after hearing her story. Her loving spirit, forward focused energy and her desire to create a positive impact was evident from the very start.

One of the real blessings in life is being able to tell your story and inspire others to make a change in their lives so I was both excited and delighted when I heard that Tammy would be writing a book about her remarkable journey. I believe this book has the power to encourage others to face each day bravely and embrace their ability to change and transform, even in the toughest of situations, knowing that the future is ours for the creating. We all come from different walks in life, but what really matters is where we are going. We can learn from Tammy's story that if someone can let go of their past, understanding that it's their inner victim that has been holding them there, then they have the power and control to create their own destiny.

Tammy delivers her message in a way that is riveting and real and exposes how your inner victim has been blocking you from opening up to the truth of who you really are while virtually depriving you of experiencing the wholeness and fullness of your life. Understand that before you make the decision to say goodbye to the victim dwelling within you, you first must recognize it, where it has been hiding and how it has falsely made you believe you cannot survive without it. This heartfelt story will encourage you to see what you may not have been able to perceive before.

Be open to the shifts and the transformation that may occur within you as you read this book and go at a rate and speed that feels good

to you, while you allow yourself time to process and release any unpleasant emotions that stir within you. Understand that this is a good thing which can empower you to fully make the decision to say goodbye to the victim dwelling within you and can ultimately aid you in feeling and following your own inner guidance. The words in this book will gently tune you in to your own loving inner voice and help you tune out the external voices, false beliefs and demands that have been overpowering it. Tammy's words will brilliantly open you up to the "More" that is inside of you, the "More" that your inner victim has so desperately trying to hide and distract you from. The choice to say goodbye to your
inner victim is truly yours and yours alone, no one else can do it for you but I believe this book will allow you to see that it can be done.

Set your mind to whatever you want to have happen in your life and move toward it. The path to get there will reveal itself every step of the way and before you know it, everything will be different. I hope you see this throughout the story and become inspired to do the same for yourself.

I am deeply honored to be a part of this book and appreciate the incredible positive impact Tammy has made in my life personally. I love watching people move into a better place in their life and we at BestLife are all incredibly proud of Tammy and all that she has accomplished. Her unique insight and ability to awaken and uplift others is a special gift. She has enriched BestLife greatly with her loving, healing energy and we encourage her to keep shining and sharing. Thank you, Tammy for sharing the gift of YOU! The impact you are making is profound and we honor and support you every step of the way.

With Love and Appreciation Always!

Jen

INTRODUCTION

I wanted to give you some insight to why the cover photo of this book is so relevant to whats on the inside of these pages as you dive into my story. This picture was taken at the top of Cucamonga Peak in Rancho Cucamonga, California. I wanted an epic photo that adequately represented what if feels like to be set free from the bondage of your inner victim once and for all. What makes this so significant is that I climed his mountain three (3) times in two months before I finally got the photo I was looking for. The first trip was on April 6th, 2019. There was still a lot of snow and ice on the trail and it was impassable. I went anyway because I wanted to see how long and how difficult this climb would be. The largest mountain I had been on previously was during a Spartan race in Ashville, NC that was 3204 feet at the highest point of the race. Cucamonga Peak is 8859 feet at the peak standing on top of the world. The Icehouse Canyon Trail Head, where I entered was 4200 foot elevation. Just past mile marker 5 is the saddle where five different hiking trails break off and the elevation there is 7600 feet. I have never experienced this elevation outside of flying in an airplane and skydiving. There was quite a bit of snow and the trail was difficult to follow but I made it in and out in about 7 hours.

My second trip up the mountain was May 4th. "May the 4th be with you" for all of my Star Wars peeps. After talking to several other hikers on the trail, they had recommended this day and said most of the snow if not all of it should be gone by then. Well, it didn't take long to figure out that was not the case. When I got to the saddle, several of the hikers said that I could make it without spikes and I should go for it after hearing this was for the epic book cover photo for the July 4th launch. As I got higher and higher, the snow got thicker. A friendly hiker named Adam, gave me his micro spikes to help me, hoping I would make it to the peak before it got too late and I would have to turn around and head down the mountain to get off the trail before night fall. It got to the point where I could no longer see the trail. I was more than knee deep in snow, going straight up the side of the mountain. I was fighting time and my safety at 4pm, heartbroken, I decided to take the safe route and turn around and head back down the mountain. I stopped at one place on the trail that looked like it might be a good spot to possibly get a cover photo shot. Another set of passerby hikers, stopped to help me take the pictures. I was concerned about time, so I didn't look at them too hard and raced back down the mountain to reach my car as the sun was setting at 6:30pm. When I got back to the hotel, eating dinner at Denny's, I looked at the pictures and realized NONE of them would work. I was heartbroken! I was so choked up, it was hard to eat my dinner. I did a Facebook live, sharing my story, my tears, and even thoughts about changing the concept of the bookcover. My friends and family were not having it. I thanked them for their support and I jumped in the shower to clean up and meditate to quiet my mind from the whirlwind of thoughts taking over. As the hot water beat down on the back of my neck and my mind was finally silent since I got back from my hike, I received the thought "your story has to come full circle." I was confused on what that meant because in my mind, it already had. I kept my mind quiet, the thought repeated with "your story has to come full circle. Your moms birthday." I immediately teared up, realizing there would be one more trip up this mountain on the weekend of my moms birthday May 24th (she would have been 70) and make the actual hike on the 25th.

I did just that. This time my photographer, Karina Cruz, went with me. This was more than a challenging hike for her. She has not been hiking in several years and had never hiked a mountain of this caliber. She was overweight and carried her backpack full of camera gear which was an additional 20lbs of weight. She fought tooth and nail to get all the way up to that mountain peak. She fought through all her fears, her demons, her doubts, elevation sickness, soreness, blisters and just pure exhaustion. She had gone through a break up the week before, so I was coaching her on this hike to help her heal. On the website is says this hike is 11.6 miles and should take roughly 10 hours round trip to the peak. I was wearing my garmin Fenix 3 with my heartrate monitor tracking the hike. It was a total of 17.5 miles and took us from 7:20am to just a few minutes before 4pm to hit the peak! But We Did It! I stood on that rock and I said a prayer with tears streaming down my face as I said: "We Did Mom! We made it to the top of the world! I Love You!" I took pictures for Karina so she could have her victory moment to carry her into the next phase of her life. I wanted her to lean on this strength when she had hard days in the future. She took my pictures, I climbed down and burst into real tears! You know, that Ugly Cry kinda tears. I looked at the time it was 4:10pm. We had haul ass to get off that mountain before dark. We both were exhausted, our knees, feet and whole body hurt. The wind was getting cold and I knew we were fighting time and exhaustion to make it back to the car before night fall. I had to push Karina way outside her comfort zone to get off that mountain. I told her, "I know your tired! I know your hurt! I am right there with you. I have one job right now and that's to get us off this damn mountain before dark. I know you want to rest, but, if you stop and your muscles get cold, they will lock up and we wont make it! I need you to just keep moving your feet until we get to the car! You can yell, scream, cuss at me and I wont be mad. But I have to keep you safe!" At 8:10pm we walked up to my car as the sun finished setting behind the mountains! We made it! I looked at her and said "Don't you ever let anyone tell you that you aren't strong! That you are not Enough! That you are not Loveable! You just climbed the biggest mountain that you have ever been on! You proved to yourself that no matter how hard things get, you can push yourself outside of your comfort zone, through all of the pain and you will make it to the other side! Don't you ever let anyone disrespect you or talk to you crazy ever again! You are Strong! You are Beautiful and You are Enough!" I hugged her and told her I loved her and how proud I am of her for what she accomplished on that mountain.

As you take this journey with me through my story, know that you too, have the power inside you to overcome whatever obstacle is in front of you and that you can create whatever life it is you want, if only you will make the decision to do so and take a step! I hope you enjoy my story and thank you for taking the time to share my life with me.

ACKNOWLEDGMENTS

First, I want to say thank you to God for giving me this amazing life to live. To my children, my son, Bradley, wife Paige and my daughter Brittnie, I want to thank you for loving me and never giving up on me. I hope the person I have become has made you proud to call me your mom. To my best friend J'son Johnson, you were the one who called me on the darkest day of my life and talked me out of something you had no idea was about to happen. Without that call, this book would not be possible. Thank you from the bottom of my heart! To my girls, Michelle, Teresa, LaTaunya & Kim. Thank you for keeping me sane during the creation of this Book! Without you, I probably wouldn't have any hair left! To my editor, Tammey Brown, thank you for all you did to help me grow as a writer during this process. You helped me to look through different lenses to produce this masterpiece, and for that, I am forever grateful! Many more books are to come because of the growth I experienced through this entire process!

1 TRAVELING DOWN MEMORY LANE

It's a beautiful sunny day here in San Diego with just the right amount of wind. The fresh smell of salt water crashing with the waves is making its way into all of my senses. What an amazing, relaxing and breathtakingly beautiful day! It's pretty amazing to me that I now live less than 30 minutes from the beach and can go any time I want to! I have always loved the beach, and it has called to me for many years and been my favorite vacation spot my entire life. After I moved here in January of 2018, I had to tell myself almost daily, *"Tammy, you live here, you're not on vacation! You have to go to work now!"*

I'm sitting here on a blanket, toes buried in the sand and a cup of peach tea from Starbucks in my hand while watching a little brother and sister play in the waves as they kick water on each other. Their mom looks on from her perched spot on the sand not far from where I'm sitting. As each new wave crashes on the shore, she smiles as they again run back to tell her how cold the water is and show what new treasures they've found. I silently smile at the warmth and love I see in their mother's eyes as she watches her children have so much fun playing in the ocean on this beautiful day.

It takes me back to my mom watching us in the same way while we were on vacation. My mom was so fair skinned, and she would just burn like a lobster any time she was in the sun, even for short periods of time, just like her mom used to do. None the less, she still loved the sun and the water. Whether it was a beach, lake or a pool, if we could get to the water, we were there. When we lived in Chicago, we would take the camper to a lake in Indiana and spend the weekends. Once we moved down to Alabama, we would occasionally get to go to Panama City Beach in Florida, to visit my aunt Sally who lived there.

The sun shining on my face and the wind blowing through my hair, as I stared off into the crashing waves, my mind was now being flooded with even more memories of the good times with my mom. Like, how when I started playing sports, she never missed a game man. Even though she hated basketball and knew absolutely nothing about it, she never missed any of my games. All she knew was I was playing, and she wasn't going to miss it! She was right there when I hurt my knee sliding into second base during a softball game, despite being very pregnant and (I'm sure) quite uncomfortable. When I got hurt, she waddled her big pregnant self right onto the field to make sure I was ok. They tried to tell her she couldn't come out on there, but she pushed her way past the ump and said: "*That is my baby out there and you are NOT stopping me from getting to her*!!" She was something else man. She didn't let anyone tell her she couldn't be there to see me at any event I was participating in.

I ended up having surgery for that injury and was released after rehab with a stamp of full recovery and permission to go back to playing all of my favorite sports. Four days later, on my 15th birthday, we had a backyard football game going at the neighbor's house. The second play of the game I got tackled and couldn't walk! It turns out I ripped everything out of my knee; all the ligaments, cartilage, etc. There was nothing left, so I had to have major reconstructive surgery on my knee, just a few short weeks later. After two hours of surgery, the doctor came out and told my mom, "I've tried doing this arthroscopically to minimize the scars on your daughters' leg, but the damage is just too extensive." My mom, being the loving protector of her daughter that she was, said "Why are you out here talking to me? She told you she didn't care about scars. Just fix it where she can walk again and she'll do the work from there! Now get back in there and get my daughter out of that surgery room as soon as possible!" She told me all about it later. She was almost 40 years old and NOT a happy pregnant woman either. But still, she stayed there and made sure I was ok. With a total of 5.5 hours of surgery and 2+ hours in the recovery room by the time it was all done, and I was back in my room.

Do you know, she slept on a cot in my room every single night of my week-long recovery so I wouldn't be up there all alone! I think about that a lot. Mom, eight months pregnant, sleeping on a cot for seven days, just for me! She never complained about how she felt, her comfort or lack thereof, but instead, she totally focused on me getting well.
During that week, she also got a nurse thrown out of my room, off my case and off the floor, after she didn't follow the doctor's orders by giving me a weaker pain medication. She claimed it was because she didn't want me to be addicted to the morphine they were giving me for pain. I am not sure if the nurse was still working there afterward, but she definitely was NOT on my floor or in my room. My mom was a force to be reckoned with when it came to her only baby girl!

Even into my adulthood, my mom still put aside her needs to take care of me. I got the flu really bad while my pregnant daughter was living with me and I was so sick, I couldn't even get out of bed. My mom took off work for an entire week to take care of me and the kids because I couldn't do it. I fell asleep in her lap every night with her wiping my head with a damp cloth. As a mother, looking back at all of these moments now, I know those were the times where I leaned into mom and thought "I love you mom, thank you for always being there!"

She never missed a call on my birthday. Always at 6am, like clockwork, she would be the first one to tell me happy birthday and she loved me. We had some pretty awesome best friend moments at different times in my life. But one thing was for sure, she always gave the best hugs, hands down.

Mom would do almost anything for me, but wow, I remember her being so afraid of everything. She was really afraid to fly. Do you know she never got on a plane while she was living on this earth? When we lived in Chicago and went to Canada to visit my step dad's parents, we drove because she wouldn't get on a plane! When my grandfather got sick, after we moved to Alabama, we drove back because she wouldn't get on a plane. She was terrified it would crash. It didn't matter that statistics showed more people died from car accidents than plane crashes. She was not getting on that damn plane man.

She was so superstitious as well. No black cats or even umbrellas were allowed in the house when we were growing up. She would say "Don't walk under ladders" and if you could stay home on Friday the 13th, well then, that's what you did. It's so crazy to me looking back on all of it now, being all "Grown Up" myself. I can say that was one thing we didn't have in common, her fear of life in general. I am always looking for every piece of excitement I can grab a hold of from flying to skydiving and anything in between. I fly every time I get the opportunity!

Mom had a heart attack in her sleep in December 2013. I had seen her just 7 short days prior where I was fussing about her not taking care of herself. I had so much I wanted to tell her. There was so much left unsaid. My heart was breaking and there was nothing I could do to stop it. When I saw her at the hospital, she was laying there on life support in ICU, with tubes everywhere and an endless beeping of machines! Right before we took her off of life support, I whispered in her ear, "Mom I promise one day, when I start traveling the world, I'm going to scatter your ashes in some faraway place so you will finally experience being on a plane!" That was my final promise to her before she took her last breath that day, December 4th of 2013.

That someday came in 2017! I went on a leadership retreat with my life coaching company. When I decided to go on the trip, I had not intended to take mom's ashes to scatter them. To be quite honest, I had forgotten I had even made the promise. It wasn't until a couple of weeks later when she came to me in a vision and said: "keep your promise." That's when I remembered what I told her on that day, which seemed so long ago. It was then the tears started trickling silently down my cheeks, I took in a deep breath, let it out slowly, and said, "It's time mom. I'm going to set you free from the box you have been living in your whole life." (I will share more about this in a later chapter.)

LIFE LESSONS LEARNED FROM MOM

I know we all have things we learn from our parents as we are growing up. Some things seem pretty simple, like how to do laundry, clean the house, cook and taking care of pets. Some things are pretty profound, even if we didn't think so at the time, like how to read a road map. At first, I thought it was stupid to learn to read a map, but because she made me do it, when I learned how to drive, I was never afraid to travel because I knew I could always find my way back home.

Once I learned, I was always the navigator when we went somewhere. Even when I grew up and moved out, before electronic GPS, I had the maps, and I navigated us wherever we needed to go. With all the electronic devices to guide us wherever we want to go now days reading a map is a lost art I still appreciate and count on as a skill in my toolbox of life.

I learned a lot from my mom. There was little if any, positive energy in our house growing up. The majority of the things I learned were from taking negative situations and making a mental note to change that in my life when I got out on my own. Life is a great teacher. When you see or feel something, you don't like, and you instantly know you want something better, even if you are not sure what that something is in the moment.

If mom taught us anything, she taught us to be strong. She taught us to depend on nobody but ourselves, especially me. I remember her saying so many times, *"Never depend on a man. Make sure you can do everything yourself and if he can add to that then great, but don't you ever wait on no man to do anything for you."*

For the most part, it was just mom and us. Outside of a couple of stepdads who left almost as quickly as they came into our lives, it was mom trying to raise 4 kids on her own. I was the oldest of four and the only girl. Looking back at my childhood, I had to grow up fast to help mom take care of all of us but because of that and l the lessons I learned growing up I am who I am today. For that, I am so very thankful.

I learned a lot about bad relationships after having a front-row view to all of hers, and I understood why she felt the way she did about not needing anyone. Looking at that statement now I realize it's super negative, and bitter, toward all men and I realize how much hurt there was in her life to get her there. Looking at it from my perspective now, I think what she was trying to teach me was to be able to take care of myself. She wanted me to know I could be happy on my own and then find a mate who would add to my happiness. She was trying to teach me if a person depends on someone else to make them happy, then they will always be disappointed. That's no way to live your life man.

From mom, I also learned I didn't like cigarettes because she was a smoker just like her parents were. I learned I wanted a better life for my kids even though I had no idea how to make it happen. I learned that no matter how hard life got children were to be protected even with your last breath if that's what it takes.

What are some of the life lessons you learned from your parents? Things that were positive you want to continue to keep in your life or the things that were negative, you learned, you want to change as you continue to grow in your life journey?

Our parents did the best they could with what they had at that time in their life. Whether it was financial, mental, emotional or spiritual. When we are living with them, we can't always see from outside our own perspective, especially as children. But now that we are older and have had some of our own life experiences, maybe even with our own children, we can look back and say "Wow, I really did learn a lot from you mom, thank you." Take a moment and write some of those things down. It will help you appreciate your parents a little more.

2 COME GET TO KNOW ME

Right after high school, I attended Herzing Institute in Birmingham, Alabama to become a legal secretary. This was not my first choice as I had applied to The University of Alabama my senior year. I really wanted to be in the medical profession and specialize as a labor and delivery nurse, but I never received any letter back in response to my application. My mom was going to Herzing at the time and she wanted me to go there with her. She convinced me that I would love being a legal secretary. In all honesty, I think she just wanted me to like something she did and do it with her, which was something new for us. We had never done anything together in all the years I can remember growing up. I played sports, she came and watched, that was the extent of our togetherness when I lived at home. Quite honestly, I was okay with that being our roles.

You know, it wasn't until a few years ago, when I was sharing this part of my story with a friend, when I had the epiphany, everyone gets a letter when you apply to college whether you are accepted or not. It was then I realized one of two things must have happened. Either mom never actually mailed my application or I got accepted, and Mom didn't want me to go away to college so she threw it away so I wouldn't find out. Even though Tuscaloosa was only about 45 minutes from where we lived, it meant I would not be at home anymore or even close to her. I was only 17 when I graduated high school and was clueless about the whole college application process. Both of those are logical answers as to what could have happened, and it makes so much sense now when I think about it.

I found Herzing pretty easy because it was a repeat of the things I just completed in my senior year of high school, which also meant I had time for a social life! During the school year, we had a party at a local bar and I met a guy, Bryan, who would turn out to be my future husband. I thought he was a nice guy and he was funny, always treated me well, and would take me out to eat and to the movies pretty regularly. He traveled all around the southeast managing the sound equipment for a local band. A couple of my girlfriends and I would go see them on the weekends when work schedules allowed.

By this time I was living with my friends, working at a waffle house, I had my own car, was paying my bills and in my mind, I was finally "all grown up." To add to the feeling of being what I considered a successful grown up at the time was going to college and graduating. I did it too! I was the first one in my family to even graduate high school, and then I topped that by graduating college with a 4.0 GPA!

Bryan and I had been dating for about a year when he asked me to marry him and I said yes. We didn't want a big wedding, more so because we really couldn't afford it, so we got married at the courthouse and had a reception with family and friends afterward. By the next year, I was pregnant with my son Bradley. I remember that pregnancy so vividly. I was blessed not to have had morning sickness, but I thoroughly believed in the theory I was eating for two! Mexican food was the love in my life, and everything spicy, no matter how bad my heartburn was afterward.

We signed up for birthing classes since it was our first child and had no idea what we were doing. My grandparents lived close to the hospital where I would be delivering, so we always stopped to see them on the way to class. This was their first great-grandchild, and my grandpa was super excited. He would have me sit in his lap until he felt the baby kick. Omg, he was so funny! He didn't care that his leg was going to sleep because I was a fat and happy pregnant woman. All he knew was his great grandbaby was almost here, and that's all he cared about. After all, I was his favorite.

What I didn't know during at the time, was that he was sick and dying. He didn't tell anyone. They put him in the hospital about two weeks before the baby was born. I made sure I went to the hospital every day to see him. They had to strap him down to the bed because he kept pulling his IV's out. One day I was sitting in there visiting with him, telling him I loved him, and I couldn't wait for him to hold Bradley after he was born. All of a sudden, he looked up at the door with this weird expression on his face. I looked over but didn't see anything. His stare was so intense, so I asked him what he was looking at.

Grandpa: Pointing with his crooked old finger from his strapped down wrist, said "You don't see him? He's right there!"

Me: "Who grandpa? I don't see anybody".

Grandpa: "The man that's on the cross above the door, he's standing in the doorway. Don't you see him? Untie me from this bed! I need to get up! If you love me, you will get me out of this bed Tammy! I don't want to be here no more!"

Me: After bursting into tears, said "Grandpa don't ask me to do that! You know I can't untie you! You keep pulling your IV's out and you need them!"

Grandpa: Looking at me, said "Get out! If you're not going to get me out of here, I don't want to see you anymore! You don't love me!"

I ran out of the room crying and straight to the waiting room where I jumped in my grandma's lap and broke down sobbing. I had realized grandpa was dying and he wasn't going to make it out of the hospital. It was Jesus he saw standing in the doorway, and I knew it meant it was time for him to go home.

Grandma was angry with him for upsetting me when I was so close to delivering. In my heart, I knew she didn't want to admit she knew his days were few and he would not be leaving the hospital to go home with her this time.

It was soon after that my beautiful son, Bradley, was born by C-Section after four days of labor, on March 19th, 1988. It was the next day when my mom shared a photo of him with grandpa and told him we were both healthy and fine. She said he had this peaceful, happy smile on his face at the news. It was then she told me the doctors had relayed to her his organs were shutting down.

I'll never forget what she said next: "Now that he knows his great-grandchild is here, they don't expect him to make it through the night." I burst into tears and screamed "Noooooooo!" She just wrapped me up in her arms and hugged me as tight as she could until I could talk again. I asked to go see him and take Bradley in an incubator so we could say goodbye. Every doctor and nurse I talked to said it wasn't safe.

The next morning at 5:27am, my hospital phone rang, and the woman on the other end of the phone said, "Mrs. McCoy, we just wanted to let you know your grandfather passed away about an hour ago. We're sorry for your loss." Then she hung up the phone.

I screamed at the phone, then threw it across the room, ripping it out of the wall causing my husband, Bryan, to about jump out of his skin! He had been asleep in the recliner bed beside me. He knew, without asking what had just happened. He got up and just held me while I cried uncontrollably.

The day after I got out of the hospital, I buried my grandfather. I was struggling with being excited about becoming a new mom and knowing I would never get to sit in my grandpa's lap ever again. It tore me up knowing my children would never get to know and love the man that played such a large part in making me the strong woman I am today. The one man who made me believe there was still some good left in this world!

I was trying so hard to be strong for my grandma. Even though, I felt like I was failing miserably. (It was the first time I ever had the conscious thought that I was a failure at anything.) I had so many questions running through my head like, how could I hold so much love and pain in my heart at the same time? How would I balance the joy and happiness of bringing my first-born child into this world, with the overwhelming sadness and grief of losing the grandfather who meant so much to me?

I am a new mom now with a new set of responsibilities. I told myself he wasn't in pain anymore and one day I wouldn't hurt anymore either. After all, the facts are that none of us make it out alive. I knew I would celebrate him through my son's life and could not let Bradley's birth be a sad time. One life ended and a new one had begun. That's why it's called the cycle of life.

With all the emotions swirling around in my heart, after the funeral, we took our son home and tried to focus on the happiness that was to come with our new family.

Six months later, I found out I was pregnant again. That pregnancy was much more difficult from the moment the doctors confirmed I was pregnant. I felt emotional and angry all the time. I went into labor about two months early. Brittnie wasn't due until July 28th. I was scared of losing her, and my only thoughts were "I can't lose my baby" as we went through seven medications before finally getting my labor to stop. The doctors put me on bed rest and told me I couldn't lift anything (including my son), do any household chores nor anything strenuous at all. The medicine made me so sick to my stomach that my hands shook all the time and I had trouble sleeping through the night. I wasn't happy about the doctors making me take so much medication while I was pregnant. But it was the only way for her lungs to have time to develop and her chances of surviving would be greater.

Thankfully, a friend came over and babysat me five days a week while my husband worked. She was such a blessing! I went into labor in less than 48 hours after they took me off the meds. July 18th, 1989 and my beautiful, perfect baby girl, Brittnie, had arrived by C-Section!

THE TRUTH REVEALED

Here I was in my early 20's with a full schedule and a very full life. Bryan and I both worked and we had a nice house, cars, two awesome children and our marriage was doing pretty well. Then I started having dreams that would wake me from a sound sleep with my heart racing. In the beginning, I couldn't recall my dreams. I didn't want to call them nightmares, I just knew I didn't like the way it left me feeling. Then one night, I saw something. It was a vague, fuzzy picture, but the feeling grew more intense with each time I had the dreams. It really bothered me that I kept waking up and didn't know why. My husband didn't understand it either. He thought I was just stressed out with work, the kids, the house and trying to keep up with everything.

Over the next few times I experienced this, I woke up in a sweat screaming for my mom and scaring the hell out of my husband! After a few nights, in my dream, I remembered my mom was in the room, and I would scream for her to help me like I was in trouble. I didn't remember anything else other than that.

Then one night later the dream became crystal clear and I re-lived that moment like it was in slow motion.

The dream started with me at the kitchen table coloring. My brother was on the floor playing. I couldn't have been more than 2.5 -3 years old as he was still in diapers, but sitting up and playing on his own on the floor. My mom and a man were having sex on the couch. The next vision I had was of my mom and him sexually abusing me together. I cried for my mom to make it stop and she replied: "*Just lay there baby it will be over with soon.*" I must've blacked out afterward as I don't remember anything else of "that night."

The nightmare came night after night after night. Louder, clearer, exactly the same each and every time. I would wake up crying, couldn't breathe, angry, and didn't know what was going on. I kept asking myself, Why am I having these stupid dreams!? My mom loves me, and we are so close, I know She would NEVER allow someone to hurt me like that.

The nightmares really upset my husband. He believed they weren't just nightmares but were suppressed memories I had blacked out until now. I told him there was no way that it really happened! My mom would Never allow that to happen to me! I was her only Daughter! What mother, in her right mind, could ever *allow* something like that to happen to any of her children, much less her only daughter! Then more dreams started coming. I remembered different times and different places, but it was all with her present and even participating.

My husband finally convinced me to ask my mom about it. He encouraged me just to ask her, and if she says it didn't happen, then he would never bring it up again. He was adamant I at least ask. All we both wanted was for the nightmares to stop. I knew he was right, but how could I bring up a conversation like this with anyone, much less my own mother? How could I suggest my mother, the woman who gave birth to me, sexually abused me when I was a child, with some random dude I didn't even recognize? And all of it from dreams I wasn't even sure I could believe myself if they were even real or not. I couldn't find the words, so I put it off for a few days. In all honesty, it quite possibly could have been weeks for all I know. It seemed as though time stood still during those days. It felt like I was in a never-ending horror film every time I closed my eyes.

I finally got up the nerve one day to call my mom. We had our normal chit chat about what was going on at work, with the kids, my brothers, etc.

Then I took a deep breath and just let the words come out as I said, "Mom, I have been having these really horrible nightmares lately, and they seem so real. They have been waking me up for nights on end. Bryan said I should ask you about it to see if you could help me figure out what it was all about."

She was quiet for a second. I really didn't think anything about her taking so long to respond at the time, but then she finally asked what the dreams were about. So, I went over the dreams in very graphic detail. I made sure I didn't leave a single detail out because I just knew, there was no way it could be true! It was just too far-fetched for any mother to allow that to happen to her only daughter.

She was radio silent for what seemed like an eternity. So, I said, "Mom, that really didn't happen… did it? You didn't do that right?! You didn't allow that to happen to me?!" Silence was the only thing I heard on the other end of the phone.
I could feel my heart racing and trying to pound through my chest as sweat was running down the back of my neck. I remember having problems catching my breath. "Mom, I really need you to answer me. I need you to tell me you didn't do this, that it's all just a bad dream and make it go away!" She took a deep breath and said "Yes! Okay! Are you happy now?! Yes, it happened Tammy! But I was a different person back then, and it doesn't matter now!"

You could have heard a pin drop with the silence coming from the other end of the phone! I'm not even sure I was breathing. Then I started crying. I got angry, and I screamed at her; "What the hell do you mean *you were a different person back then*? Really?! Are you Fucking Serious right now?"

The rest of the conversation was like an out of body experience. I yelled and screamed at her at the top of my lungs. I couldn't even process what she had said. I yelled at her, "How In the HELL could you Allow this to Happen to Your Only DAUGHTER!!! What the Fuck were you thinking!?!? You even participated Mom!!! Really?! And you just expect me to be OKAY with your lame ass excuses that you were a different person then! That It Doesn't Matter Now! Let me help you with what I think about that! I NEVER want to see you again for as long as I live!!"

I told her she would never see her grandchildren as long as there was air left in my lungs! As far as I was concerned, she was dead to me! I slammed the phone down! I was throwing things, screaming and finally just crumpled to the floor crying. I was home alone, so there was no one to console me, no one for me to rant to, just me, myself and I, with a million out of control thoughts. I don't remember much after that except my husband came home and I broke down all over again to him.

I want you to know I am not sharing this part of my story for you to feel sorry for me. That is not my intention at all. Actually, it is the exact opposite. I want you to feel empowered by all of this! You may be wondering how anyone who reads this could find something to be empowered by, but it's here, just keep reading.

What I want you to experience when you read this is that I never knew this happened to me as a child. I never remembered any of this until my children were the same age I was when these traumatic events occurred. Also, thankfully, I don't remember any of the physical pain or trauma. I know, beyond a shadow of a doubt, God protected me as a child and even as an adult from the physical pain by blacking out my memory. That tells me there was a purpose in all of the things that happened. I wasn't aware of what that purpose was until just a few years ago. I had to grow into my purpose, just like we all do.

To not feel the pain and to separate the person from the act helped me to look back on this with a different perspective. As you continue to read on from this point, I want you to look at it as this child went through these things and she, as an adult, **overcame** them.

I used this as fuel in my life to help show people we are NOT the acts that happen to us. If you experienced something traumatic and survived (which you have because you are here reading this book), there is a purpose in that! You have a purpose on this earth to complete. *That act is only a building block in the stairs leading to your destiny!* There is a purpose in the emotional pain experienced in a lifetime. I promise you that! Just keep reading and I will show you what I mean.

Being a mom myself, I couldn't begin to imagine (or even wanted to try) letting anyone hurt my children, much less participate! Who in the hell, in their right mind, does that?! I tried to rationalize it from every different angle. I didn't recognize the man in my dreams. It wasn't until years later when I figured out who he was. After asking a lot of questions and putting the pieces of the puzzle together, I figured out he was my biological father; which mortified me even more. I was so angry, hurt, confused, sad, depressed and I am sure a whole host of other emotions I couldn't even give a name to while I was experiencing the living hell inside my mind and the broken heart it produced.

I felt so lost. My husband, Bryan, didn't know what to say, much less do, to make me feel better or how to take any of my pain away. He just knew my mother was never going to be a part of our children's life ever again. The nightmares kept coming. I was hardly sleeping without taking something or drinking enough alcohol just to make me pass out. I was about 23 years old at the time. As I am looking back at all of this now, it's easy to see I had zero coping skills and all I knew was I wanted to be numb. I wanted the pain in my heart and soul to stop! I wanted the voices in my head to shut up! I needed to find some peace, somehow, some way! I had no clue how that was ever going to happen with all the voices echoing in my head.

Months went by. Mom tried to call me several times, but I wouldn't talk to her. Back then there was no way to block phone numbers from calling, so I just didn't answer, I had nothing left to say to her, and she finally gave up. Bryan and I, we were so young when all of this happened, and we were doing the best we could trying to figure it all out. We buried ourselves in the kids as that was the only thing that gave us any sense of normalcy. We loved on them every minute we had available and played with them until they passed out every night. We would hang out with friends and family, just trying to stay busy. Anything we could, just so we didn't have to think about it.

The *subject* was off limits to any and everyone. I, myself, didn't want to think about it, much less, talk about it. After all, who could even begin to understand how I felt or what I was going through emotionally! (Hell, looking back at it now, I didn't even understand what was going on inside me! I just knew I was hurting and I didn't see any way to make it stop!) What kind of conversation can you have when your opening line is "Oh yeah, by the way, I've been having nightmares about my mom and some random dude having sex with me when I was like three years old"! Talk about sucking the air out of a room and killing any kind of Happy mood there may have been. Besides, if I'm being perfectly honest, I wasn't even sure anyone would believe me if I told them anyway. Hell, I wasn't sure I believed it myself, and it happened to me.

I don't remember ever being consciously aware of not wanting to be home. I just didn't want to be there, which I'm sure probably led to mom and I never doing anything together. When those nightmares came, it was like Pandora's box was opened up and my whole world came crashing down around me. Mom was always verbally, emotionally and even physically abusive to us as children. When I was 13, my stepfather raped me. We went to court, and his attorney convinced a jury that "I liked it." He got probation for three years and couldn't be in the same county I was living in.

Anger was always my go-to emotion as a kid. Looking back at all of these events as an adult, it makes perfect sense now. There were other things too, like the time my youngest brothers' father taught me to drive a straight shift when I was 16. He looked over at me with this creepy ass look and said: "I sure would like to get in between your thighs where that Mt. Dew bottle is". My quick response was, "It'll be over your dead body." I was always angry at him. I always had my guard up because I didn't trust him at all. Hell, I hardly trusted anyone, including my own mother.

I remember coming home one afternoon, and he had my mom pinned down on the floor and was punching her in the face. Without thinking, I grabbed a butcher knife off the counter and put it to his throat. I probably would have killed him if my mom hadn't screamed to snap me out of my blind rage and begged for his life. The police officer who showed up was, thankfully, my best friends dad, and he told the other officer they would not be pressing charges against me because it was self-defense. To be perfectly honest, I am not sure killing him is something I could have lived with for the rest of my life.

A few years ago, I talked to a few of my high school friends during our 30-year class reunion and they don't remember me being an angry kid. They always described me as strong and determined. There was only one friend who knew what was going on at home and I pretty much lived at her house my senior year.

The parts of my childhood I don't remember, are the normal events of my life, which seems odd to me. I believe that's because what society would call normal, was abnormal in our home. There were not very many happy things going on at home, so all the standout moments were related to the abuse I lived throughout daily life. When my friends from school want to recall past events, most of the time, I have to admit openly, I simply just don't remember. When we were all in school, I focused on the things that made me happy, which were sports and school work. I knew those were the two things that would get me out of my mother's house which was my only goal!

FORGIVING THE UNFORGIVABLE

Time seemed to pass without a second thought of how it affected anyone. It has one job to do and that's to never stop letting the seconds stop ticking away. Minute by minute, hour after hour, day by day, month after month and year after year, time marched on with little regard for my feelings or the emotional hell I was living in every waking hour of my days. I wish I could tell you how much time had actually passed without me talking to my mom again, but I really don't have a clue.

I started feeling the all too familiar knots in my stomach again and hearing this ringing in my ears. When I say ringing, I mean this phrase was on repeat day in and day out; *if you don't forgive, you won't be forgiven*. It seemed never to stop! I would wake up in the middle of the night in a cold sweat, crying and calling out for my mom. Then I would hear it again; *if you don't forgive, you won't be forgiven*. I just wanted it ALL to stop! I couldn't take the nightmares coming back and reliving that all over again!

Bryan and I were attending his brother-in-law's church at the time. I had "claimed" to be a Christian for many years. I went to church with my grandmother as a child growing up in Chicago. Then after she passed away, my mom never made us go back to church, but we were allowed to go with friends if we wanted to. I had said, "the prayer" (many times in fact), got my free bible and everyone patted me on the back like I had won some kind of prize to which I had no clue as to what that prize was at the time. Nobody ever told me what being a Christian meant. No one ever taught me how to pray, read or study the Bible or even told me I had to go back to church. There were no "next steps" or classes to take to help me learn about Jesus or God or even how they could help me get through all the ups and downs life had thrown at me thus far and was going to throw at me from that point forward.

When the dreams came back full force, I talked to the pastor in confidence, without even letting my husband know. I shared everything I was going through and the phrase on repeat in my head: "*if you don't forgive you won't be forgiven*" and I asked him if it was true.

He showed me the verse in the Bible and told me in order for our sins to be forgiven then we had to forgive those who hurt us. I shared I wasn't sure I could forgive her, and I never wanted to see her again. I said I felt what she had done to me was unforgivable, end of the story. He didn't disagree with how I felt at all. He understood my feelings about the situation, the best he could anyway, and said he couldn't even imagine how I felt.

He did take the time to try and help me to understand forgiveness is not about letting her off the hook for what she had done. It was about freeing God's hands to heal our heart and soul from the wrongs that were done against us. He said forgiveness doesn't mean I have to go to her and say "I forgive you" although it would be awesome if I could find the strength within my heart to do so. What it meant was telling God you forgive her in your heart, and you are giving your heart to him to heal so you can be set free from your own hurt and pain. To let him deal with the people who hurt you, so you don't have to anymore. He also wanted to be sure I knew that just because I forgave my mom, it didn't mean I had to let her back into my life. It just means you want to be set free from the pain that's tearing you up from the inside out.

Looking back at that conversation as I am writing this book, knowing what I know now about forgiveness, I believe the pastor was teaching me that forgiveness is a decision, not an emotion. Decisions are choices we are faced with day in and day out. Each of them affects our lives in the now and in the future. Are all of our decisions easy when facing things that have hurt us, either emotionally or physically or both? Absolutely not!

What I can share with you from my own personal experiences and perspective is that in the place, I am right now, mentally, emotionally and spiritually; Forgiveness for me is an acknowledgment to myself that I am upset or hurt in some way by what has occurred. That is followed by taking an inventory of my emotions, thoughts and/or feelings as to why I feel the way I do about that particular situation. What was my role in the situation? And then forgiving the person, the situation and myself.

It's important that I ask what my role in the situation was. If I'm honest with myself, I know I contributed in some way in every situation. When I learned the art of forgiveness and self-awareness, I found freedom within my soul like I had never known before.

Now... let's get back to the story....

I would love to say that conversation liberated me in some way and I walked away the perfect little Christian girl who was able to say: "I forgive you and let's live happily ever after as one big happy family!" But, that's not what happened at all. Instead, I kept going to church and got baptized "again." This time I wanted to do this Christian thing the right way, so I chose to dig into my Bible more, prayed more, and cried a lot more. I was working on becoming a better person while attempting to building a relationship with Jesus. Even with all of this, I still felt very angry and hurt by my mom. I knew I still had a really long way to go with this forgiveness stuff where my mom was concerned, even though I felt better about her and the situation overall.

Then, one day, I finally mustered up the nerve to call her. I wasn't sure what I would say, but what the words that came spewing out of my mouth were, "I don't want you to say shit, I just need you to shut up and listen! I am going to say this out loud, but I am not doing this for you, I am doing it for me because I need some peace and some sleep! I forgive you for what you did! You are my mom, and I do realize you are not the same person you were back then. There are parts of me that still love you, only because you are my mother. I don't know if I will ever be able to have a relationship with you, nor do I know if I will ever let you have a relationship with my children. But I am forgiving you because I know that if I don't forgive you, I won't be forgiven by God. So, I am taking the selfish route to save myself by forgiving you and letting him deal with you from here on out!" Then I hung up the phone and burst into tears again. I'm not sure if I even took a breath while I was rattling off ALL of the anger that erupted out of my heart at the woman who had given birth to me. After I hung up on my mom, I prayed the pastor was right, and I would finally find some peace by forgiving the unforgivable!

I can tell you the dreams took a shift after some time. I started remembering the good times I had with my mom. I remembered the mom who never missed any of my sporting events, who even as an adult, she came to all of my softball games and cheered me on until I retired from the game. I recalled when I tore up my knee sliding into second base, and she waddled her pregnant self out on to the softball field to make sure I was okay. I thought about the time she spent the night in the hospital on a cot for 7 days at 8.5 months pregnant when I had reconstructive surgery on my knee.

When she called and wanted to be the first to wish me a happy birthday or to be safe on Friday the 13th. She was the mom, that even though she had a jacked-up way of showing it sometimes, made sure we knew she was proud of us and she loved us endlessly. God found a way to soften my heart toward her.

My husband, on the other hand, was NOT happy at all when I started talking to my mom again. It took a lot longer for him to see she was not the same person from my childhood and then to get him even to entertain the idea of letting her back into our life. It took some time, but, we eventually did let her back in our lives, little by little, step by step. We let her see the kids again, and she began rebuilding a relationship with them. It was hard for all of us. I was terrified to leave my kids alone with her, but she stuck to it and eventually got to be around whenever she wanted to. Even though our emotional relationship was still more than a little strained, my children knew their grandmother, and that was very important to me. I knew they would never have to suffer the things I had as a child. I had broken the chains and curses that had been handed down for who knows how many generations.

DIVORCED AND HURTING

As I said earlier, time has a way of passing by without a second thought as to how it's affecting anyone. I can't even really put my finger on any one thing that happened, but my husband and I slowly grew apart. We had not been happy in a really long time. We were arguing and fighting all the time, so I asked him to go to counseling, but he always refused. His words were "If we can't fix it ourselves, then it's not going to happen." I even went to the extreme and got his parents involved trying to get them to convince him to at least talk to the pastor and get marriage counseling through the church. Nothing seemed to work. So, eventually, I gave up and told him I wanted a divorce. On the one hand, I didn't want to get divorced because my mom had done it six times and God knows my one mission in this life has always been to do everything in my power to not be anything like her. On the other hand, I didn't want my children growing up to think a marriage as dysfunctional as ours had become was normal. All the arguing, no love to be found anywhere, our life had become distant and basically lifeless. I was so torn with how I felt about the decision I made. In my heart, all I wanted was for them to have a better chance of getting it right when they entered into the adult world. In my mind, this was just not something that couldn't be avoided. I prayed I was making the right decision, not only for me but for my children.

I was now a single mom. My son was about to turn five, and my daughter was just three. Our divorce was finalized in March 1993. They were predicting a big blizzard in Alabama that year. I was moving into my new place that weekend when they announced how bad they expected the blizzard to be. In Alabama, you could never really tell by the forecast what was going to happen. They could tell you 20" of snow is coming, and you see 20 snowflakes instead. My new place was total electric, so Bryan convinced me to stay at the house at least through the night to make sure the power and everything was going to stay on. If we stayed at the house, at least we would be safe, dry, warm and have a way to cook over the fireplace if the predictions were right.

I was so thankful we chose to stay at the house overnight. We ended up getting over 18" of snow which included snow drifts that were over 30" high. The 4 of us stayed in the den which was a 12x16 room. We sectioned it off in order to keep in the heat from the fireplace. For 5 days, we had no power, no phone, no water or any of the usual comforts of life. I slept on the couch, Bryan and the kids slept on the floor on a pallet made out of bedding from the bedrooms. We kept the food from the fridge, buried in the snow on the front porch, to keep it from spoiling. If the truth were told, we probably could have kept the food in the fridge because the house was so cold. One morning, I got up to get the milk to make the kids some cereal and saw footprints in the snow coming from the road to the porch. Someone had walked through the snow all the way down this country road, and stole our food off the porch!

We were a couple who were divorced and snowed in together for 5 days. We were huddled up in a 12x16 room, with 2 children under the age of 5, with no power, phone, TV/cable or water. Looking back at it now, we can laugh about the events of that week, even though in those moments, we weren't laughing about too much of anything.

I met my second husband shortly after my divorce while playing softball. I was living not far from my kids' dad at the time, so it would be convenient for both of us. I wanted him to be a part of the kid's life and see them as often as he wanted to. After all, it wasn't the kid's fault we couldn't make our marriage work. Me and Chip hit it off pretty fast. He seemed to be a good guy. He spent money on me, took me out to eat and was good with the kids. We got married in November. Bryan, my kid's dad, was already re-married and soon after, a custody battle over the kids began. This whole thing drained every ounce of the life I had left in me. The judge split the custody of the kids with no reason given other than it was in the "best interest of the children." My son lived with his dad and my daughter lived with me. That was one of the hardest things I ever had to go through. Not having both of my kids living with me all the time took all the air out of my lungs. I honestly thought my heart would stop beating.

Chip and I bought a nice house in Pinson and owned the pool league for the Birmingham area. I was a legal secretary doing real estate closings making good money, and he worked for a local printing company. We made well over six figures between our two jobs and owning the pool league.

One day I looked in the mirror and realized I had gained a bunch of weight. I never paid any attention to what I was doing after the custody battle. I was just mindlessly eating all the time, and I wore baggy clothes trying to cover it up. I also hadn't realized my husband seemed to like the fact I was fat until I joined an all women's gym weighing in at 174.8lbs my first day. I then lost over forty pounds to get back down to 133lbs, which was just 5lbs over what I weighed when we got married. He was so angry and wanted to know who I was losing the weight for because it wasn't him. Looking back at our relationship now, I realized I was never actually in love with him. In all honesty, we should not have gotten married. It wasn't his fault because in his mind we were in love. Subconsciously, I believed I was doing the right thing and thought I loved him enough and we could make it work. Eventually, our marriage fell apart and there was no salvaging it. We divorced in 1998. In the back of my mind, I heard the voices say "you are on the way to being just like "Mom"! Divorce number two. Marriage fail number two! Now, what the hell are you going to do Tammy!?"

After that I started going out with friends on the weekends, partying all the time, experimenting with drugs and drinking a lot of alcohol. After about a year of this, I met a guy at my favorite club. We had amazing sexual chemistry right from the beginning and ended up going to a hotel that night. I went home the next morning and didn't see him again for close to six months when I ran into him at a pool hall. It took a few minutes of chatting before we realized who each other was. It wasn't long after we started dating. The sex was amazing and I was struck by what I believed was true love.

It didn't take long to realize I was stupid in love with this man. I bought him gifts, spent time with him, met his family, and then out of the blue, his crazy ex-girlfriends start showing up. Yes, that should have been my first clue to get the hell out, but I couldn't see past the "we are in love" part. He gave me every lame excuse in the book. I believed the lies, even though my gut was telling me to run. I chose to stay because a bad relationship was better than being alone. Subconsciously, I believed that if I was alone, I wasn't loveable.

During the time I lost the pool league business and then the house I had purchased with my second husband was foreclosed on. This was followed by the car and two motorcycles being repossessed. I stayed even after being evicted from two more apartments, because "at least

I'm not alone," is what I told myself. Finally, after five BS years of hell, this merry-go-round relationship crashed and burned. It took finding out he had been cheating on me with three other women and had married one of them in secret while still with me! His wife found a text message on his phone from me and called to find out why I was telling her husband "I Love You." I just wasted 5 years with a man that didn't give a rats ass about me! All because I believed I was "In Love" when the reality was I let this man used me because I desperately wanted to be loved. I didn't want to be alone. In my mind, if I was alone, that meant I wasn't loved. I believed I could "buy his love." I just got my heart busted wide open because, subconsciously, a bad relationship was better than being alone.

There was a serious cycle in motion here. I just wanted to be "loved." I wanted to Feel Loved! To be honest, I had no clue what real love was or what it was supposed to look or feel like. I never had an example of what "Real Love" was supposed to look like growing up. When I looked at both of my marriages, they were not a picture of what I "Thought" love was supposed to be.

What I didn't know at the time, was that because of all of the sexual abuse I went through as a child, subconsciously, I believed if you had sex with me, that meant you loved me. My whole childhood, the only way an adult male showed me "love" was by having sex with me. So that is what I was conditioned to believe. If you left me, well that was because my sex wasn't good enough. Or I had to buy your love because as a child, the men would give me money and tell me "this is our secret okay?"

My relationships from a subconscious standpoint were doomed to fail, and I had no idea I was on this sinking ship with no life jacket. I felt unloved, worthless, betrayed and abandoned by everyone. The very real thought in my head was I would be alone for the rest of my life. I had these overpowering feelings of loneliness, and they were crushing me inside. So I just drank more, did more drugs and I put on my mask of a happy face for everyone else to see. Nobody heard my cries at night. I never let anyone see me hurt. I had to be strong, not realizing the path I was on was very dark and slippery with no roadmap on how to get out.

3 DEPRESSION TAKING OVER

After all of the smoke cleared from the devastation of that relationship ending, I landed a good job working at a barbeque spot in town. I really loved that job and felt happy for the first time in a long time. It was great because I got to wear jeans and t-shirts to work every day, plus, waiting tables meant I had cash money in my pocket. I had just moved into a nice townhouse just up the street from work.

My son was now married and had given me my first granddaughter. I loved his wife, Paige, and was excited to have another daughter in the family after growing up with all brothers. Then in 2008, my daughter delivered my second granddaughter that spring.

Life looked pretty good on the outside. I was still doing a lot of partying with drugs and alcohol, especially on the weekends. I was functional, so I didn't see the problem with any of it. Nobody else knew all the pain I felt inside that I was trying to hide. I never missed work, and I made sure all my bills were paid. At the end of the day, that was all that mattered, as far as I was concerned. I just put on my fake happy face for everyone to see and did my job making everyone believe I was "Okay."

I was so lost in my own little world; my belief was that if you hung out with me at the bar or you partied with me, you were my "Friend." If I called you my friend, that meant I could trust you. Consciously, I was clueless about what a "Real Friend" was because I just wanted everyone to like me. I was the poster child for "People Pleaser." I trusted some friends I had no business trusting. In my very shallow way of thinking, I trusted you until you gave me a reason not too. (That was the dumbest idea I've ever had!)

During this time a "friend" asked me to take him to meet his cousin to pick up some money and a gift for his mom. He said he would give me $100 for my trouble and fill my car with gas in return, seemed legit, so we headed out.

I was tired and ready to go home after meeting the cousin who lived much further away than I'd originally been told. I got pulled over for speeding by a county sheriff. The officer asked for everyone's ID, and my so-called friend whispered: "don't let them search the car." It turns out he had a warrant for his arrest! When the officer asked if I had anything in the car, I told him no, I had taken my friend to pick up a vacuum cleaner for his mom and he put in the trunk. They searched the car and found 4,000 pills in that box. Thankfully, they let my daughter go, and me and my so-called friend, well, we went to jail. I was so angry and hurt that he lied and used me as a mule for his drug running. When I finally got to speak to the detectives after spending the weekend in jail, I told them the whole story and cooperated with all of their requests. My charges got knocked down, but it was still on my record.

During this time, I am just trying to hold my life together and feeling like the air is getting sucked out of me. Just six short months later another friend asked me if I would help him cash some checks because he didn't have a drivers' license or photo ID. After the last escapade, I wanted to be sure I didn't make another stupid mistake. So I called the company to verify the checks were legit, and I even got the girl at the bank to call for additional verification as well. Both responded the checks were good, so I cashed them. He gave me 10% of what the check amount was as thanks for helping out, so hey, extra income right? I did this for four different checks. I think in total my cut of the checks was roughly $1,000. A few weeks later the police come knocking on my door, and I learn there is a warrant for my arrest. I actually knew this police officer and I told him I didn't know what he was talking about. He called back to the station just to verify the warrant was for me. I asked, how do you arrest someone for cashing a check that's forged when they have no idea they were forged to begin with? He didn't disagree with me, but he had to do his job, and I got arrested…. again.

I spoke with the county sheriff after spending the weekend in jail. He made it clear he had made his own determination that I had a major drug problem and running a check cashing ring. He attempted to bully me into confessing to that story. I looked at him like he was crazy and was very direct when I told him "If you want to drug test me, go right ahead! I don't have a damn drug problem. I am not running any check cashing ring. I had no idea those checks were forged. I called to verify it was ok for me to cash them and had the cashier at the bank do the same. I will happily give you all the information you need, to get the people who did this to me, but you are not going to bully me into confessing anything that I didn't do. If that's all you came down here to do, I want an attorney and Now. Thank you and have a nice day! Our conversation is now over!" I demanded an attorney and was bailed out that night, thanks to my son and his wife.

I was appointed a public defender, and over the next year, I cooperated with the police to get my charges knocked down. During my year of court drama, I was doing my best to live something that resembled a normal life. Whatever the hell "Normal" was supposed to be. It had been so long since I experienced anything normal that I really had no idea if it was even possible anymore. I decided to attempt the online dating thing. Obviously, nobody in Birmingham was worth having, so it was time to try something different. With all the trouble I had been having for what seemed like my entire life here in Alabama, I was looking to find an escape out of this damn state. If I found a good guy somewhere else, I was out!

It wasn't long into my online search when I met this really cool dude named J'son. There was 11+ years difference in our age, but he didn't have an issue with it. I had a few concerns about the age difference because I wanted a relationship. I wasn't sure someone that much younger than me would even want a relationship with someone like me.

I will give him this, he was super persistent from the time we started talking in September, right after my second arrest, all the way to January. I never let him know he got extra brownie points for being so persistent during those first few months of chatting. There was just something different about him. I couldn't put my finger on it, but I was willing to chat with him for a little while longer to see if I could figure it out. I just knew I liked him, a lot.

Right after New Year's, he came to Birmingham from Atlanta to surprise me. He called me and told me to come pick him up on my way to go shoot pool. I was shocked and a little excited he did that. We went and had the most amazing night. We laughed, had a great time, all of my friends loved him (traders lol) and told me I needed to keep him around. I was feeling a little tipsy, and I didn't want to drive home like that, so after taking him back to his hotel, I hung out for a little while. We laughed and cut up some more while we were watching ESPN. We started cuddling, which lead to a hot make-out session, which kept me there until I had to get up to go to work the next morning. I really loved our connection from the last few months of talking and from the entire night, but I was super disappointed in myself. Spending the night with him was not my intention at all. In my mind, after the last relationship failure, I already knew how sleeping with someone on a first date turned out...Bad! In my head, I tried to justify it, to make it seem like it really wasn't the first date because we had been talking for four months.

He made many trips to see me over the following months. I really didn't want to fall in love with this man because I just didn't see any future in it, but there was something different about him, and my heart was not letting me off the hook so easily. He was living in Atlanta, and I was living in Alabama. I didn't want to do long distance since we were still just getting to know each other on a deeper level, so it was too early to consider moving there. But that thought did run across the back of my mind as it would get me the hell out of Alabama.

A few months later I lost my job at the bar-b-que place, then the house with the car to follow right behind that. I was trying to figure it all out, and I didn't know what I was going to do. This was the fourth time since 2002 that I had lost everything I owned! Now I was going to be evicted out of my home… Again! Every night I would cry myself to sleep, trying to figure out what in the hell I was going to do. I was desperately trying to hold it all together, and I knew I was failing miserably.

I moved in with my son and daughter-in-law for a few months until I could get back on my feet. That was my goal anyway. My mom and my brother were helping me sell everything out of the townhouse so I could try and at least save my car. I needed it to get to and from work. If I could work, I knew everything would be okay. They helped me sell over $900 worth of stuff out of the house in two days.

I started a new job at a steakhouse and was borrowing my son's car to get back and forth until I could get my car back. I sent my mom a text letting her know I was coming by to pick up my money on the way to work.

She answered the door, says, "Hey! What are you doing here?" I said, "I text you before I left Brad's house, I need to get that money from everything you sold, it's like $900 right? I have to go make my car payment so I can get to my car back and get everything going back in the right direction." She just looks at me like she didn't understand a word I just said. So I said it again, "Mom, come on, I need to get that money, I need to get to work." She looks me, dead in my face, and says she doesn't have it. I took a deep breath and said: "What in the Hell do you mean, You don't have it?! I Need My Money and Now! Go Get it!"

It was then I found out she had used all of the money to buy a bunch of pain pills to feed her drug habit. I was so angry I punched the window instead of punching her in the face, which was what I really wanted to do. All she could say was "This is the first time I've ever done this to you, so you will be okay." I got in the car mad as hell and went to work. My mind was now racing with how to come up with that kind of money, knowing the clock was ticking and fast. Needless to say, I didn't speak to her for a very long time after that... Again!

Then my son's car broke down, which meant I couldn't get to work, and I lost another job. So, here I was, no money coming in, living with my son, and no car or way to get to and from work (if I was to find another job that is). I was frantically looking for anything I could do to help bring money into the house. So, in the middle of the night, while everyone was asleep, I started doing webcam shows. I told myself the lie, "it's just a show, the money will make it better." I was so ashamed that I couldn't even look at myself in the mirror. I lied and told everyone I was making money playing a game online.

J'son had been coming to see me while I was living at Brad's house. We got into our first big fight not long after I lost my 2nd job since I had met him. It wasn't until then we realized we had fallen in love. We talked a lot over the following days. We ended up working it out so that we stayed together. I was so happy J'son chose to stay with me! In my mind, that was really the only positive thing that had happened in my life All Year! I talked to J'son a lot leading up to my court date. I was trying my best to stay positive, but deep down I was worried I wasn't coming back from that hearing.

My court hearing was October 10th, 2009. I had talked to J'son right before I left the house. I didn't have a phone, so all of our communication was on Yahoo messenger. My daughter-in-law, Paige, promised she would let him know what happened if I didn't get to come home. The sheriff wasn't willing to do any additional work, because they had me on video cashing the checks. So, for him and the D.A., it was a slam dunk case. When it came time for sentencing and because of my prior arrest, I could have been facing 10-20 years in prison. The judge read my case and saw I went above and beyond to give the sheriff all the information they needed to clear my name. She said she couldn't, in good consciousness, sentence me to a prison term when the judicial system failed to do their part to get to the truth of the matter. She also couldn't let me off because they did have me on camera cashing the checks. Because of that, I had to pay all of the money back from all of the checks, and I would have the additional felony on my record. In my mind, my "Fake Happy Life" was crashing down around me and fast. There was nothing else I could do about any of this, other than accept the consequences of my actions of trusting people too freely. Obviously, I liked to learn my lessons the hard way. It felt like this was becoming a way of life for me.

We were all relieved about the judge's decision to let me go home. My son and daughter-in-law had just found out they were pregnant with their second child. It was shortly after that when I moved out to give them room for the new baby.

I rented a room from my friend down in Roebuck. A few weeks later J'son came to see me, and we had another big fight. We broke up during that visit. I was so devastated and felt like my heart had just been put through a meat grinder. I put on my fake happy face each day when I went to work. Every weekend, I was out partying again, drinking and doing drugs. I cried myself to sleep every night, alone where no one could see me. I was gaining weight; I absolutely hated what I was doing and who I was becoming.

My kids were mad at me and not speaking to me from some stupid argument that I can't even remember what it was about. All I knew was that I couldn't see my granddaughters. My heart was shattered, and it felt like I had to force the air in and out of my lungs with every breath. Nobody could know I was hurting because that was a sign of weakness, so I did what I always did, put on my fake happy face for everyone to see. Get up, go to work, smile, go home, cry myself to sleep, get to the weekend, party, and do it all over again.

THESE VOICES ARE SO LOUD

If there was ever a picture in the dictionary of what miserable was supposed to look like, I was it!! I was angry all the time! I hated who I was, what I was doing, and who I had become. The voices in my head were telling me I was a horrible mother. Who was I to argue that, after all, neither of my kids were talking to me, told me they hated me, and they wouldn't allow me to see my grandchildren. In my mind, that was proof positive I was just as horrible as the voices in my head said I was. On top of the webcam shows, I was dancing at private parties to make money just not to be homeless. I was drinking and doing drugs just so I could be numb enough to even do the jobs I hated so much. I didn't want to think about the reality of the living hell I called my life!

It was right around the holidays. The voices in my head kept getting louder and louder. The only time I didn't hear them was when I was asleep. I was crying and angry all the time. I put on my best face around the few people I would allow to hang out with me. I didn't want them to know the truth about what was going on with me. I was so ashamed about everything going on in my life. I didn't know what to say to them about how I was feeling. And I definitely was uncertain about what they would say if they knew the truth about how I felt or the very real thoughts running through my head. At that time in my life, I was more worried about what everyone else thought about me because if my thoughts were this horrible, then everyone else had to believe the worst about me too!

There was this one day where I cried a lot, was throwing stuff around, arguing with myself, and then crying some more from not knowing what was going to happen next. The only time I didn't hear the voices screaming in my head was when I was asleep. I bought a bottle of sleeping pills when I was at the store earlier in the week. Sleep was not my friend these days, and that's all I wanted more than anything, to sleep! I didn't know any other way to make them stop. The sleeping pills were sitting beside my bed with a bottle of water. They were just staring at me, as if telling me it was okay, I would be saving everyone that knew me, if I just went to sleep. I told myself they didn't want me in their life anyway so they wouldn't even miss me if I was to just go to sleep and never wake up. The only time I didn't hear those voices in my head, telling me what a horrible person I was, was when I was asleep. So that was going to be my solution. I was going to go to sleep, permanently. I told myself, nobody was talking to me anyway. Nobody loved me. Nobody would ever love me again. If my kids hated me, then in my head and my very hurt heart, there was no reason to be alive anymore. Those were the **Lies** screaming inside my head.

My roommate was just going to come home and find me asleep. I didn't know how long it would take her to figure out I wasn't going to wake up. Quite honestly, at that point, I didn't care anymore. She was just using me for her own purposes anyway so why did I care about her feelings or anything else for that matter. I'm not sure how long I sat there arguing with myself. Part of me wanted to fight for my life, and the other part of me just wanted all the pain to end! It had to stop, and I didn't know any other way to make that happen.

I was sitting there, on the side of my bed, with tears streaming down my face, just staring at the bottle of pills beside my bed. I picked up the bottle of water and the phone rang. I don't know what made me look at it, but I saw it was J'son. We had not talked in a couple of months. I really didn't want to talk to him because he had hurt me, but something made me answer the phone anyway. What is odd about this is that he *never* calls anyone. He had always text me before when we were together, so I guess I answered just because it was so out of the norm for him to actually call.

Me: What do you need? I am busy right now.
J'son: What is wrong with you?
Me: Nothing. I told you I'm busy. I only answered because you never call. So, what do you want J'son? (He hated it when I called him by his name. He knew I was angry when I did that) I really don't have anything to say to you right now.
J'son: I don't know WTF is going on with you right now but you need to get your head out of your ass! You don't ever talk to me like that and I know there is something going on! You're not the woman I fell in love with and I need you to get your shit together and Now!
Me: (I was crying uncontrollably) Why are you yelling at me?!?!
J'son: Because you're not listening to me. And another thing…..

He rambled on for I don't even know how long. I cried, then he made me laugh, then I cried again

Me: you made me cry again! are you happy? Are you done now!!?
(screaming at the top of my lungs)
J'son: No I'm Not happy! No,! I'm not done and another thing….

I don't remember the rest of the conversation to be perfectly honest. Out of all of that, the only words I heard were "I LOVE YOU!" My heart was pounding uncontrollably, and my head whispered *He Loves Me.* By the end of the call, he had me calm for the first time in what seemed like months, hell, maybe even years. I wasn't crying anymore, and we even laughed a little bit. I did feel a little better, even though I didn't know why. He asked me in a gentle voice;

J'son: T, come on now, for real, what's wrong? Will you talk to me please? Let me help you. I am always here for you no matter what. I need you to know that.

Me: Actually, you already made it better, just by calling. Thank you for that.

J'son: For real T, promise me you're ok.

Me: I promise, I'm good. Thanks again for calling me ok. It means a lot.

J'son: No problem. I will always be here for you. I don't care who's in my life or yours if you need me, I'm a phone call away. You know that, right?

Me: Okay…

We hung up the phone. J'son had no idea how bad my day was nor how bad it was about to be when he picked up the phone to call me. I starred at that bottle of pills for a while and it was then I noticed that for the first time, in as long as I could remember, the voices in my head were quiet. It was the first time in Weeks (maybe even months) I didn't hear anything screaming inside my head. I was breathing normally again, and there were no more tears flowing, no feelings, no anything. There was silence in my head and in my heart. It felt like I was numb, inside and out. I know that probably sounds terrible, but it was a level up from where I was just at an hour earlier and even weeks/months before. It was then I picked up the bottle of sleeping pills and walked to the bathroom on the other side of the house. I opened the bottle and watched every single pill fall into the toilet. The tears started flowing uncontrollably down my cheeks again, one at a time, as I flushed the sleeping pills and watched them go down with the water until there was nothing left.

I don't know how long I stood there, just staring at an empty toilet. Tears were trickling down my cheeks. I'm not sure when it was that I realized my breathing was quiet and normal. There was a silence in my mind I didn't recognize. For the first time in a long time, I could actually Breathe just a little deeper. I wasn't sure what that meant, or what my next move would be, I just knew something had to change.

There may not be another phone call to save me a second time.

FIGHTING TO WANT TO LIVE!

I fought with my emotions every day. I knew the dark places were still way too close for comfort. I was nowhere close to being out of the woods. I had no idea what to do, but I knew I had to do something. It was a harsh reality to swallow knowing I was so close to ending my own life, Forever! I never wanted to feel that way again. I had a family, and even though they weren't talking to me, I knew one day we would be a family again. I was not going to give up until I made that a reality! That was the little bit of hope that sparked in my heart to keep me fighting to want to live! Even if I wasn't sure how to feel better or even if I could, I just knew I had to try, if not for me… for *them*!

I joined the gym within walking distance. I was the heaviest I had ever been in my life, including either of the times I was pregnant! I was an angry 186lbs! Angry I let myself get in that condition. Angry I was in the situation I was in, and it was all my fault. Even though I would never admit that out loud to anyone, including myself, I was blaming everyone but ME for all the Bullshit I had been through. I was playing the victim role every opportunity I got, and those around me sided with me, told me it was ok, that I had every right to feel the way I did. So, that made it easier! They didn't even know the whole truth about where I was emotionally or that I had every intention of taking my own life. It was time to put on that fake "Happy" face for everyone to see again. All they needed to know was I was tired of being FAT! They didn't ask any questions, so I didn't offer any information.

I hated looking at myself in the mirror. I had always been an athlete growing up, so I knew my way around a gym. I needed something to focus on and working out filled the gap. I had done it before, so I knew I could do it again. I started to train myself hard a couple of hours every day. Sometimes even two times a day. Then my best friend, Michelle, wanted to lose some weight too and started joining me at the gym. When my roommate saw I was really making progress and losing weight, she joined me for a few weeks too. Between the three of us, we lost almost 150 lbs. in less than three months. I went from 186 lbs, down to 135lbs. I worked out angry every day because angry felt better than sad and I knew where feeling sad lead to and I never wanted to go there again!

The gym manager asked me if I was a trainer. I told her no, I just knew my way around the gym because I had been an athlete my whole life. She told me she had several people asking for me to train them and said if I got certified, then I would have a built-in client base there at the gym. I was so surprised that I said: "I can get paid to do this? For real?" That was a light switch moment for me. I wasn't sure if I believed I could really pull it off or not, but I liked the idea of doing something where I got to keep my clothes on. It would be a real job I would be proud to tell people I was doing.

I walked home by myself that morning. All I was thinking about was the possibility of becoming a personal trainer. Michelle thought it was a great idea and said it was perfect for me! She was the only sane person in my life and I trusted her. So I did some research and found an online course that was cheap. For the first time in my life, I made a decision to do something for me. I had no idea if it was the right decision, but I knew I had to take a chance in hopes that it just might really work. I filled out the information, as my heart felt like it was beating out of my chest. I took a deep breath, closed my eyes and hit the "Finish Transaction" button to start. It was time to take the next step on my new journey.

Emotionally, I knew I wasn't out of the woods. I still didn't feel right. It felt like there was something still very wrong with me. I felt so empty and alone, even though I had people around me all the time. I may have looked really good on the outside, but on the inside, the voices were still there, even though I could tune them out sometimes, I could still hear them, and that worried me. I was still dancing, and hating what I was doing. I still felt very alone. I was drinking a LOT and still doing my party drugs on the weekends. When I was high, I did not have to face the reality of the bullshit life I had created for myself.

Me and my roommate got into a fight one weekend. I had found a club up in Huntsville to work at and was already commuting back and forth to dance at clubs up there. So, when the lease was up in Birmingham, I just went ahead and moved up to Huntsville to save the commuting. I didn't want to see anybody that I knew anyway. I had danced at a small club in Birmingham for a little while, and when people would come in that knew me, it made me sick to my stomach. I put on this fake ass happy face, got super drunk and acted like it was all fun and games. I didn't know anyone in Huntsville, so the chances were smaller of anyone I knew walking into the club. That seemed to make it a little easier to do the job I hated so much.

I lived in a hotel up there for close to a year. I kept my head down, danced, drank, did my drugs to sober up so I could make it home, slept and did it all over again. That was my cycle of life. I didn't even tell anyone my real name. I made my dance name a "real" person's name and told everyone that was it. Period. I knew a "Dancer" was not who I was on the inside. In my mind, I had a belief that if I told someone my real name, then that so-called "life" became my reality! Hell would freeze over before I let that happen! I didn't even care to remember any of the other dancer's names. I didn't want to remember any of them. I didn't care about anything but making my money and getting the hell out of there. Nothing more, nothing less!

But there was this one chic, and her name was Teresa. She was the first person to be nice to me up there. To be honest, I still didn't want to be friends with her or anyone. I was still trying, so hard, to get to the light at the end of my dark tunnel, that was so dim. I felt like I was crawling on my hands and knees through the hell I had created, toward that light, every day, one step at a time. Then, one day, I felt someone reach out and grab a hold of my soul and whisper, "You're not leaving here without taking me with you." I wasn't sure I knew how to get me out of there, how the hell was I supposed to get someone else out of there too? In my heart I knew, beyond a shadow of a doubt, she was supposed to go with me. It wasn't easy to make friends in that place, but we did. Someone needed me. I just knew she was now my only friend in there and that was ALL I needed to know.

TIME TO GET THE HELL OUT OF ALABAMA

I had been driving back and forth to see J'son almost every week. After that day with the sleeping pills, which he still knew nothing about, we had started talking again. There was something that drew me to him. He must have felt it too because he kept saying, "I don't know what it is about you; you're not like the rest." He had asked me several times in the previous weeks when I was going to move to Atlanta. In my heart, I turned that into believing he asked me to move to Atlanta to be closer to him. When in actuality, he said nothing like that at all. Did he subconsciously convey that to me, because he didn't know how to express it any other way? Maybe? I honestly don't know the answer to that question, and I didn't care to know. All I knew was he asked me to move to Atlanta, so I was following my heart, and my heart was where J'son was. April of 2011, I decided to move to Atlanta. I went and interviewed at a couple of the clubs there to see what I could find. If I got offered a job by just one club, Atlanta would become my new home, and I would be closer to my heart.

I was still studying for my personal trainer exam, or at least that was the lie I told myself, and anyone else who asked me. I said it was a lot of information and it was harder than I thought it was going to be. I said I had been out of school for a long time and my study habits were not as good as they were when I was younger. Those were the excuses I made up to convince everyone else I was studying. I said those words so much I actually think I started to believe them myself. If I am completely transparent, as I look back now, I can see I didn't have a lot of belief that I could break free from the dark world that was trying to chain me down. A very real thought was, If I didn't believe I could break free, was it even a possibility I could do it? I had no self-esteem in any area of my life, and I didn't know if I was even smart enough to pass that damn test. I bought into the thought I was too old. Plus, I wasn't sure I could make enough money to survive as a personal trainer, and I still had a lot of crazy thoughts running around in my head all the time. One thing I knew for sure was that J'son was in Atlanta. If I was there, and he was near, then I would feel safe again. I would try harder because he was there. After all, he said he loved me, right?

I moved the day after all of the tornadoes tore up Alabama on April 27, 2011. I watched funnel cloud after funnel cloud form like I was watching some sort of Sci-Fi movie. Siren after siren going off that started way before I even woke up that morning. I had worked the night before and had turned the ringer off on my phone. My daughter, Brittnie, had been calling me all morning after she watched the news. The sirens started before 10am that morning and went on until long after 11pm that night.

I went to Walmart to pick up some essentials just in case the power went off. The sirens went off while I'm inside and they rushed everyone to the designated Store Area for safety. The lights start flickering and we hear what sounds like a train on top of the building. It starts shaking, parts of the ceiling started falling, people are screaming and huddling together. I stood in the doorframe and for the 1st time in a long time I Prayed! I asked God to please get me back to the hotel safely and to save all of the people in that space with me. I told him I was trying so hard to become a better person, and I just wasn't sure if I even knew how to anymore. But could he please, just one more time, give me another chance to get it right this time. I didn't know how, I didn't know when, but I would do ALL I could to make him proud of me someday if he would just Save me…One…More…Time! The sirens stopped and I made it back to the hotel after nearly an hour in Walmart, and they said it was safe to let everyone leave. There was no power. Sirens were still going off every 10-15 min. I made the decision to just go to sleep and wait it out. Staying awake and trying to wait it out was too much for my nerves to handle at this point. I said my prayers and the rest was left in God's hands. That was the belief I chose to stand on in that moment. I had not a clue what he had in store for my life from that day forward. I just knew it had to be better than the mess I had made of my life to date.

When I woke up the next morning, I was just so thankful to still be alive. There were times during the night. I wasn't sure what would happen. I only hoped that when the sun came up in the morning, I would be opening my eyes to a new day. I made peace with whatever my fate would be that night. I was giving up trying to control things I knew I could do nothing about. It was time to hit the reset button on my life and hope there was something better on the other side.

The sun was coming through the blinds, shining on my face. I felt the warmth as I started rubbing my eyes as I was waking up. I laid there for a minute and realized, there were no more sirens going off. I made it through the night! I was Alive! To me, that was a sign something better was coming, even if it was a faint sign, it was still a sign. After all, when you're at rock bottom, you only have two directions you can go. I can either use it to catapult me to a new level, or I can wallow in my own self-pity and slither along on the floor sideways and keep recreating the life I'm currently living. To me, recreating the Bullshit I had in my life was not an option. I wanted something different. It was time to see if leaving this state, that had shown me nothing but hurt, pain, and sorrow would change my current circumstances. I didn't know if it would or not, but I truly believed if I stayed in this God-forsaken state, that I would Die! And I knew I desperately wanted to Live!

The power was out when I woke up, so I found something that didn't require cooking so I could eat really quick, then loaded everything that would fit into my car. Atlanta, Here I come. I drove the long way through Birmingham because I knew the back roads would be impassible after listening to the reports on the radio of how bad the destruction from the tornadoes had been. Plus I wanted to make sure I could get gas when I needed it. All of the stations in Huntsville that were lucky enough to have power were sold out of gas. Cullman had reported over 30 tornadoes that day. Phil Campbell got leveled. Athens looked like a war zone. The devastation I saw as I drove down I-65 South headed towards Birmingham, was not only mind-blowing, it was heart-wrenching. I heard story after story on the radio of towns that were completely wiped out. Families who lost everything. Loved ones that would never get to hug the ones they loved again. There were a lot of tears that fell as I drove all those hours, running away from all the pain I felt. Not from the tornadoes that day, but from the life-long hurt, I went through from the day I set foot in this state. I was headed to a town I knew nothing about and prayed the next chapter would be better than the last.

I had a lot of thoughts running through my head (and heart) as I was on this long drive and they were on, what seemed to be, a never-ending loop. I lived through the night with tornadoes dropping all around me. I see all this devastation and wonder why I was one of the survivors? How did I deserve to live, with the life I was living? What was the purpose in me still being here? Did I have a purpose for being on this earth at all? I didn't have answers to any of those questions. The one thing I did know was that I was on my way to Atlanta. I had lived in Alabama for 33+ years! That is ALL I had known my whole life! I was 11 when I moved there in 1978, and now I'm in my 40's, driving with Everything I could fit in my car, to Atlanta, Ga. A new state where I knew 1 person; J'son! That was it! I had a job in a strip club on the south side of town. It was a bikini bar, so that made me feel a little better even though it was still the same atmosphere of dancing. I just had a little more clothes on, that was all.

I told myself, this is my chance! I was going to be somewhere that nobody knew me and I could start over. I would make the changes I so desperately wanted and needed to make. I just had to keep going. I had to keep my sight focused on that little glimmer of light off in the distance. The one I believed that if I reached it, I would change my stars! I would change the legacy of my family to something I would be proud of. J'son was there, and he was my safe space. He would be just a phone call away. I just needed to stay focused and hold my shit together!!

It took me over five hours to get there. I was so happy to be out of Alabama and closer to J'son. I hustled my ass off for two months after moving to Atlanta and moved into my own apartment! I was so excited!! I finally had something to call my own! I felt better not living in a hotel anymore. I was still dancing, and the alcohol and drug use wasn't any better if anything they were getting worse, but I was alive, and I was out of Alabama. I knew I was not studying like I needed to be. I still wasn't sure I could pass that damn test to become a trainer. The lie I kept telling myself was that I was "okay." The trouble was, there were nights I didn't remember driving home. I woke up in my bed, sometimes with all of my clothes still on. The door was locked, and everything was in its place, but I had zero memory of the drive home, which was not cool at all. Something had to give man.

Despite how much I had hoped for it, me and J'son were not a couple. Even though I thought after I moved there, we would move toward that goal. It just didn't seem like that was going to happen. Since I was finally in my own place, and feeling a little more secure, I decided to be more active in the online dating scene and joined a site called Tango. It was interesting, and there were games available to interact with other members, like buying other people's profiles as your pets. They also had one called the *Match Game*. I think this was probably how the idea of Tinder and the whole "Swipe Right" thing came about. In this particular game, it was either a "Match" or "No." I rarely, if ever, played the Match Game. There was one Sunday night though when I was mindlessly playing in the app when I decided to see what came up. I was painfully aware of how single I was, so I thought; why not? I started clicking, and about the third click, there was this tall, gorgeous, light skinned guy who was built like a brick house, smiling up at me. I couldn't hit Match fast enough, even before I went and stalked his profile to see what he was all about! I was like WOW! I thought, even if we don't click, he sure is pretty to look at!

After clicking, I went and fixed me something to drink. When I got back to my laptop, I had a "You have a Match" on my screen and an immediate Inbox from him. We chatted on there for a few minutes then migrated to Yahoo Messenger. We chatted and laughed for hours. Before I knew it, it was 1:30am. He had to go to work and I was tired. He wouldn't let me off of there until I gave him my phone number though. Then he had to text me to see if it was my real phone number. I can't explain what I was feeling, but it was fun and more exciting than the singleness that was weighing me down, so I went with it.

I woke up to a *Good Morning Gorgeous* text from him. That was something new for me. He was at work but on my phone ALL morning long. I felt like a high school girl with a crush on the star quarterback. I got up the nerve and asked him if he wanted to meet in person since we were clicking so well already. I really didn't see any point in wasting time, if we met and the chemistry was not as good in person, then we would be done. He agreed, and we planned a date at a local sports bar that night.

Let me tell you, I was so nervous and had a stomach full of butterflies! I didn't know what to think about all of that. J'son was the only other person that had made me feel that way. I had all of these emotions going on inside still where he was concerned, but I knew I needed to push them to the side and I had to do this for me. This was something new for me. I had always put other people first and put my needs to the side. So, I wasn't sure how it would turn out, but I knew if I didn't go, there would be no way to find out. I put on my favorite pair of Miss Me Jeans, a cute top, and some sandals to show off my awesome pedicure. Every hair was in place, and my makeup was flawless. I wore my favorite cologne, Dolce & Gabbana's Light Blue, to top it off.

We were scheduled to meet at 5:30pm, but I didn't want to get stuck in traffic, and I wanted to have a glass of wine (or three) before he got there to calm the butterflies, so I got to the restaurant around 4:30pm and sat up at the bar. I chatted it up with the bartender and told her about my blind date, and I didn't expect there to be any issues but still asked if there was an escape route for me if something went wrong. She laughed and said yes, there was a way to go out the back and she would make sure I was safe. I text Dee, my hot date, and told him that I got there early to avoid traffic and to take his time and I would see him soon. He laughed because I was over an hour early. I still felt like this little high school girl going out on her first date. I had no idea what to expect, but I hoped he at least looked like in his pictures. Then, if his personality was anything close to what I had experienced over the last 24 hours, this was going to be a win in the dating world for me!

The other guys I had met were not looking for anything serious. I wanted so desperately to be loved and to feel loved. I wanted someone that wanted to be with only me and who wanted to spend time with me because there was no place else they would rather be. I wasn't sure that even existed anymore, not for a girl like me anyway. A girl from Alabama, who was a stripper, who was always "trying" to pass a personal trainer certification…"someday"… to get her out of the dancer life. Deep down I still had some pretty big doubts of that ever happening.

Dee responded: "Hey Beautiful! I'm stuck in traffic, but I'm less than 10 minutes away!" I chugged what was left of my wine and touched up my makeup right there at the bar. I ordered another glass. My heart was racing 900mph. I thought to myself "WTF is wrong with you?! It's just some dude! He's probably just like all the rest anyway! Chill out already!" I took a deep breath, and I just waited.

I was facing the window so I could see him walk up. I heard the door open and turned around, and there he stood! Holy shit! He was 6'4" with shoulders as wide as half a football field, this big beautiful smile, and ALL eyes on *me*! I really had to catch my breath when I saw him because he was so gorgeous! He walked straight to me, gave me a huge bear hug and said "Wow! Your pictures don't even come close to how beautiful you really are baby!"

We sat at the bar and talked for a while, then moved to a booth, ordered some food and laughed… A Lot. It felt like we had known each other forever. I really just didn't know what to think, other than I wanted to know more! The connection and chemistry were undeniable. He was a perfect gentleman and had this deep, sexy voice that just melted me from the inside out. He was funny, had a great job, his own house, and a car! All the things I said I wanted in my next mate. I had a fleeting thought "What did I do to deserve this perfect specimen of a man?" I wasn't sure what would happen next, but I was willing to take a chance to find out.

Our relationship moved super-fast. We talked every day, several times a day in fact. I woke up to text messages from him every morning, and I talked to him on the phone every night before I went to bed. He knew I was a dancer and he didn't bat an eye about it. He said he understood I was working toward something better and if that's what I needed to do until I passed my test, then he was okay with it. It was right then I had a gut check. This man right here didn't judge me by what I was doing. He didn't assume that because I was a stripper, I was tricking out of the club, like so many of the girls did.

He said he trusted me. Wow! Who was this man and where did he come from? Was he for real? Did he really believe the words that were coming out of his mouth? Was this a trick to get me to let my guard down? All of these thoughts felt like they ran through my head simultaneously and probably about 1000 times more.

He seemed to accept me for who I was and that made me want to be a better person. If I am honest with myself (and all of you reading this right now), I didn't accept me and hated who I was! I knew If I didn't do something to change, I could quite possibly lose the only man who had shown me something that resembled "LOVE." At least what I thought love was supposed to look and feel like! So, I made the decision to really dig into studying for my personal trainer exam. In February 2012, I interviewed for a trainer position, and they hired me pending passing my exam. They asked me when I was scheduled to take it, and I bold face lied and said it was on March 8th. I had not even looked at a calendar to see what day that was or even if there were any spots available to take it on that day. I had to give them something, so I did.

When I got home, I looked up all the exam dates, places and times available. I took my exam on March 8, 2012, just like I had told them, but I drove to Birmingham because all of the test centers in Atlanta were full until April. I was so nervous when I pulled up to the test center that morning. My test was scheduled for 10 am. I had three hours to answer 150 questions. I had no idea if I was ready to pass that test! I had prepared the best I could and now it was show time! I honestly thought I would have to throw up before I walked in there.

I walked into the room, sat down at my cubicle in front of a computer that would decide my fate in the next 3 hours. Would I change my life today or was I destined to remain the sad, pitiful person I had grown to be? My hands were shaking so much it was hard to type. I think I read every multiple-choice question 10 times before I answered. My heart was pounding so hard in my chest I thought I might actually have some bruised ribs and I was sweating as if I'd just worked out for two hours.

It only took me 90 minutes to finish the test. I thought I had done something wrong because I finished so fast. I started going back through my answers again, and something just told me, "You're done Tammy, it's okay to get up now." I hit the finish button, desperately watching the screen and waiting to see my score as it was supposed to pop up immediately after the test. I needed to have a score of 70% in order to pass.

The screen was blank! I just stared at the screen with my stomach in my throat! I walked out of the room and I asked the girl at the testing center three times if I'd passed. I told her the screen was blank. She showed me on her screen, and I burst into tears right there on the spot! It was at that moment I KNEW, beyond a shadow of a doubt, I had just changed my life forever!

I called my daughter, Brittnie, as soon as I walked out of the room, full of tears! I am not even sure she was able to understand a word that came out of my mouth! All I know that I said clearly was "I Did It! I Passed! I am officially a Certified Personal Trainer Now!!"

I had been talking to my son, Bradley, about all of the changes I was making to become a better person. I let him know I wasn't dancing anymore; I was going to be a personal trainer. I had my own apartment, a car and everything in my life was getting better! I told him I would really love if we could get together someday soon and start over with a clean slate. I was willing to do whatever I could to make that happen. I missed him, Paige and Brantlee so much. I met Bradley and his whole family for lunch where I got to meet my beautiful, amazing grandson, Cruce, for the first time! I also got to see my oldest granddaughter, Brantlee! She ran and jumped in my arms, screaming GG when she saw me walk in. I hugged my son so tight I thought I would stop breathing. Then I did the same with Paige and told each how much I loved them.

My life was truly changing for the better! I can honestly say, I did not know the magnitude of what I had just done for myself. I knew going back to that dark life was not an option! This was the first real positive movement where I consciously realized I had control over what happened in my life.

I was headed home to Atlanta! I was so damn Happy man! I don't know how many tears fell that weekend, but there were a lot! For the 1st time in a long time, they were happy tears! No sadness, no hurt, just tears of joy and happiness. This was a new feeling for me. I had not felt this way in so long it was strange. For a change, it felt good to have those tears fall this time. I texted Dee and said "I Did It Baby! I passed my Test! It's Official! Ya Girl is a Certified Personal Trainer!!!"

Of course, he was happy for me too! He knew how hard I had been studying. I had really been working at it and was up all hours of the night and then getting up early and right back at the books. As I learned something new, I would share it with him. He would always respond by saying he was proud of me and he knew I would make an excellent personal trainer.

I even texted J'son and told him I passed, but I wasn't sure what he would say or if he would even respond. He was still my friend, and he meant a lot to me even though I don't think he was aware of how much he was still a part of my heart. He had no idea what he did for me on the dark day he called me. If I wanted anyone to be proud of me, it was him. He had seen me in the darkest time of my life, that nobody (not even him) knew about. Deep down, I needed him to be proud of me. It was almost immediately after I sent the text when I got his response "Good job! I knew you would do it!" but no "I'm proud of you." Then my thoughts start spinning out of control with "What does that even mean?" I had to shake my head. He said he knew I would do it which means he believed in me. That's kind of the same thing. I don't even know why it matters, Dee is proud of me, and he is my man now, so quit fucking worrying about him!

The Monday morning after I passed my test, I started my new job at Snap Fitness. I proudly walked into my new future, and I walked away from all the darkness, money, drugs, alcohol and the dancing world and I never looked back. I didn't care what I had to do, but I was never going back to that life. I knew if I was going to continue to become a better person, not only for myself but for my children and my grandchildren, I was going to have to change Me!

I wasn't sure what changes I needed to make, or if I even knew how to do it. Deep down I knew I needed to start with getting back in church. I asked my son, Bradley, if he would help me find a church like the one we had attended together in Birmingham. He suggested looking online for churches that were non-denominational and come as you are. After I researched several choices, I sent him my top three and we settled on Cumberland Community Church. It wasn't far from where I lived, and they had the same principles listed on their website as our old church back home. Bradley suggested I go visit the church for a couple of services to see how I liked it. If it didn't feel good, we would keep searching until we found me a good church that I could call home. I was so excited that Bradley was helping me with finding a church home in Atlanta. He was really involved with the church back home and loved working with the youth groups.

I was excited and knew with all my heart this was the next step in my journey. It was time to get my heart and soul right again. I wasn't even sure what that meant or what it would take. Quite honestly, I wasn't sure God was going to want me back after the life I had lived, especially with the darkness of the last 5 years. That was a very real thought in my heart, and it terrified me to think I could be right. I had made a promise to God the night of the tornadoes, and I was going to keep it.

4 GOD HAD A BIGGER PLAN

The first Sunday I planned to go, I locked my keys in the house! I had to call a locksmith to get me into the apartment and obviously missed the church services that day. I was super frustrated with the whole situation, but I didn't let it get me down. Instead, I found Joel Osteen on TV to watch instead. I chose to believe there was a reason things happened, even if I didn't understand it at the time. The next week when I got to the church there was no one there because they were doing what they called "FIA," or Faith in Action, weekend. They were out in the community doing things for God. I went home a little disappointed and more than a little frustrated after a second failed attempt to go to this church. I told Satan, "You are NOT going to stop me from going to church!"

Luckily, week number three I finally got to go inside the church, which was way bigger than what I was used to. I wasn't sure how I felt about it being such a large church but, I was here, and I wasn't leaving until after service was over. I was nervous and excited all at the same time. I knew absolutely nobody there. I walked up the stairs to the front door, and when I walked in, I felt like I was at home! People were walking around; some were chatting after the previous service had ended as others came in for the next service milling around and were joining the conversations.

They didn't seem very friendly from my initial observation, but in all honesty, it was probably just my perception because of the insecurity I felt about being there in the first place. I knew this was going to be a new experience with me stepping out of my comfort zone, in a new place, and a new town. I didn't know anyone here and this place was Huge compared to my other tiny church back home in Birmingham. In my mind I was saying to myself "just smile and act like you belong here, nobody will say anything to you, and you can get out of here as soon as service is over." I was very nervous and unsure of what to say to anyone, even if they had tried to talk to me. I just wanted to be there, in church, close to where God lived. I believed at the time that he lived in the church and we went there to be with him. I wanted to see how it felt to be in his presence and if I would feel different once there or if I would even feel anything at all. I was excited and terrified all at the same time. I had to keep telling myself I wasn't leaving until service was over! Period. I walked up to the coffee stand and fixed a cup of coffee before I walked into the sanctuary. I felt like getting back in a church was what I was "supposed" to do, whether this was the right church or not, it was the right one for today.

I sat down in the back, the music started, and I almost burst into tears right there. I knew God had a plan for me right then and there. I was excitedly terrified at what was going to happen next in my life. I was ashamed of who I was and who I had become, and I had run from him for so long. I really didn't think I deserved to be in his presence or that I was worthy of his love at all, but he showed me something more. From that chair in the back of that huge church full of strangers, he showed me forgiveness, grace, and mercy! He shined a light into the dark room I called my soul. He didn't say anything, he just shined the light and waited for me to take the next step toward him and what he had in store for me. I knew his path had to be better than the one I had been traveling. I didn't know how easy or hard it would be, but I had just enough faith and hope that it would somehow be better.

Week after week, I was on the altar crying and asking for forgiveness and cleansing. I wanted to finally be free from all of the nasty, negative voices inside my head. In August the pastor preached on Philippians 3:13-14 about letting go of the past and moving forward toward the future. When he read that verse out loud, I burst into tears right there in my seat, and I knew that was my sign!

I made the conscious decision to rededicate my life to Christ! I gave my purse and phone to the friends I was sitting with, walked down to the altar, said the prayer again, walked up on stage and got baptized right on the spot!!! It was one of the most freeing days I had experienced in my spiritual journey while taking steps to make a better life for myself! When I came up out of the water, it was like I was filled with a new kind of Air I had not experienced before. It felt like Freedom! I felt Weightless! For the first time in my life, I felt like my life was going to be Different! It was going to be Better! I didn't know how it was going to change, I just knew that life as I knew it, was about to change for the better. And that my friends, was what

Freedom meant to me at that very moment! I was walking away from the Past and Creating a Bright New Future!

The next week after service was over, I asked the pastor to put me with a mentor. I had learned from past experiences, going to different churches over the years, where all they did was hand you a Bible, pat you on the back and say good luck on your new journey. I knew I wanted to do it right this time, even though I didn't know what that truly meant. I just knew I didn't want to try and figure it out on my own. I knew my way of thinking took me down paths I didn't want to travel ever again. I knew if I wanted to grow in my faith, I needed someone to guide me. I wanted someone who knew God, who was experienced in prayer and knew how to teach me how to study the bible. I wanted to make God proud of me! (For a split second I had a thought "There's that phrase again, what is that? Why do I keep saying I want someone to be proud of me? Who cares?")

He put me with this awesome woman named Michelle! Ironically, that was my best friends name, so I just knew this was going to be an amazing connection. I felt myself growing stronger emotionally and especially spiritually week after week as we continued to study and talk through the Bible lessons. I cleared away more hurts and found some more forgiveness I was unaware I needed. The biggest part of the forgiveness that was given was for me! When I had found out about the childhood sexual abuse by my mother, I was taught by my old pastor forgiveness isn't an emotion, it's a "Decision." I didn't think about me needing to forgive myself for anything or that I needed to make the decision to do so. I learned there is a beautiful power in making a conscious decision to forgive myself. I had to learn to accept that we are all human. We make choices that take us down paths we probably wouldn't have chosen, had we known the outcome ahead of time. Without those crooked roads, we wouldn't grow into the person we needed to be in order to complete our purpose here on this earth.

I talked to my son Bradley, and I told him I never wanted to go back down that dark road I was once on and asked what books he recommended to help me become a better me. He gave me several to start with. One of them was about learning to pray and how it works by Doug Sheets. The other one (seriously life changing for me!) was The Traveler's Gift and Mastering the Seven Decisions by Andy Andrews. Both of these books changed my life forever! I will share more details a little later on in my story, about how digging into personal development and self-growth was pivotal in me becoming the person I am today.

FINDING FREEDOM THROUGH FORGIVENESS

I continued working with my mentor, Michelle, and we did a weekly bible study to help me gain a better understanding of the Bible. She also opened my eyes to things in my life I had not previously confronted. It was during this study I truly grasped that I could not conquer what I would not confront. One thing I carry with me, even today, and share with anyone willing to listen is that Forgiveness is the Key that unlocks the door to the Freedom of your Future.

I clearly remember the day we were sitting on my couch during our bible study and Michelle had our session on forgiveness all planned out. I had already shared my past sexual abuse story with her and about my mom. I don't think either of us was completely prepared for what happened next.

After reading the scriptures we were studying that week, we got to the discussion questions. Michelle asked if I'd forgiven the people who had hurt me in my life, especially those involved with my childhood abuse? I said "Yes. It was something I did a long time ago and continue to do. It was the only way I had found any sort of peace in my life that had allowed me to move forward. It also allowed me to have a relationship with my mother, which I didn't think would be possible at one point in time."

Then she asked me if I knew that God had forgiven me for the things I'd done in my life. I said, absolutely! She looked at me curiously and asked how did I know?

I felt something welling up inside me, where I was almost defensive for some reason. I said "If he had not forgiven me, I might not even be alive right now. I for sure would not be in this apartment, my utilities would not be on, and I would most likely be homeless on the streets. The truth of the matter is, since I quit dancing, I haven't made enough money as a trainer to pay for this apartment. I owe over $5000 in back rent to my landlord at the moment. I have told him what I was doing, and he agreed to work with me. In my mind, that is all God. I don't know of any other landlord on the face of the planet that is going to let someone stay in his apartment and not get paid, especially to the tune of thousands of dollars that I don't know that I will ever be able to pay at this rate. I haven't been evicted, my utilities haven't been cut off, I don't have a car, but I make it to work every day. I have food on the table, and I never miss church. The only answer in my mind for this is that it's All by the grace of God."

Then she said something I'll never forget. "Wow! I had no idea you had all of that going on. Well, let me ask you one more question. Have you forgiven yourself for the things you've felt that you did wrong?"

It was at that moment it felt like someone had opened up the flood gates in my eyeballs!! I immediately broke down into uncontrollable, sobbing! She was shocked! Hell, we both were! She did her best to try to console me, but the truth was, I thought the things I had put myself through with the choices and decisions I had made, were unforgivable. That's what I believed in my heart anyway.

I can look back now and see there really are no wrong decisions. People make choices based off of where they are mentally and emotionally at that moment. Sometimes those choices lead to places we don't like and to experiences we'd rather not have had. But, without those experiences, then we wouldn't be who we are today. They shaped us, me, into the awesome people we, I have become. Each one got me one step closer to my purpose in this life. Once I realized I had not forgiven myself, the healing process truly began. In all honesty, I was unaware of what a huge step this truly was at the time I went through it. After she left, I went into the bathroom, looked myself in the mirror and said the following words out loud!

"Tammy, I forgive you! I forgive you for all of the stupid shit you've ever done in your life. For all of the people you hurt and the paths, you went down that put

your life in danger. Tammy, I love You! I Love you just the way you are. You are human, and it's okay because we all make mistakes. Tammy, I am so very proud of you for making it this far! You are a beautiful work in progress and everything is going to be okay. From here on out you are going to do everything you can to make the rest of your life better than it has been before today. You can do this! I Love You!"

I want to take a break from the story momentarily to ask you a few questions and for you to do this same mirror exercise for yourself. If you have never in your life, looked at yourself in the mirror and said the words out loud: I forgive you, I love you, and I am proud of you, then you don't know what real emotional healing truly is!! I want to challenge you to take just 5 minutes right now to go say one (or all three of those statements) while looking at yourself in the mirror.

Be open to the emotions when they come and let them flow! Then really feel the freedom that results from within your soul when all the tears have faded away. You will sleep better than you probably have ever slept in your entire life. I can tell you this, most likely, will not be an easy exercise to say just one of those statements. But, what I can promise you is, if you will use the courage I know you have inside you, and say the words "I Love You" or "I forgive you" and/or "I'm Proud of You", that you will change your circumstances and your future beyond anything you can possibly imagine.

Now let's get back to the story…

I even went deeper into the forgiveness by reaching out to some of my close friends I'd said things to that hurts my heart to even think about now. Actually, I don't even know how they are still my friends today. I was journaling *all* the time back then, it was the only way for me to find some kind of peace most days, so I had a written record of the hurtful things I had said or done. When I went back through my journal, I broke down in tears again, and I knew I had to give them a formal apology. All of them were so understanding and thought I was being silly for even saying anything. Some were even agitated with me because they didn't want me re-living those experiences. One of them in particular, J'son, said forgiveness was a blanket around me from him and he never wanted to hear about it again because I was not that person anymore. End of story. My friends are pretty freaking awesome, even if I do say so myself.

Was that all there was to my forgiveness? Absolutely not! I had some really rough days where I had to push through the negative thoughts and self-talk. I cried a lot and wrote in my journal sometimes 2-3 times a day to let it all out. My best friends, J'son, Teresa, Michelle & LaTaunya, were my safe places. When I needed to talk, cry, scream, yell, pray or whatever, they all had their role in getting me to where I needed to be. They all were invested in my life to make sure that forward was the only direction I was going. To each of them, I will be forever grateful on a level I don't think they will completely comprehend! #FriendsToTheEnd

LETTING GO OF ME

When I say "Letting Go of Me," I mean the person I had become over my 44 plus years of living. I was always a smart kid in school. I never had to try very hard to make A's and B's. I was great at sports. I was good at lifting weights. I was good at fighting. I was good at working. That is all I had ever done.

I knew my current way of thinking and me being "ME" had lead me to where I was, and I wasn't too proud of the person I had become. My kids were grown, and now I had grandchildren. I wanted all of them to be proud of me. I wanted them to love me unconditionally without having to think about it. I didn't want them to be ashamed to introduce me to their friends or invite me over for family functions. And quite honestly, if I were them back then, I wouldn't have wanted me around very often, if at all. That really made my heart hurt, caused a lot of tears and was probably the biggest catalyst to the deep seeded desire I had to want to change my life for the better. I put on a good front for the outside world, but inside I was still very broken, and I wasn't sure how or if I could fix it.

When I was in school, I could follow directions and do extremely well at whatever it was I set my mind to. Now, however, I had to be my own teacher. I had to teach myself how to be a better me. Talk

about scaring the hell out of yourself! Sheesh! I had gotten myself here and now I had to figure out how to make it better on my own by reading and applying things out of books. I had to hold myself accountable. I had to grade myself. I had to be brutally honest with myself and say "Tammy, you Pass" or "Tammy you fail!"
I wasn't sure what to expect, much less, what I was doing when I decided to start reading the personal development books. I had absolutely no idea what would happen or better yet, If anything would happen, that would make my future better than my past. The only thing I did know, was the way that I'd been doing things, got me results I didn't like. I'm not sure if at that time if I had heard the saying, "If you want things to change then you have to change" or "You can't keep doing the same thing and expect a different result." I just knew I was willing to try something different in hopes that where I was headed was going to be better than the hell I was emerging from.

This was my first experience with personal development without going to a school where someone else was telling me what to do and how to do it. Failing in school was never an option, so failing now really wasn't an option! The only report card I had was this thing called life! I was either going to be a success in life, or I was going to fail and repeat the same stupid mistakes over again and never be anything better than who my mother was to my brothers and me. That in itself was enough motivation to go all in and do everything I could to become the best mom, GG (grandmother), friend, personal trainer and entrepreneur that my imagination could inspire in me. Looking back at my life then, my imagination was not very imaginative. I had small dreams at that time, but they were dreams none the less, and they were a start! Even though they were small, they felt huge to me at the time. Not dreaming, not having a vision, and not planning for the future almost killed me! So, dreaming of any kind, no matter how small, felt good! I learned from all of this, and now I like to tell my clients; crawl until you can walk, walk until you can run and when you can run, run as fast and as far as you can! I've been there. I understand. I'm their biggest fan!

Everyone has different triggers that motivate them to push through hard times. My biggest triggers were I didn't want to be like my mom or that I wanted my children to be proud of me. My children never experienced any of the childhood traumas I endured growing up, and if I accomplished nothing else in this life, that was a win I was proud of. My children loved me, but there were a lot of times; they were not so proud of me, and I desperately wanted that to change. Growing up it was my mom's belief that you work as hard as you can, pay your bills on time (when you can), make sure the kids have what they need, and when you retire, you live off of social security until you die. She never had any kind of savings. I don't know if she ever even considered it. I do know she lived with a lot of fear; fear of flying, fear of trying new things, fear of dying alone, etc. Any time I wanted to do something new, she had a fear she wanted to share about it. She lived inside a box her whole life man. She was never able to break free from her self-imposed prison and I didn't want to be like any of that.

No matter how uncomfortable an emotion, thought, situation or circumstance was to deal with, I told myself I was not going to be my mother! So, I would do WTF ever I had to do to make that shit happen! There were good days and bad days, but once I started, I never looked back! I was peeling away the layers of the onion that was my soul, hoping and praying when I reached the center, there was going to be a whole new me for the world to see. Most of all, I was going to make my family proud of me. I was going to be proud of me …someday.

Learning how to pray, for me at least, was an important part of my journey. I felt like I was doing it wrong. When in all honesty, there isn't really a wrong way to pray, so long as you do. Prayer is about belief, sincerity and being thankful/grateful for the grace given to us within our prayer. At least that is my belief. I'm not here to debate spiritual beliefs or what not. So, as I mentioned earlier, I started with the Doug Sheets book "Authority in Prayer" all about learning how to pray. It was a small book and it was an easy read. I read that book with a highlighter and a pen in hand. I was underlining and highlighting anything that was important (which was almost the entire book when I was done lol). I was engulfed in learning everything I could about how to pray. When I had questions, I was on the phone with my son, Bradley. He had given me the book and was really open to helping me develop spiritually. I was so thankful for him and for all his patience with me. He wanted me to "want" to pray, which I believe made it easier for him to invest so much time, love and attention to what I was learning. For the first time in a long time, I felt good on the inside! Things were waking up inside me that I am not sure I had ever felt before. I wasn't sure what all this meant, but what I did know, was that I felt better than I had in a really long time!

I was so excited and loved all the new information. I was feeling closer to God with each day, and I was really starting to feel him during my prayers. I was praying for friends and things were happening. My best friend, Teresa, would call me and ask if I'd been praying for her that day because she could feel it, or something would happen that let her know I was in focused prayer about her.

I truly believe starting here is where the foundation was laid for all the successes that followed. Did everything become easy when I started praying? Absolutely Not! Did I have hard days and challenges? Yes I did! Are all of my days perfect now? No they're not! But I can tell you I have fewer hard days now because I had learned how to guide myself in a way where those challenges no longer ran my life and beat me up like they used to. I see challenges as opportunities to grow instead of thinking "why is this happening to me?" which was a phrase I used very often in my life before now.

I want to take just a moment to share a time with you from our 24/7 prayer week at church. I was so excited about having the sanctuary all to myself for an hour to be with God. It was my first ever experience of this kind, so I was stoked, to say the least. I scheduled three days during that week to go! After reading Doug Sheets book, and learning in church that 3-5am was prime time for talks with God, I made my first day at 3am, my second day at 4am and my last day was on Saturday at 5am. They had prayer stations set up all around the sanctuary for everyone to pray at. As I said, this was new to me, so I really didn't know what to expect. I just knew I had to be there.

I walked around to each of the prayer stations, read what they were for, said a quick prayer and moved on to the next one. Near the stage was a ladder covered with index cards, each one had written prayers and/or goals from the people of the community, and each step had a designated time frame (1 year all the way up to 20 years). I read some of the cards and was very moved by what was written. I just put my hands on the ladder to pray with the people who had written these cards and I had this feeling come over me that physically moved me. I had tingling all over my body and was light-headed, and yet I felt so at peace at the same time. I had no idea what to think, so I just went to the altar and finished praying, full on tears streaming down my cheeks, but amazingly I still felt at peace. Then I went back home and got ready for work. The next day I asked all my friends if they wanted me to pray for anything while I was at church. They gave me some things to pray about and I finished off with some prayers of my own. I cried as I prayed and again, I was filled with this beautiful peace. Then Saturday was when I had an amazing realization that God truly had a plan for me. That morning I walked straight to the altar, took communion, grabbed a whole box of tissues, and sat down in my usual spot to pray. I said "*God, I am not here to ask you for anything this morning, only to thank you for allowing me to be in your presence and hearing my prayers during our last two sessions together. I just want to be in your presence and soak you in this morning.*"

I sat there in silence for a few minutes. Then I started getting all of these messages in my head. What I now like to call 'downloads' when I get them. I had very specific messages for my friend Teresa, my son Bradley, my daughter in law Paige, my friend LaTaunya, my daughter Brittnie and my friend Michelle. He was telling me to text them right then. I silently argued I would text them when I leave. I felt the urgency in the words, "No, Now!"

My next memory was looking up and seeing the next person walking in for their time. There was a stack of Kleenex beside my feet, and tears streaming down my face. I looked at my phone to check for messages to see if I had been texting, but I saw none. It was all so strange to me at the time, so I blew it off, cleaned up my snot rags and went home.

A couple of hours later I got a text from my son. He said, "Mom, what were you doing at the church at 5am, on a Saturday?" I reminded him it was 24/7 prayer and it was my last day to have my hour in the sanctuary. He asked me how I knew about what I had texted him and Paige about that morning? I was confused and asked what he was talking about as I hadn't sent them texts.

He simply sent me a screenshot showing I sent them both a very clear message, and it showed it was from me, but those messages were not on my phone. I told him about my experience at the church that morning. Then I got calls from Teresa & LaTaunaya. Again, messages about things that there was No Way, I could know anything about. Again, they were NOT on my phone. That day I realized I am a messenger and I have a very special Gift. I wasn't sure why I had it, what I was supposed to do with it, or even If it was really real, but it was too beautiful to ignore. At that moment I had no fear, only peace. The proof was right in front of me and all of the people that were closest to me.

NEW LIFE LOADING…. PLEASE STAND BY

After I finished "Authority in Prayer," I picked up my next assignment for my personal growth. That was "*The Travelers Gift, Mastering the Seven Decisions*" by Andy Andrews. I liked the fact that The Travelers Gift was a fictional story with a purpose. It too was an extremely easy book to read. Once I picked it up, I wasn't able to put it down. If I stopped reading it at all, it was only because I fell asleep with it on my chest. I could so relate to the lead character, David Ponder. I was in the dark place he was in for a very long time. It was still very fresh in my mind and still a little too close for comfort. I wasn't 100% sure I could keep myself from the shadows if I didn't stay focused on what was in front of me. I believe with everything within me, that is why I was so caught up in this book.

After I finished The Traveler's Gift, I started the workbook "Mastering the Seven Decisions." I thought this would be a super simple process. After reading the Traveler's Gift, I had the gist of what was going on. I understood why all of these things were important. I knew I could make those changes. Man, was I in for a rude awakening lol.

I started with the first decision, the Responsible Decision. That meant taking responsibility for my life and taking responsibility for where I was and quit blaming my past for my current circumstances. I felt that was exactly what I was doing by reading the book and putting the principles into action.

If I am 100% transparent, when I went through all of the exercises in that chapter, I wasn't all in. I was very topical with answering the probing questions. I wasn't taking 100% responsibility for my past or the things that had happened to me. Nor had I taken full responsibility for the choices and/or decisions I had made in my life that had me in the position I was in. Did I do enough to create change? Yes I did! But it wasn't until I started Teaching these principles that I realized I had not played full on the first time around.

Fast forward a few weeks, to when I finished Mastering the Seven Decisions. I can honestly say I completed all of the exercises at the level of comprehension I was consciously able to during that time in my life. Afterward, I found myself more excited about life. I wanted to set goals and make plans so that I could make them happen. I was 44 years old and had never consciously set a goal in my life until I finished this book! What was more amazing to me was that I was excited about life, my goals, where I was going, what I had planned, etc. I shared with everyone I came across what I had planned and God was helping me do it. I didn't even care about opinions of whether or not they thought I could accomplish them. I was excited about life and I was going to scream it from the rooftops. I don't know how I knew, but there was no doubt I just knew, with everything that was within me, I was making those dreams and goals happen!

I am not sure when the realization truly hit me, "I Did It!" I had changed my stars! I had chosen a new path and changed who I thought I was into who I thought I wanted to be!

Step one was passing the personal trainer certification and was probably one of the biggest life changes that I ever orchestrated "on purpose." I knew things would be different and better after that, (or at least I was praying and believing with all my heart it would be better). There were still a lot of hurdles I would have to jump and somewhere deep inside me I knew that. I still had a deep seeded fear that I wasn't good enough, and asked myself almost daily, "How was I going to make this new life work?" I kept thinking about, I was 44 years old and embarking on a new career I really knew nothing about, other than I knew how to work out myself. I was praying that it was going to be enough. That I could fake it until I made it. I wasn't sure how the money was going to work or if I would make enough to pay the bills or anything. All I knew was that I was *not* going back to that damn strip club! I didn't care if I had to work 20 hours a day at the gym, somehow, some way this was going to work!

Every time I heard those little negative voices trying to get loud in the back of my head, I would tell them to Shut TF Up! I told myself I was an awesome trainer and there were no other options! This is what I affectionately call having a decided heart! I burned the boats and bridges behind me so that the only options I had was to face what was in front of me and make it happen.

I was really blessed that I had a really great boss! His name was Bobby Fournier, Jr. and he took a big chance on hiring me being a brand spanking new trainer at the age of 44 with only my own success story in tow. He was always willing to help me be successful. The other trainers at the gym also took me under their wings and showed me the ropes. It was really like a family there and it felt good! What was great was that the other trainers helped me with workouts for my clients. They knew I was brand new and there was no competition between us. There was never any cutthroat atmosphere there like I had heard from so many people about what "trainer life" at the gym would be like. Several people told me to watch my back and not to trust anyone I worked with. (In my mind, if I couldn't trust you, why would I continue to work with you.) I got to work out with them, and they taught me so much about training and about myself. We also worked together as a team. Soon I was getting good results with clients, which felt great and was more validation that I knew what I was doing.

I had a good man, Dee, a good job and I was happy, everything seemed to be working out for me. I think this is where I really started trying to change how I thought about myself and the way I looked at the world in general.

The voices in my head would bring up the past, reminding me how trusting people had gotten me into some pretty shitty situations. I chose to stay focused on what I had going on in front of me this time. I knew I had changed my circle of people; my circle of influence and I even changed my whole location on the map as an added safety net. There was nobody in my life now that was a contributing factor to the downfall of my past. I refused to let history repeat itself again. I learned to trust my intuition and if I got any red flags, I was out. There were no second chances at this point! I had one main objective, and that was to become a better me and win at this thing called life. The only grades available were, I was going to be a successful trainer, or I was going to be a failure! Failure was not an option, period! I was my teacher, my own accountability partner, and my own competition!

WHEN YOUR FAITH GETS TESTED

April 5th, 2012, I was on my way to the water company to pay my water bill and avoid getting it cut off. Money was tight and I had just missed the bill payment. I was stopped and waiting to turn into the water company, when I looked in my rearview mirror and saw there was a pickup truck barreling toward me, without any signs of slowing down. I braced for the impact because there was nowhere for me to go. I let off the brake so that hopefully, the impact wouldn't be as intense and prayed I didn't get pushed into oncoming traffic.

The driver saw me at the last minute and jerked the wheel to the right in an attempt to miss me, clipping the right rear quarter panel of my car. I just remember screaming "Noooooooooo!" at the top of my lungs right before impact. There was at least 15-20' of skid marks from his truck. I was rattled, and my right shoulder, thumb, and right hip were all battered. My car was drivable even though my fear was it would be totaled by the insurance company. I didn't make it into the water company before they closed, so I was without water all weekend. To me, that was roughing it! I had to go outside to get water from the pipe on the side of the building. I filled up every bucket and pot that I owned and used that to flush the toilet and cook. I still had power, gas and most importantly, my life after the accident. So as frustrated as I was for the inconvenience, I settled into being thankful for all the blessings I had. I realized I had to take responsibility for my part in not having water. It wasn't because of the accident. It was because I hadn't paid my bill on time. At the end of the day, I was where I was at because of the way I thought! My perception of everything gave me the circumstances to match.

After I got the water turned back on, that Monday, I saw an attorney about my accident. My fear was confirmed, my car was totaled. Since it was an older model, I didn't get enough insurance money to buy another car. My credit wasn't great, so I went to a place that offered loans despite bad credit, but that meant my payments were high. I thought to myself; I am alive! I had a car! I had a job that I loved. I had a man that I loved and who loved me. That is what I chose to focus on. Busy season was ending at the gym, and I wasn't even sure I would be able to continue to make the payments. In my heart, I just hoped and prayed it all would work itself out.

Money was getting super tight with each passing day. I had stopped working at the strip club in January. That was the last payment I made on my rent. I never told anyone I was behind, much less the amount I owed. I talked to the owner and told him what I was doing, and if he would be patient with me, I would get it all caught up as soon as I could. He said he was proud of me for what I was attempting to do and he would work with me as best he could. I prayed he would keep his word and I would keep the roof over my head. I was not sure I could take going through another eviction. I was going through a major stage of life changes, and the fear of losing everything again had my thoughts spinning out of control. The very real thought of the past repeating itself was ringing loud and clear in the back of my mind.

Then Summertime at the gym hit! That's when my will to keep going was tested and my Faith in a God that, to be honest, I was still getting to know. Looking through my human eyes, I wasn't sure there was any way I could make this work!

June came around and I made a total of $150 at the gym for the entire month. My rent was $750 and my car payment was $352 every two weeks. Add in gas to get to and from work, food, utilities, phone, etc. and I was under more than a little stress! I had no idea how I was going to make it another day, much less through the entire month. With the escalation of stress came the escalation of drinking; again. I was working longer hours at the gym selling as much Advocare as I could. I had just started going to church, and I was still more than a little shaky in my faith. I kept writing in my journal every day, just trying to find some kind of relief from the pressure I was feeling. It felt like the walls were closing in on me and there was nothing I could do about it. I kept talking to God and sharing how stressed I was about my financial situation. I didn't share it with anyone else, not even Dee, the man I so desperately wanted to keep in my life. We had started having problems, in my heart, I knew we were growing further and further apart. He was traveling so much as he was helping his family, so money was tight for him as well. I couldn't bring myself to ask him for help. I believed if he knew my real financial situation, he would dump me for good and I would be standing there all alone…Again.

I woke up angry every morning, went to bed even more frustrated and full of tears every night. Sleep was not my friend during these days. One morning I woke up pissed off at myself for the situation I was in again! It was then I made the decision I was going to figure this shit out come hell or high water! I was getting ready for work in the bathroom and looked in the mirror and screamed at myself "I am sick and fucking tired of all this struggling Bull Shit!" I knew the only person responsible for me was staring back at me! There was nobody else, just me! Nobody owed me anything. If this was going to happen, it was going to be because I figured it out. I refused to go through this shit anymore! So, I spent more hours in the gym. I was in straight grind mode. I was talking about vitamins to anyone who would listen to me. Money was going to come in, and I was going to see to it!

No matter what, I didn't miss a Sunday at church. My belief in God and what was possible was more than a little shaky, but I knew without him, things had not turned out so well for me in the past. I wasn't willing to take the chance on the past repeating itself again. So I kept praying, reading my Bible, journaling and writing my goals down. It was a rough first summer as a trainer. Bobby had told me in the beginning if I could make it through the first slow season, then I would make it as a trainer. I was never much of a quitter, so I turned that into a challenge and literally just refused to give up! The only way through this struggle was the path right in front of me! Period!

Well, I made it through the slow summer season, and I was moved to a new gym that was a little closer to where I lived. It was the Sage Hill location of Snap Fitness, over by Emory College in North Druid Hills. It was super small compared to the other gym, but it was my new home, and now it was time to make it my own. I started there in August and picking up clients at first was slow and seemed harder than it should be to me. Money was tight and I had to make this work. The voices in my head were starting to get loud again. They kept whispering louder and louder, "I make more money dancing. I could just go back so easy and solve all these money problems today." I got Angry! I refused to Go Back! I made the Decision that training was the only option period!

I started by talking to more people, no matter how uncomfortable it felt. I was going to make friends here and somehow; I was going to make a living at this job I loved so much! Meghan was one of my very first clients there. She came in to sign up for a membership, and I remember I wouldn't let her leave until she scheduled her fitness assessment with me. She was nervous and scared, but after the first hour with me, she became a regular client! Meghan worked so hard every week, and we had so much fun during her training sessions. She was one of the ones who let me know training was a gift I had and encouraged me never to stop doing it. I really started believing in myself, and that is when my business started to grow. You know, she was still with me when I left five years later!

November came around and I was getting ready to go home for the holidays. Money was tight, but I was managing to rob Peter to pay Paul to keep things going for the time being. The Tuesday before Thanksgiving, I had a fairly new client that weighed over 500lbs. His appointment was scheduled at 10:30am. I called to confirm because he had canceled his last 3 appointments and I didn't want to make a trip to the gym if he wasn't going to make it. As I pulled into the parking lot, he texts me, "Hey, sorry for the late notice but I can't make it today, just charge me for it." Needless to say, I was more than a little frustrated. I just chalked it to the game, it was a free $37 for 30 minutes that I didn't have to work. I paid my car insurance online before I left, stopped at the grocery store then headed home to beat the traffic.

I'm on I-20W listening to the radio and enjoying the beautiful weather, while I'm trying not to think about how I just drove all the way to work for no reason. Next thing I know, the pickup beside me drifted into my lane and clipped my front end, which caused me to fight for control of my car! I hit the inside wall, was rear-ended by another car which caused me to slam into the pickup truck again. I remember spinning out of control across four lanes of Atlanta rush hour traffic and hitting the guard rail head-on. I learned later that guard rail was the only thing that stopped me from going over the embankment and onto the street below! During the spin, I hit the side my head on the driver's side window. I'm dazed and trying to focus. I remember thinking "ugh, everything hurts." I shook my head, grabbing the place that was hurting, as I leaned up to look for my phone.

Once everything settled down, a lady opened my car door and asked if I was alright. I kept asking her if my car was okay and she kept telling me to be still and help was on the way. I remember looking around and seeing cars everywhere, some were stopped, and others were driving by slowly to get a better view. The police were the first on the scene, then the fire trucks and ambulance. I couldn't tell anyone what had happened as I wasn't sure, I just knew my car was in a guard rail, and my entire body hurt.

Once the paramedics arrived, they did their best to ease me out of the car. My legs and back hurt like crazy and my head was throbbing. I remember screaming and crying as they twisted me to get me out of the car and onto the backboard and secured into place. As they were lifting me into the ambulance, I asked if my car was okay and they guy said it looked like I would be getting a new car soon. I knew he was trying to cheer me up, but my heart sank with the knowledge I'd had two car accidents in six months that resulted in the cars being totaled. My mind was racing! My whole body hurt so bad, from the impact of the accident, and there was no stopping the tears from flowing down my cheeks now. I just started praying in my mind. I didn't understand what was happening to me or why I had to go through all these struggles again. I knew there had to be a reason, and I was pretty sure I wasn't going to like the answer if I ever figured it out.

On the way to the hospital, I called Paige and Bradley. I told them what had happened, I was in pain, but I thought I was okay. I had hit my head pretty hard when the car spun out of control and they were taking me to Grady Memorial to get it checked out. After I arrived at the hospital, I texted Dee and told him I was in a car accident with all the major details. What hurt me so much, was he sounded more exasperated that I had an accident than he seemed to care about whether or not I was injured.

I was released from the hospital with a mild concussion and whiplash. My best friend, LaTaunya, picked me up and had me stay with her that night to keep an eye on me. She didn't want me staying home alone with a concussion. Dee was in South Carolina and said he couldn't leave work to come home to take care of me. That was the first time I found myself wondering if he loved me at all or if it was all a lie. I put on that fake happy face for everyone while I made excuses for him again. I told myself we weren't married, so his job didn't have to give him time off for anything concerning me, but deep down inside, I knew our relationship was falling apart. I was desperately holding on in hopes that it would somehow work itself out and we would be okay. I didn't think I could take another failed relationship and especially not on top of everything else going on. The weight on my shoulders was really becoming more than I could bear. Now what? What was I going to do without a car and a way to get to work? I couldn't lose another job! I had to figure out a way to get to and from work without a car until I could get another one.

On the way to LaTaunya's house from the ER, we stopped to fill some prescriptions. I had just left the hospital after being in a horrific accident and my best friend, who is from Miami, loves to drive FAST! She drives like Mario Andretti on race day. I think that was the first time I ever Screamed at her, "You do realize I could have just Died in a damn car accident! You just picked me up from the hospital 5 minutes ago right?!" lol. She just laughed, and said, "just put your head down and text you will be okay in a minute." I did manage to get her slow down to Mac 1 from 5, so I didn't throw up in her car.

TIME TO CHOOSE... FAITH OR FEAR?

J'son had called to check on me as soon as I got back to LaTaunya's house. He wasn't even my man and he called to check on me. He asked the same question she had asked, "where is Dee?" I told everyone who was nagging me, he was in S.C. and he would be home as soon as he could. All J'son said, was we will talk about this more when you feel better. She, on the other hand, gave me a raised eyebrow and looked at me sideways. You know the kind that says everything while saying nothing at all. She and her husband were as subtle as a train wreck, about how that was not acceptable. They expressed their thoughts that if you Love someone, married or not if they are in a car accident, you get your ass home to check on them, Period! I heard them loud and clear. I wanted to avoid any more conversation, so I began complaining about my head hurting and wanting to sleep. The truth was, I didn't want to talk about it anymore because I knew they were right. I agreed Dee should have been there. I knew something was wrong between us and I was holding on to him and us so tight! I didn't want to lose another relationship. I knew I was still coming out of my dark places and it felt like they were starting to close in on me again and fast. My heart was hurting as bad as my body was from the accident and I just wasn't sure my heart could take another hit right now.

I knew the reality of my financial situation, and somehow, I believed that just being in a relationship was a good thing and it would make my financial situation better, or quite possibly, even go away. In all honesty, I knew deep down, I was looking for him to save me. I wanted him to sweep me off my feet and just take me away from it all and us to live happily ever after. I was a victim in my own mind, looking for someone else to blame and looking for someone else to save me from myself and what seemed to be a never-ending saga of trouble. What I didn't realize then, was that I needed to save myself. I needed to be my own hero.

When I picked up my accident report, I learned the police officer wrote the accident citing everyone at fault. The guy who was driving the pick-up was an off-duty police officer. I knew enough about the code "We protect our own," to know there was nothing I could do about it now. My insurance paid my car off and paid all of my medical bills, but that was it. There wasn't any extra money for a car or lost wages. I had no way to get to work other than to use the public transit system. I had Never in my life used a public transit system before, so this was going to be an interesting learning experience for me. All the years I've been alive, and I've never been on any bus but a school bus. How pathetic was that!

All of my friends were more concerned about me being on the bus than I was. I knew I didn't have a choice! I had to figure it out, get on the damn bus, or lose everything! I wasn't losing Nothing! I didn't give a damn about riding a damn bus or anything else. I was going to make it to work every single day and on time! Period! The closest bus stop I knew of was two miles from my apartment, and there were a lot of hills on that long road, but I didn't care! I got my ass up early enough to be there to catch the first bus at 5:30am every single day! I had a 7:30am client and refused to be late! I left the gym at 6pm every night just to make the three-hour ride home. I knew if I missed one connection it could add another hour plus to my ride home. I did that for an entire Year! I refused to quit! I wasn't giving up on shit! I was going to make this work! I refused to let fear take me down a road I knew I wasn't going to like! I was NOT going backward! If it meant I had to ride the damn bus everywhere I went, then that is what I was going to do! I burned all those other bridges! I had Dreams! I had Goals! And Damnit, They were going to Happen!

Even with all the heartaches, I'd experienced since becoming a personal trainer, I still had a hope in new beginnings. I had a belief that somehow this was going to work itself out. Dee and I weathered a lot of storms over that year. We were on and off again. When we were apart, we realized that is not what our hearts wanted. I shed a lot of tears when he wasn't around. I didn't want him to see how much I was hurting. Something told me he was hurting too and neither of us knew what to do. We just knew when we were together, the rest of the world seemed to just melt away. After one of our big fights, we had a long heart to heart and decided to try one more time. We agreed if it didn't work out, we would walk away knowing we did everything we could to try and make it work.

Not long after that Dee was up for a promotion which would require him to relocate to Puerto Rico, he asked me if I would go with him if he took the position. At first, I told him that I didn't know because our last year had been so rocky, and I wasn't sure moving was a good idea. If we didn't make it, then I would be down there all by myself. For the next couple of weeks, we would randomly talk about it, but no decisions were made. The more I thought about a tropical island and being there with him, the more excited I got, and soon I really wanted to go, so I began looking up things about the island. The next time he came home I told him if he wanted me to go, that I would go under one condition. I would go if we were married because I wasn't going to go down there as just his girlfriend. He agreed that it was the right way to do it. He told me he loved me and we would work it out if the position was offered to him.

Deep down, I was thinking about all the back rent I owed. The girl at the office who had been helping me was leaving the company. I wasn't sure how much longer I had before they were going to tell me I had to get out or be evicted. Going to Puerto Rico with Dee would Save Me! I would figure the rest out later.

I was excited at the thought of moving and shared with a few of my clients. I found out one of them was from Puerto Rico and she offered to let me move in with her until we moved, which would allow me to save money and pay off some bills. It was also a blessing because it put me closer to the gym and she had an extra car I could drive! That meant I could work more hours and make more money, which meant I could pay off some debt! I thought this was a perfect plan, but when I talked to Dee about it, he was a little taken aback by me making such a bold move. I told him, I had two choices; either take her up on her generous offer or potentially risk getting evicted. So, unless he wanted to help me pay the back rent of over $7,000, then this was a better option. There really wasn't a whole lot he could say other than okay. I got it all worked out, and I moved in with her the middle of September, just before my birthday.

Shortly after I moved in with my client, I began to see a change in Dee's and my relationship. As he was getting ready to head down to P.R., to get things ready for us to move, he became more distant. He wasn't calling or texting hardly at all. I was actually surprised I got a call on my birthday with the changes in his behavior. His birthday was just 5 days after mine and I called him early that morning and several times throughout the day. He never answered or returned any of my calls or text messages. He even missed our 2 year anniversary, which was super out of character for him.

He always got mad over little things like me calling, texting, or asking questions about what was going on. I even offered to go to P.R. first and find us somewhere to live and get everything set up for us. He would just respond by telling me he would handle it! When I asked how his new job was going, he said they treated him like a rock star. I knew what a rock star got treated like and I didn't like the feelings that were welling up in my gut. I was trying so hard to hold on, and I didn't talk about us to anyone. The last night he came home was on October 15th, and we had a long talk about us and our future. He just didn't seem himself.

I asked him if money were no object and he knew he couldn't fail, what would he do? He sat there staring off in the distance and finally said: "that's a deep question T. I really don't know what I would do." As I watched him walk out the door that night, I realized nothing had been resolved and honestly had no idea what would happen to us. I was standing on my faith that everything would work out for me no matter what. I wasn't sure if we would make it or not, but I knew I would be okay either way. At least that is what I tried to make myself believe. Little did I know it would be the last time I would see him.

5 R.I.P. MOM

THE ULTIMATE CHALLENGE

After Dee left that night, I stayed focused on what I needed to do for me. I had just moved out of my apartment, sold everything I owned, and moved in with a client I barely knew. I was pinning it all on my hopes of "Happily Ever After" with Dee. When deep down, I knew his heart wasn't with me anymore, and I was going to have another challenge, sooner rather than later, when it finally came to an end. For now, it was just easier to keep hoping.

Thanksgiving showed up like it always does, and I went home to see my family. I was missing them a lot and really looking forward to getting to spend time with them. My brother had let me know mom had not been feeling well. Mom had asked me to stay with her and my brother, Scott, so I did. I went to see the kids and grands while I was there which is always awesome. Scott shared with me that mom had been having dizzy spells and she wouldn't go to the doctor. He wanted me to try and talk some sense into her to see if she would go for me. She listened to me a little bit more than she did anyone else, at least that is what he said. I really didn't believe that too much because she would be doing better than what she was if that were the case.

I was leaving that morning and sat down to talk to her as I was packing my bag. I said, "Mom, you know I live in Atlanta now. I can't get here in 5 minutes if something was to happen to you. I need you to please take your meds like you are supposed to okay? Please!? I also need you to start eating more regularly. You can't make a bag of ramen noodles last all day long and call that eating! What are you doing with your money? I know you get a discounted rate to stay here, so this shouldn't be that hard ma. Come on mom, I Love You! I really want you to be around for a while ok; please do this stuff for me? You gotta budget your money better so that your food last you for the entire month from now on. Cook stuff and freeze it in portions if you have to so it lasts you all month long. Can you do that for me? Please?"

She teared up as she said okay, then she gave me a big mama hug and told me she loved me. I also made her promise that if she had another dizzy spell, she would go to the doctor. I knew there was more going on with her that she nor Scott would tell me. But I could only go off of what they were willing to share.

What I didn't know, was that when I left that night, it would be the last time I would ever hear her say the words "I Love You" and it would be the last "Mama Hug" she would ever give me. The last conversation I ever had with her was with me fussing at her about taking her meds and eating better. That was the Tuesday before Thanksgiving 2013. The following Monday, December 3rd, I got a call from my brother, Scott. He was crying and panicked, and it was hard to understand him. "I came home and found mom not breathing, she was blue in the face. I called 911, and when the paramedics got here, they revived her then rushed her to the hospital. They said she had a heart attack in her sleep. Her kidneys were shutting down along with the rest of her organs. They told me I needed to call the family in because there was not much time left! Tammy, mom, is dying! You gotta get here! What am I gonna do?"

I hung up the phone and just crumpled to the floor crying, and then I went in the den where Sarah (my roommate) was and just put my head in her lap and cried some more. I asked her if I could take the car to go say one last goodbye to my mom. She was really afraid of me driving in that state, but she knew if I waited, I probably wouldn't make it in time. She didn't want to be the reason I didn't get to say goodbye to my mom. So instead, while I was in my room getting ready to go, she packed me a travel bag of goodies and even gave me cash to travel with. She was so sweet and loving. She stayed pretty much in constant contact with me while I was gone. She knew this was going to be one of the hardest weeks of my life. She had already lost both of her parents and her husband, She knew the grief I was about to experience and was being the best friend to me that she could possibly be, for the short time she had known me.

I tried calling Dee several times, with no answer again, so I left him voicemails and sent him text messages letting him know what was going on. I told him I needed him because I couldn't do this alone.

Next, I text J'son, because I knew he was always up late and I knew he would answer as soon as he read my text. I knew it was a long shot, but I asked him to drive me to Birmingham and drop me off and told him I would take a bus back later on in the week. I wasn't thinking about his Asperger's, and being with me in such an emotional state would be too hard for him. He did the next best thing he could, and he followed me more than halfway there to make sure I was ok. He was in constant contact with me the entire week, and he held on to me the best way he knew how. Just like he always did, my safe space.

I got in touch with the rest of my family so they could come say their goodbye's to mom. I called my best friend, Teresa, while I was driving. She talked to me and kept me sane on the longest 2.5-hour drive of my life! The drive to make it in time to say goodbye to the woman who had given birth to me! I had just seen mom six days earlier and the last conversation was me fussing at her. As I think back to that night, it all seems like a blur. My eyes have tears in them now, remembering all the details as they unfolded that night.

I had so many emotions welled up inside of me, but the one thing I knew for sure, was that I was going to make it to that hospital in time come hell or high water! I was going to say Goodbye to my mom before she let go of her time here on this earth. I had missed the opportunity to say goodbye to each of my grandparents and that was not going to happen here. I stopped for gas and tried to call J'son.

He texted back and asked where I was and if I was ok? I said "I've stopped for gas and I just really needed a hug from you right now. I need to find some air because my lungs can't seem to find any on their own." He knew how I felt about getting to mom in time and he picked up the phone to talk to me this time. He actually called to talk to me and reassure me. "Tammy, you can't waste any time waiting on me. You have to get there in time or you will never forgive yourself. I will always be around to give you a hug when you get back. Turn your flashers on and go as fast as you can to Birmingham! If you get pulled over, tell them what is going on with your mom and ask for a police escort the rest of the way! Okay? I will be right here, on the phone, via text, all you want or need okay, I promise, now get your ass in the car and go!"

My angels were watching over me that night because I made it with only one stop to get gas. Time was ticking away, as the seconds seemed to be going faster than I could count, I just kept saying "Hold on mama, I'm on the way, please just hold on until I get there!"

I arrived at UAB hospital safe and sound. My emotional state, on the other hand, is what was more than a little questionable. I knew my brother, Scott, was in no condition to handle anything concerning Mom. Billy, my oldest brother, just had another back surgery a few weeks prior and was still in a back brace. He had told the doctors before I got there that I was in charge and any decisions to be made would be handled when I arrived. I was the oldest, and it was my job. I was now going to be the head of the family. Internally, I didn't want that job, not now, I wasn't ready! I had so much more planned and was still getting my life together. I wanted to make them all proud before this day came. Those were the thoughts running through the back of my mind.

When I walked in and saw everyone sitting around, Scott, Billy, Heather (my sister in law) and my daughter Brittnie. She had been on a girls night out and cut it short when I called her about her grandma. After I arrived, she wasn't leaving my side. We didn't always get along, but if ever there was a time I needed her, she was always right by my side. I hugged everyone as I walked in and asked if there was any other news or if anyone had seen her since we had last talked? Nothing new was reported, so I went to the nurse's desk, told them who I was and requested to see my mom. They already knew who I was and welcomed me as best they could under the circumstances. They said they were running some more tests on her, so they would come get me when she was ready for visitors. I boldly asked if she was still alive. They responded with an emphatic yes ma'am and said the doctors just wanted to run some more tests and then they would call me back.

My perception of time now, was that it had slowed down to a crawl. I was anxious and I felt as though they were not telling me everything.

Time seems to have stopped moving at all now. As I look around at everyone, I feel as though everything is moving in slow motion. I am forcing the air in and out of my lungs. I know the outcome, but I somehow want to stop time so we can hold on just a little bit longer. I know there is nothing we can do but accept the inevitable task to set her free, to find peace from the pain and suffering of her physical life here on this earth. Leaving all of us behind only to remember and wish we had done things differently. In my mind, I'm trying to rewind the time, wanting to say all the things I needed to say, do all that I could do to make this day not be happening today! Because right now, there is no time left to change the outcome of it all.

Finally, the doctors called us back and they took us to a consultation room. We all looked at each other as we felt this sinking in our hearts. We knew the news they were about to give us was not going to be what we wanted to hear. I just needed her to still be alive! I needed to say goodbye! The doctor came in, looked at me and said: "you must be the one that is in charge we have been waiting on, Tammy, is it?" I nodded, then asked when I could see my mom. I told him I'd been there almost an hour, drove all the way from Atlanta to get here in time, and really needed to see her, please.

He explained her kidneys, bladder and other organs were shutting down. They had cooled her body down to keep her alive, but she was on a respirator to help her breathe because she was not breathing on her own. She had had another heart attack right before I had arrived and they were able to revive her again. They wanted us to allow them to transfer her up to the second floor, so they could watch her over the next couple of days while they warmed her body back up to a normal temperature, to see if she would come out of her coma. If she didn't, then at that time we could make the decision as to how long we wanted to keep her on life support, in her comatose state or just let her go.

The whole family turned and looked at me. The rest of this conversation truly felt like an out of body experience, but I remember it like it was yesterday.
Me: "Correct me if I am wrong, as I am not a medical professional, but my understanding of anatomy, is that if the kidneys and bladder

have shut down, even if she was to miraculously, wake up from this coma right now, she would have to be on dialysis in order to survive Correct?"

Doctor: "Yes ma'am, it is correct that her kidneys would not come back from this. Her bladder and liver could possibly recover and start functioning again, but her mortality rate is so low she wouldn't be eligible for dialysis."

Me: "So, without dialysis, she would make it what, maybe one or two days at most?"

Doctor: "Yes, that is correct."

Me: "We promised our mom a long time ago, if she ever got so sick that she had to live on machines, we would not let her live that way. I can tell you right now, as a matter of fact, if she was to wake up out of that coma, being on all of those machines, she would be kicking my ass as soon as she was able to get off that table. I am keeping that promise I made to my mom! It's now 5:30am doctor. If she has shown no signs that she is fighting to stay alive, at 7:30am, we are taking her off ALL of those damn machines, and we are letting her go in peace! ALL I ask is that we get to go back there and spend as much time with her as we can, and she is given whatever pain meds necessary to keep her from feeling anything. She has spent her whole life in pain and these last two hours of her life will not be painful in any way for her! Can you give me, no…not me, ALL of us that, as our last wish for my mom, doctor?"

Doctor: "Yes, we will make sure she doesn't have any pain. Can we move her to a private room so that you don't get caught in shift change?"

Me: "NO! You are not moving her anywhere! I honestly don't care about your damn shift change! I want to see my mom! Now Please!"

Doctor: "Give us a few minutes to prepare the room for all of you. Would you like us to call the staff priest down for the family?"

Me: "Yes and thank you." (Deep breath)

He turned and walked out of the room and we all burst into tears! There were no more words left to be spoken. All I heard was tick…tick… tick off the clock… the heartache all around me and there was nothing I could do to make it stop.

SAYING GOODBYE

When a loved one is in his or her last days or hours, before they transition into the afterlife, it's easy to believe you have it all under control that you are following their last wishes and making it as peaceful for them as possible. When in all actuality, it's hard, if not impossible, to find any inner peace to get you through. I am speaking for myself primarily here.

Standing there in the hospital with my mom dying in the other room, I knew I was still fighting off the shadows of darkness from the depression I was still emerging out of and losing my mom at this juncture was bringing a lot of those thoughts and feelings to the surface. Consciously I believed I had healed all of my broken pieces and everything was just "Fine." At least that is the lie I told myself Deep down, there was a fear I refused to admit existed. I knew if I gave it any energy or any conscious thought, it would grow like some sort of super weed that feels impossible to kill, no matter how hard you try.

So, I chose the safest path I knew, and that was to just focus on mom. I focused on making sure she was comfortable. I focused on everybody else in the family. I made sure everyone who wanted to say goodbye got to. I made sure the priest came down to pray with us before we unplugged her from the life support. I took time alone with her to tell her how very much I loved her, and I told her I forgave her, I told her it was okay to go in peace now. I told her that we all were going to be okay. I told her everything was okay! I'm not sure I believed any of the words I was saying, but I had to put on a good front, not only for her but everyone else.

I looked up at the clock, and my heart was beating so hard in my chest that I'm not sure I could take much more, as it said 7:30am, which meant it was time to keep the promise I/we had made to my mother so many years ago. I went to the head nurse, told her it was time, she hugged my neck and went to get the doctor. He came in one last time and made sure this is what we wanted to do before he took her off of the machines that were keeping her alive. We all just nodded in silence. I asked him one last time "she can't feel anything, right?" He said "she can feel no pain, I promise. She can hear you until her heart stops beating after we have taken her off of the respirator. I want you to be aware it could take up to 30-45 minutes before she takes her last breath. She may even gasp for air as her lungs deflate. It's a normal occurrence, and it's not her fighting for air, it's her letting go. I am giving her another shot to make sure her body is relaxed. Do you have any last questions before I take her off of the machines and start unhooking everything? Once we unhook the respirator, we will let you and your family have all the time you need to say your last goodbyes."

With tears streaming down my face, I looked at my brothers, and we all nodded in agreement and said: "It's time."

After they unhooked her from the machines, we all went up one by one, held her hand, kissed her forehead, whispered our last thoughts in her ear and said "Rest in peace Mom. We love you."

Mom took her last breath at 8:46am on December 4, 2013.

I want to take a moment here and acknowledge the staff who were on duty in the ICU at UAB Hospital in Birmingham, Alabama that day. They stayed in that room with us. They went above and beyond to make mom comfortable, but most of all, they made us as comfortable as they could during the hardest day of our lives. They laughed when we were sharing funny stories of times with mom, in our feeble attempt to take the edge off of the situation. They hugged us, cried with us, and loved on us in our darkest hour! They wiped our tears and helped us understand every step of the process. I can't imagine going through this time without them there! I don't remember any of their names, but their faces are forever etched in my heart! So, if any of you happen to read this book, and you were working the ICU at UAB on December 4th, 2013, from my family and myself, from the bottom of our hearts, thank you for all you did and all you continue to do to help the many families who go through this each and every day! You are amazing and appreciated.

THE FAMILY DYNAMICS

I am only here to share my perspective through the lenses I was looking through at this time in my life. My mom had her own inner demons that she was never strong enough to battle, much less beat them. I know this may be hard to understand after reading about my life growing up with my mom, but even today, I still love her very much.

If you talked to each of my brothers and myself individually, we all have very different thoughts about our childhood and the life we shared with our mom. I can't speak for my brothers, but as for myself, there were a lot of troubled times at home while we were growing up. Our family was definitely divided when it came to mom. Me and my oldest brother caught the brunt of mom's abusive ways as children because we were the oldest. We were also a lot stronger than our younger brothers, and maybe in some way, she thought she was making us better so we would somehow create a good life when we left home. My two youngest brothers were definitely favored, at least that's how Billy and I saw it.

There was one time, while we were still living in Chicago and after my grandmother had died, we had been outside playing, and mom told us to come in so we could get our bath for the night. As I went upstairs, she told me to make sure I washed my knees and elbows because they were black. I did as she said, but what she didn't realize was they were black because I was just that tan. When I came downstairs, and she saw me, she was instantly angry. She spanked me, drug me back upstairs by my hair and threw me in a hot bathtub. She took a brush that you would normally scrub your nails with and started scrubbing my knees and elbows with it. I was crying and screaming that she was hurting me. It wasn't until she saw blood come from my elbow she realized that was the actual color of my skin. See, my mom was super pale from all the Irish blood on her mom's side of the family. My grandmother, her mom, was a carrot top redhead, who would burn in the shade. I must have taken after my father because I was the only one in the family who would get tan. Mom felt so bad after that, and she let me have ice cream for dinner every day for a week.

There was another time, I remember after we moved to Alabama and we were living in Trussville, on Sweeny Hollow Road, I think. Mom was waiting tables somewhere, and she usually didn't get home until after 11pm. I was probably about 13 then. She had told Billy and me to have the house clean by the time she got home. Everything was done but the kitchen. He was finishing up his part so I got in the shower and told him I would finish my part when I got out. I was in the shower when all of a sudden, the curtain flies open and Mom is standing there screaming at me! She grabs me by my hair and drags me naked into the kitchen. She starts throwing dishes at me, breaking them on my body, while screaming at me the house was supposed to be done before she got home. I was crying and my legs were all cut up. I asked her if I could get dressed so I could clean up the mess. She said no and to get it done before I got more. She was drunk. You could smell the alcohol reeking from her as she yelled. There was no point in trying to argue or do anything else. Naked or not, I knew I needed just to hurry up and get it done, then we could lock ourselves in our room for the rest of the night.

I remember mom saying one time, "I just don't want to die alone. "She had my youngest brother, Daniel when I was 16. Scott always lived either with mom or close to her. She kept him close by and would make him feel guilty if he didn't help take care of her. Daniel was diagnosed with severe ADHD as a child. Mom was in her late 30's when she had him. Her patience was not where it needed to be in order to handle a rambunctious child. He was on Ritalin for his condition and was only supposed to take it while he was in school. Mom couldn't handle him if he wasn't on it, so she gave it to him 24/7. He was pretty much a zombie during his whole entire childhood.

The last fight I remember having with my mom was when I was 17, right before I moved out. I came home from softball practice at 4 pm. I went into the fridge and started warming up what I had brought home from work the night before. She said she was cooking dinner. I told her that was fine. I was starving and I would eat what she cooked too. For whatever reason, she freaked out and said: "If you can't eat what I fix then you can just pack your shit and get out!"

I said "Mom, I said I was going to eat what you fixed! I haven't eaten since lunch at 11:30 this morning! I am hungry and can't wait until you fix dinner! You haven't even started cooking yet!" She started throwing stuff and cussing at me. I threw my food back into the fridge, went upstairs and started packing. I had had enough. I had a job, a car and somewhere to go until graduation. She came upstairs, and that is when all hell broke loose!

Mom: "Where the hell do you think you are going?!"
Me: "You told me if I don't want to eat what you fix then pack my shit and get out. You don't want to hear anything else I have to say, so I'm doing exactly what you told me to do!" (as I was throwing clothes in an overnight bag)
Mom: "You're not going anywhere! Unpack right this minute!"
Me: "You just told me to leave. I'm going with that! It will save us all a lot of problems later!"
Mom: "Tammy, I said you're not going anywhere!" And she tried to pull my stuff out of my hands.
Me: "And why should I listen to you now? You can't seem to make up your mind about what you want. So, I'm leaving!"
Mom: "No you're not!" and she pushed me away from my suitcase
Me: "Don't put your hands on me again! Now go back downstairs and let me finish what I'm doing!"
Mom: "You had better listen to me!"
Me: "Why exactly should I do that now?"
Mom: "Because I'm your mother and I said so!"
Me: "Oh and now that's supposed to mean something?"
(She took a swing and slapped my face so hard she snapped my head back)

I don't even think I realized what was happening as I grabbed her up by the throat and shoved her into the wall! I was squeezing her throat so tight that she was having a hard time breathing. I got in her face, nose to nose and said under my breath, almost in a growl.."If you ever put your hands on me or any one of my brothers again, I will kill you with my bare hands! Are we clear!?"

I eased up the grip off of her throat, with fear in her eyes, she nodded. I moved my hand, and she just stood there and looked at me. I think that was the first time since she had children, that she realized she had gone too far and we were not going to take it anymore. From that day forward, if I was around, she never put her hands on any of us. Although, I've heard stories from my brothers of things she did when I wasn't there. They admit it started out as punishment for what they did most of the time, but she had a hard time stopping when she got started.

Mom was a drug addict for as long as I can remember. I know from the time I was born, according to my grandma, she was already in way too deep. She had an abusive boyfriend, who was my biological father. He kept her strung out on drugs, while they were together, from the stories I was told from my grandfather before he passed. I remember he had beat her so bad one time; she was in the hospital for three whole months. Part of that time she was on life support because he almost killed her. She still went back to him one more time after that before she finally escaped his hold on her. The sad part was she never was able to beat the drug habits that came out of that relationship. I am not sure of what drugs she used when we were young, but when we were older and could see what was happening, it was prescription drugs that had her imprisoned until she died.

On my Facebook memories recently, I saw the memory where my mom had asked me to help her find a church to go to that was close to where she lived. I remember how happy I felt because one, she wanted to get back in church and two, that she came to me to help her. I believed she truly wanted to change and hoped she could finally set herself free and find healing and freedom from her inner demons. It wasn't long after that when she passed away.

Most children, as they grow up, decide at some point they either want to be like their mom or their dad, depending on the family dynamics. Their parents were an inspiration in some way, shape or form and showed them how to live through the example they set for them. In our case, we didn't have a father to look up to. All we had was our mom. My oldest brother, Billy, and I quickly learned what we didn't want in our life. We didn't want our children to have to experience any of the things we went through. We didn't want to live anything like she did as an adult. We didn't want to struggle, living pay check to pay check, but hadn't learned any other way to live. We had so many things listed under what we didn't want to experience anymore in life, but we had no clue what we wanted. We just wanted different than what we were living. We just knew we wanted better a better life.

We were never taught how to set goals or make a plan, not even in school. Our dreams were shut down because we came from the other side of the tracks. We were poor, and we had nothing. We were always on school aid with free lunches. We didn't know what having money looked like. As adults now, we are in a better place than mom was, but for the most part, we all still struggled living paycheck to paycheck. It's time to make a change! A change, not only for myself but for the legacy I want for my family.

After losing my mom and all the heartache that brought, I knew, beyond a shadow of a doubt, I didn't want my children and grandchildren to grow up to only struggle living paycheck to paycheck like the generations before them. I wanted them to have an abundant life and to have a legacy of financial freedom. With that would come more choices to be able to do whatever they wanted in life. I wasn't sure how to make this happen, but I did know I was going to change my family's history from this day forward…No matter what it took!

BRINGING THE FAMILY TOGETHER

My best friend Michelle had gotten my message about mom about 6am that morning. After giving her all the details about moms final hours, she told me she wanted me to come to her house as soon as I was done at the hospital. She said I could stay there all week and she would be there for me. I don't think I have ever been as thankful for our friendship as I was at that moment.

When I got to her house, she met me on the porch, and I just crumbled in her arms full of tears. She hugged me until she could feel me breathing somewhat normal again. We went inside, and I filled her in on everything that had happened over the last week, but mainly focused on the last 48 hours. She asked what the family was doing and if we were going to get together for dinner later. I said: "I honestly don't know Chelle, I am just too tired to think anymore right now." She had me call everyone with a set time to get together over an awesome meal she cooked. She remains such a huge blessing in my life and is always so giving. That is her gift!

This was the first time in many years my entire family (minus Daniel who was in prison) was eating dinner together. I was so happy to have us all under the same roof as I had been praying for that day for a very long time. We ate, got caught up on life, laughed, told old stories, watched the kids play and just enjoyed being with each other, in spite of the tragedy of the morning.

My brother, Scott, was out on the porch chain smoking. He had been a heavy smoker for years, and with the drugs, his smoking habit only increased over the years. We were all really worried about him. He lived with mom and was the one who found her after her heart attack. None of us were sure he would be able to make it without mom. I had no idea how bad his drug habit had gotten, only that he had not said hardly anything since we left the hospital that morning. It was obvious to us all he was in shock, and I just prayed he would make it out of this alive. Mom had turned him and Daniel into addicts when they were younger. I don't think she consciously knew that's what she was doing. I believe her overwhelming fear of being alone when she died, kept her from thinking clearly about the consequences of her decisions where they were concerned.

At this point, I had been up for more than 42 hours. We were drinking wine with dinner and every time Michelle saw my glass a little empty, and she filled it to the rim again. She had tried to get me to lay down earlier, but I couldn't sleep. Every time I closed my eyes, my mind would just spin out of control. I kept seeing mom's face, and then I would see Dee. It was better for me to be awake and stay busy. Michelle, being the awesome friend she was made sure I was going to sleep that night, even if it meant she had to make me drunk enough to pass out. Spending all this time with the family took my mind off Dee and the fact I had only spoken with him one time since I found out about mom. I was thankful for my family, for Michelle and her generosity. I was also very thankful for J'son. He was on my phone via text every single time I text him without fail. Just like he promised.

We ended up cremating mom because she had no life insurance or any funds of any kind to take care of her burial. Michelle took me to the crematory in Southside to pick up moms remains on Saturday. I knew I would not be able to handle doing this alone. I went inside, handled all of the paperwork and paid the man behind the desk. He asked if I wanted to open the box? I said "no, I am sure everything is in order," took it and quickly left. I held it together until I sat down in the car and just burst into tears again. Mom was really gone. A box full of ashes was all that was left. I would never hear my mom's voice again. No "I Love You," "Happy Birthday." No more big mama hugs. I was now the head of the family. How could I take on that role and I could barely take care of myself!? All of these thoughts raced through my mind and flowed out as tears down my cheeks. Michelle just hugged me tight & cried with me until I could force the air back into my lungs to breathe again. We drove back to her house with the radio on, but I didn't hear anything that was playing. I just felt numb.

I was leaving later on that afternoon to head back home. The rest of the family felt weird about having her remains, so they went back to Atlanta with me. I had told mom after we took her off life support when I started traveling the world I was going to scatter her ashes in some far away beautiful place and set her free. I had no idea when or if that would really happen when I made that promise, but it was my intention with everything that was in my heart when I said my goodbyes to her that day. Little did I know, with those words, I set a plan in action that would manifest itself just four short years later.

When I left Birmingham Saturday night, I drove home with Mom in the back seat. My mind kept wandering aimlessly, as I drove down that long stretch of I-20 east headed home. I couldn't believe I had just seen her the week before and now she was really gone. If I learned anything from this one trying experience in my life, it's that time is short. We never know when the last time is that we will see someone. So, always forgive quickly, love completely and never let the nightfall on you with an angry heart. Be sure to tell the people you love how you feel. Hug them every chance you get. And most of all, Always, Always, live your life with no regrets!

As I drove, I was replaying in my mind the fact that I had only heard from Dee one time the entire week. My mom had passed away, and I couldn't get a phone call every day? My roommate couldn't believe it either. I saw the look on her face when I recounted all of the events (or lack thereof) from the week. I knew she wanted to say more, but that was not the time. Sometime late Sunday night Dee sent me a text that said:

"I'm sorry I wasn't there for you when your mom died. I feel lost. I don't know what to tell you about us."

I was in shock and speechless! I just sat there and stared at it in disbelief, reading it over and over again. I really didn't know what to say or what he even meant. The words that came flying out of my mouth were "you're going to send this to me the day after I pick up moms ashes? Really?!" I couldn't believe with all that had happened, the text he finally did send me was about him feeling lost. I had to go to work and felt like I couldn't deal with the situation then, so I didn't. I was already so emotional that it was difficult to focus, much less function and it felt like all of the walls were closing in on me again. The voices in my head were starting to get louder. I was NOT going back to that darkness! That is all I knew! I just shook my head, mumbled something under my breath and walked out the door. I had clients at the gym, I was studying for my national certification exam, my mom was in a box in the back seat of the car and the man I loved, who I thought loved me, didn't know what to tell me about ' us.' WTF does that even mean?

All of my friends and family called to check in with me and make sure I was okay and if I needed anything. Teresa was such a Godsend. I talked to her several times every day. I could yell, cry, cuss, laugh, whatever I needed. I am quite sure if she could have crawled through that phone to be there to give me a hug, she would have done that too. J'son was in constant contact too. He was there during my darkest times, and I believe he felt the shadows were still haunting me, even though he never brought it up in any of our conversations. He asked me where Dee was and when he was going to make it home to take care of me. I couldn't bring myself to tell him about the text, so I just told him me and Dee had broken up. I knew what he would say, especially with mom just passing. This had to be my decision. I knew if I told him the truth, he would be disappointed in me if I allowed Dee to stay in my life after that. So, it wasn't long after that conversation, I sent Dee a text since he wouldn't answer any of my calls.

"You don't know what to tell me about us? Let me help you with that! We are done! You don't have to worry about me or us anymore! Go back to being a "rock star" in Puerto Rico! That is obviously what makes you happy, so don't let me hold you back! I will be just fine without you!"

In the last 7 days, I've lost my mom and my man of 2.5 years. Whatever air I had left in my lungs, just got sucker punched out! Now what, I thought? I had given up everything to move in with my client, for a short period of time, because I was supposed to be moving to the beautiful tropical island of Puerto Rico with Dee. Obviously, now all the plans had changed. My roommate wasn't pushing me for answers, but I knew the conversation was going to come sooner than I was ready for. She was very loving and understanding. If it wasn't for her, I wouldn't have made it in time to say goodbye to mom. For that, I will be forever grateful. I am not sure I could have handled that with all the other pressures surrounding me at the time. I felt like the walls were closing in on me again and I had to find a way to stop them before it was too late.

6 REINVENTING A NEW ME

The holidays were just three short weeks after mom had passed away. My family got back together for Christmas for the first time since I was married. I had been praying to have my family back together for a very long time, and even though it was losing mom that brought us back together as a family, I was happy we were all together. We had dinner over at Billy's house, which is also where I stayed for the long weekend. It was so great being there, laughing, cutting up with my nephews, and getting to know Billy all over again. I had my big brother back! I told him I had missed having him in my life, and I gave him a big bear hug! Nobody had heard from Scott since mom died. We had no way to get in touch with him. Someone had told Brittnie he was living on the streets and begging for money. This broke my heart, but there was nothing I could do about it. He had to want to get clean and want his life to change before it would happen. Plus, I was barely taking care of myself, so I didn't even see a way I could help even if I wanted to try.

I knew my eating was getting out of control. When I was upset about mom, I ate, a lot. If I was upset about Dee, I couldn't eat, so I drank…a lot. The added stress of studying for my exam and unstable living situation was not helping my emotional state at all, and I was a yo-yo all over the place. All of my clothes were getting tight. My face was getting fat. Nobody would say anything about it though. In their mind, it was all justified. The last time I saw mom, I was 146lbs. When January rolled around, I was 169lbs. I gained 23lbs in less than 30 days! WTH! I needed to quit throwing my little pity party and get my shit together! Nobody is going to hire a fat personal trainer. I don't care what personal stuff you got going on, in my mind, it shows a lack of control. I had been out of control for the majority of my life, and this was a tailspin I was not willing to experience a second time. It was time to knuckle up and get things back on the right track.

So, I did what I coached all of my clients to do. I took my before pictures (which I hated), my measurements, body fat & BMI totals. I ordered a 24 Day Challenge from my Advocare site and set my start date! It was time to start feeling better. Working out was always a release for me, and I knew this time would be no different. It was a way I could get all of my hurt and anger out to help me emotionally heal. When I felt the pain in my muscles, I knew I was on the right track. I started meal prepping again, eating 5-6 times a day, drinking a gallon of water and making sure I got a minimum of 6.5 hours of sleep a night.

During this transition, my clients and the members and staff at Sage Hill Snap Fitness were so supportive and amazing! They were my rock and loved and supported me during my loss, and they also cheered me on during my weight loss journey after losing my mom. They never wavered and always helped me keep a smile on my face! That was my home for six years of my personal training career, and they all had become my family. To Meghan, Lea Barrett, Becky, Colleen, Kim, Fernando, Blake So'Brien, Bobby Fournier, Corkie, Crystal Waters, David, Rich, Deborah, Dionna, Evan, Greg, Ms. Faye, Joey, Jacob, John C, Louie, Lydia, Pia & Tal Frank, Susan & Jim just to name a few and I know there are so many more; I love you guys so much and thank you from the bottom of my heart for making Atlanta my home for so very long.

I was getting stronger and healthier, and I had passed my national certification exam in March! Then, Mom's birthday rolled around in May. That was a hard day for me, along with all the other holiday's that year. It was also a time of healing, not only for me but most of my family as well. We were closer, spending more time together, growing and beginning to enjoy life together! I had some serious concerns about my two youngest brothers. They both were still buried deep in their drug habits. I did what I could, but I knew from my own experiences, they had to want to change and take those steps on their own. No amount of me asking, begging or even attempting to help them would set them free. I was not going to enable them to continue down that dark path by contributing to their habits. It was a hard decision for me, but I knew it was the only way I could help them the most.

ENTERING UNCHARTED WATERS

My life was definitely looking up! I was feeling and looking better than I ever had before. I was in church and growing spiritually as much as I was personally. I still had this feeling like there was something more coming. I had no idea what that was, but I knew I needed to come up with a plan. Me living with my current roommate was only to be a short-term situation. I needed a car and a plan for a new place to live, and soon.

At this point in my life journey, I didn't know what a life coach was, much less that it would become a part of my future. All I knew, was that I really enjoyed helping people. I absolutely loved being a personal trainer, but for some reason, I had a feeling this was not all there was to my future. I didn't know what that meant, I just felt like there was something missing, but I didn't know what so I just stayed focused on what I was already doing and let it all develop on its own.

My best friend Teresa was living in Tampa and there was a period when I couldn't get in touch with her. Her phone was off, and I got no response from messages on Facebook, nothing from emails, I mean radio silence! This was way out of character for us. If I didn't talk to her several times a day, it was unusual. She was living with her boyfriend of 12+ years. I knew their relationship was a turbulent one. He never really liked me from the first time I met him, even though I'm not really sure why. She told me she had to memorize my number and take it out of her phone so he wouldn't know she was talking to me. So, to go days to almost 2 weeks with Zero contact, made me super nervous. I got in touch with her mom on Facebook. I asked her if she had heard from Teresa? I told Dona, it was super unusual for me not to be able to reach Teresa. After a long conversation, I found out her boyfriend was in the hospital, and she had no phone, nowhere to go, he had threatened to send her home in a body bag to her kids. I knew I had to do something.

I called my other best friend, LaTaunya, and her sister, Charmaine. We were and are all Prayer Warriors. We did a 3-way call, and we prayed over and for Teresa's safe return home to her family and children. We all set a time we would pray for her every day that week, and even though we were not on the phone together, we dedicated concentrated prayer time to her. In less than a week of this, I got a call from Dona, "Teresa is Home! She is in bed resting right now, but she is home safe! I don't know what you did or how you made it happen, but Thank you for getting my baby home to us!" I was so happy and thankful! I told Dona, "I prayed for her relentlessly with my other friends and prayer warriors! That is all I knew to do! God brought her home, and I just helped get him the message she needed his help to get her there!"

From that day to today, Dona has called me Teresa's "Guardian Angel"! I would love to say Teresa's abusive relationship ended right here, but it didn't. It took a 2 year battle for her to free herself, not only from the torment he bestowed upon her on a regular basis but from her own inner demons. Her own thoughts are telling her that she didn't deserve anything better than what she had right in front of her and that she wasn't worthy of having someone, who would love her without his fists.

This time was probably some of the hardest times we have ever experienced as friends. I held strong to the belief that I could help her. Or better put, I wouldn't give up until I did! I held strong in my faith that God would use me to breathe life back into her soul and to give her the inner strength to say enough and find herself again. No, not only find, but create the person she wanted to be and to believe she not only deserved a better life but she was worthy of a life that was so extraordinary that words couldn't even find their way to her lips at that moment.

After every church service, I gave her my take away's from the sermon. If I saw something inspirational on YouTube or TV, I shared it with her. I prayed for her at every service. There were times when she would text me and ask if I'd been praying for her at a specific time. Usually, she was right as I prayed for her every day. I saw her getting stronger every day, but he still had this damn hold over her. To this day, I am not sure what it was, other than a deep seeded fear of the unknown. Fear of what he would do if she tried to leave. Fear of the blank page in the new chapter she was attempting to create.

He had such a hold on her emotionally and physically. He ended up talking her into taking him back and letting him move up to Minnesota with her. She had been there for a while and was doing well on her own. At least that was the appearances she put on for the rest of the world to see. When she cried at night, I could feel her tears drip into my heart. I was upset she took him back, but it wasn't my place in life to make decisions for her. I was her friend. The only thing I could do was support her and love her and pray for her. She knew how I felt and accepted how much I loved her, but she felt she needed him. I, by no means, kept my thoughts to myself about the situation. Our friendship has always been the type where we could speak our minds and truth even if those truths were hard to say. We knew they came out of love and to this day, our bond is unbreakable because of the journey we traveled to get to where we are.

They both had a job at the same restaurant, he worked in the kitchen, and she waited tables. She was going to school to be a nurse and was really working toward leveling up her life. She was reading her bible, and she was not only speaking in a more positive way, but she saw a better future for her and her children. Then, her daughter began having anxiety issues and was in and out of the hospital. That really added to her stress and turned up the heat on Teresa's anxiety. We rarely spoke about her boyfriend. I would ask how things were, and she would give one-word, brief answers. Deep down, I knew what that meant. I just prayed more and focused on her healing from the inside and for her to see and feel her true worth, to know she deserved so much more than the self-imposed prison that she had caged herself in, with him as her gatekeeper!

Then one day, she called to let me know she'd just got back from the ER and had three broken ribs. My first question was if he'd done it. She said no, she was chasing the dog and slipped on some ice on the stairs leading up to the apartment and fell. I knew she was lying. She didn't want me to know the truth. She was afraid if he found out she told somebody the truth about what had happened to her ribs, that next time he might kill her. I don't remember exactly how long it took for her to come clean about what happened. I believe it was only a couple of days because I kept asking questions. Then one night in a dream, I got a vision. It was a fuzzy picture, but in my heart what I saw was him kicking her, and that was how her ribs were broken. When I told her about the dream, she broke down and told me the truth about what really happened that day.

Teresa: "I was running to get away from him. I was trying to get into the house and lock the door behind me before he got to me, but he was just too big and strong. He kicked in the door and started in on me. It was the first time in all of the years we had been together that I screamed for help! I knew the neighbors were home and would hear me. I just prayed they would come help me. There was something different in his eyes this time, and I was truly afraid he would kill me that day if I didn't cry out for help."

She was still in danger because he was there. Even though he was trying to be nice to her like he always did after he beat her up, we both knew this time was somehow different. I knew she had done enough changing that this could finally be the last straw. The one that made sure she left him for good. I called LaTaunya, and we prayed for and over her for a solid week to help her heal and to give her strength.

Dona, Teresa's mom, called me. She asked if I had heard what happened to her? I told her she fell on the stairs chasing the dog because that was the story she told everyone. Dona already knew the truth. She knew Teresa was lying to protect him, when the reality was, she was lying to save herself. hey had a family event coming up and they were going to do an intervention to try and help get her away from him so she would finally be free and safe. Teresa had a serious inner battle going on. He had told her on many occasions, if she ever left him, he would hurt and/or kill her family. She would take all the pain he dished out to save them. Even if it meant she lost her life, her family was more important. And I knew that is how she felt about it even though she would never say it out loud.

What he didn't know, was that she was not the same person that left him in Tampa. She had changed and was still changing for the better. She wasn't where she wanted or needed to be, but she was definitely different. She was now plotting and planning how to make this breakup happen and how to escape and save her family too. With her anxiety at an all-time high, there were days we couldn't even communicate. Those days were terrifying to me because I didn't know where he was, what he was doing or if she was okay or not. I managed to get her to at least text me one time a day to let me know she was okay to give me a little peace of mind about the situation.

He ended up getting fired from his job. The short version of what happened next is she told him she was done, he left, and he moved to Vegas. She was finally free! He was gone! I thought she would finally feel free, but as much as she tried to say she was glad, I felt the pain and emptiness screaming from her heart, feeling lost and hurt. She had not been alone in over 12 years. He was always there. Even with all the bullshit, he put her through, and she wasn't sure how to do life without him in it. I was going to do everything within my power to help her create her life by design from this point forward.

Helping Her Grow

April of 2015 rolled around, and she was moving back down to Minneapolis with her mom. I told her I would come help her move if she wanted, so she bought me a plane ticket, and I went up to help them make the move down from Grand Maris. We spent the night up there then drove back down the next morning. You know, what makes this so significant is this was the first time since we met in 2011, that we had hung out together outside of work.

We had become best friends via phone calls, text messages, and Facebook. We knew each other's thoughts, fears, dreams, hurts, joys, and tears. As I said earlier, her ex hated me, so she had to memorize my phone number, delete text messages and phone calls or there would be repercussions. I think somehow he knew if she stayed friends with me, she would finally leave him.

While we were up there that night, loading everything in the truck and getting packed up, he called. Teresa couldn't take the dog with her because Dona's homeowners' insurance wouldn't cover a pit bull being in the house. Of course, he tried to use this as a way to get Teresa to bring the dog to him. I saw the terror in her eyes, and I knew she wasn't ready to be around him again. She wasn't strong enough to just go drop the dog off and come back.

It was during this time, as we continued to talk, and our bond became even stronger. There was one day, in particular, I don't remember the time frame or what was going on, but there was this overwhelming feeling that had come over me. We were on the phone and I asked her if I could pray with her before we hung up. She said yes, and as I started praying, this peace just flooded through me, and there was a different flow to my words and the prayer. I just let it all come out, however it chose too. We both were in full on cry mode by the time I finished praying. I told her I loved her and no matter what happened I was going to be there for her. Everything is going to be okay!

Shortly after that day, she ended up taking the dog to Vegas. We talked pretty much her whole way there. I was prepared for her not to go back to Minnesota, but I never let on to her. Instead, I kept talking to her and building her up, hoping beyond all hope that something I said would stick, and she would just go back home to her kids. I know words don't teach, only life experiences do. Words can inspire, motivate and empower a person to take action if they are ready to change their current circumstances. The words also, could quite possibly, help to give you a different perspective in which to look at your current situation. But, until a person is ready for change, sick and tired of being sick and tired; tired of being used, hurt and abused, there are no amount of words on the planet that can move them to better their own life.

I saw her Snapchat and Facebook posts, and I knew his hooks were once again set into her heart. There was nothing else I could do. She had to go through this on her own. When I say on her own, I mean, I cut off our friendship. I was not going to be a crutch or an enabler for her to continue running back to. We had the conversation previously if she went back to him, I was done, and our friendship was over because I couldn't just stand by and watch her kill herself. I felt that by going back to him one more time after him breaking her ribs, it gave him even more confidence and power to do whatever he wanted to and get away with it. If he lost his temper again and decided to beat her, she admitted that she would probably not survive his unrelenting punishment. Still, she willingly chose to go back again. The next 3 months broke my heart. I blocked her on Facebook, deleted her out of my phone and refused to take any calls from her. I stayed friends with her mom, so I could keep tabs on her. I continued to pray for her relentlessly, but I could not pretend everything was okay while she was still with him.

Time passed so quickly, my exact memory of what happened next is a little fuzzy. Either there was a post or her daughter text me that it had happened again. I sent her a message that said simply, "Really Teresa." She sent me videos and pictures to show me she was okay. We argued and I just stopped responding. I loved her like a sister but she was still with him and it was all out of my control. Over the next couple of weeks, she kept texting trying to get me to talk to her. Then one day she sent a text that said: "The difference between you and me is I still want you, my best friend, in my life ...sigh". She won. I could no longer keep her out of my life and not talk to her. I desperately missed our daily chats. I missed our laughs and just doing nothing with each other on the phone, as silly as that sounds.

They were living with his sister and her husband. She was still reading her Bible every day, and I could see and feel she was different. She was stronger than I had ever seen her. I could see all the work we had done together, had become well-watered seeds and now the roots were growing into trees. I couldn't say anything though, and I was just there to support her in whatever way that I could from so far away. I knew how he felt about me. She had told him he was not going to choose her friends anymore and that included me.

She called me one day, not long after that conversation and said they were looking at apartments. He wanted them to get their own place again. I think my heart was stuck in my throat when my exact words "Teresa, I really don't think it's a good idea. You are safe as long as you are with his family. He doesn't want them to see who he really is. Are you sure you want to do this? Are you sure history is not going to repeat itself? Do me a favor ...reach down and feel your ribs? How do they feel right about now?" All I heard was silence on the other side of the phone. When she replied all, she said was "I will be careful. I promise. The first sign of trouble and I'm out of there." The first night in their new apartment, she couldn't even sleep in the bedroom with him. She had flashbacks of Grand Maris. I want to say it was less than two weeks later when she texts me with "It's time for me to go! I'm packing my shit now, and my friend from work is coming to get me tonight". This was super late for me on the east coast. I was still living in Atlanta at the time, so I didn't see the message until I got up the next morning for work. She had thrown all of her stuff in a garbage bag and was waiting outside when her girlfriend from work came to get her. When I talked to her the next day, I found out he had told her in no uncertain terms "get your shit and get out or it's going to be a bad night for you."

The day finally came when she left him and she never looked back. She knew it was over and she never wanted to experience the pain that he inflicted on her soul ever again. She still had doubts and some fears, but she knew, this time, there was no going back. She had finally had enough and she was Done. It was time to turn the page.

A NEW DREAM WAS BORN

Not too long after she walked out of that apartment and really, the only life she had known for over 14 years, she had to learn how to live on her own again. She had to stand on her own two feet, look at herself in the mirror and learn to love who she saw staring back at her. She had to learn she was worthy of so much more than what she had allowed herself to experience. She also had to learn to forgive herself. I know it sounds crazy to someone who has never been in or experienced an abusive relationship before. But I can tell you there is a level of guilt the abuser puts on their victim that is hard to comprehend. That weight can manifest itself in so many ways, that its unfathomable to the rest of the world. She had to forgive herself for trusting him over and over again, for going back believing it would be different; for putting herself in the situations that could have taken her life and most of all, for allowing him to keep her from not only her friends but most importantly from her family and children.

I poured love into her every day. We talked several times each day as she went through this self-healing and growth process. She had to trust herself to choose a new life that would be better and a man who would see her from the inside out. Someone who wouldn't look at who she was not, but who she chose to become after walking through the fires of abuse, hurt, turmoil and lies. The woman who emerged on the other side, a totally different than who she was when she went in. The pain she went through was not only inflicted by another but also by her own self-inflicted thoughts she still had to fight through in order to learn to believe in herself, her purpose and regain her self-esteem once again. The length of this road would be determined by how willing she was to change and how teachable she would have to be in order to make the changes, not only in her thoughts but her beliefs and deep within her heart and soul.

She was staying with her friend from work, and this was a safe haven for her at the time. Her friend had been through similar things and had a level of understanding that not many other people had of the circumstances she had just freed herself from. I encouraged Teresa to start getting out of the house and find something fun to do to take her mind off of the past and start really focusing on a future she gets to create now. It was new territory for her to work on herself and to find out what it was that really made her happy! This wasn't about anyone else any more...it was now about her!

Not long after, Teresa started going out with her friend just to get out of the house so that she could clear her head. We both have always loved to shoot pool and we were also pretty good at it. There is this local little sports bar in San Diego that had pool tables and she really liked the atmosphere at this place. One Friday night, this HOT guy walks in. Tall, bald, built and gorgeous. I do believe it was love at first sight for her, well maybe lust, but it was definitely a start in the right direction. If you ever get to hear her tell this story, you would know exactly what I mean. They hit it off right away and pretty much became attached at the hip. They spent time together doing things during the week, after work and finding fun things to do on the weekend, like hiking and going to the comedy clubs.

For the first time in over 14 years, Teresa had found someone who valued her. He saw who was standing right in front of him. He wasn't looking behind her to see where she had been. He would build her up and tell her she could do anything if she put her mind to it. He also helped her to find her self-worth again and believe that she deserved this new life she was creating. He always showed her how she was supposed to be treated by a man. He opened doors for her, and he loved on her, he helped her in any way that he possibly could. It was a new way of life for her. She had never experienced this type of treatment from any man she had ever been with.

There were conversations where I helped coach her through her thoughts and feelings about him and the fear she was experiencing. There was one night, in particular, she told me about when he walked up behind her too fast and it scared the hell out of her. She jumped, he saw the fear in her eyes and saw she was physically shaking. He was so shocked by her response and asked her what was wrong. She blew it off by telling him she didn't hear him behind her and just avoided the whole conversation.

She was afraid to tell him the truth about her past, with the abuse, and for how long it had gone on. She had a deep seeded fear that he would think less of her and walk away. She told me she wasn't sure she could handle that so soon after escaping from her dark life. I let her know her feelings were valid but assured her that once she was able to get it out and give herself the grace of forgiveness, it would take her through her healing process deeper and faster than she could even imagine. She trusted me, knowing the things I had been through in my life. Though different, just as traumatic. She knew if I could do that for myself, then I had the tools to help her do the same.

It took some time, but she finally got up the nerve to tell him about her past relationship. She was right about the fact that he just couldn't understand, one, how any man could do that to a woman and two, why anyone would stay under those circumstances. It was outside the reality of what he believed a relationship should be like. He assured her he was nothing like her ex and she had nothing to fear from him. He was a strong and a gentleman. He would walk away before he ever would stoop so low as to put his hands on her or any female for that matter. There was something in his words and in his smile that made her start to believe this could quite possibly be the start of something real. Something she had only dreamed about before, like a fairytale, she never believed could come true. Would this be her fairytale ending? Could he be the one to open her eyes to a new life and a loving relationship like she had never known or experienced before? Only time would tell, but the seeds of hope had been planted and were being watered every day.

We had planned for me to come out to Cali in September for her birthday. We were scheduled to run a Spartan Beast at Pala Raceway. This was going to be my sixth race of the year. I was on the quest for my double trifecta. I had just passed my test in August to become a Spartan SGX Coach, and this would be my first race after that. My clients at the gym, who are awesome by the way, had put together a GoFundMe account to send me to Dallas to take the Spartan course in June. I had two more races to run after this Beast in SoCal. One that took me back to Dallas on Halloween weekend and the last race was the week after my big public speaking event in November. The race was on Teresa's birthday which was the 17th, her new boyfriend's birthday was the 16th and mine was the 22nd. We had a lot to celebrate while I was in Cali for the first time ever in my life. I was excited about the adventure we were embarking on and getting to do this race together and getting to meet her new man with the bonus of all of us hanging out together.

I was the only one of her friends ever to meet her new man in person. She didn't trust herself to completely let go of her fears in order to trust someone again with her heart. She knew my intuition, and my connection with God would tip me off if anything was not as it should be with him. I had breakfast with him one morning while she was at work. As we ate, we talked about her birthday and the gifts we wanted to get her. He helped me to figure out where to go to find my gifts for her since I didn't know my way around. We talked about her previous relationship for a really long time. I tried to help him understand it from her point of view and to try to get him to look at it outside his own perception.

My hope was that I had planted enough seeds for him to at least get it and think about the situation differently. After spending time with him, I truly believed he was genuinely a really good guy. I knew from that conversation, and the night we went out to shoot pool, and he really cared about her way more than she knew or that either of them were willing to admit. Even though they had a hard time expressing their feelings, I saw right through both of them. Two hurt people who were hiding the fact that they quite possibly had fallen in love and fearful of the rejection if they were wrong. Was he her soul mate? Had she really found "The One"? Or was he just the one who was supposed to bridge the gap from a bitter past to a bright new beautiful and better future, so the next man could have his happily ever after, with her as his wife? I didn't know the answers to any of those questions running through my mind and it didn't matter. I wanted her to find happiness within herself and if he could add to that, then all the better. She deserved to be treated like the queen I saw in her, but she needed to see it in herself and accept it. She deserved to be loved for who she was, lifted up, encouraged and to have someone she could lock arms with, so they could build a legacy together. Did I think it really could be him? I don't know, but I saw a lot of potential for that. They both had a lot of healing and growing to do, individually and together. Only time would tell exactly how this part of her story would play out.

We took a long walk on the beach before I had to head back to Atlanta. I told her, "I think he is really a good guy, Teresa. I can see he really cares about you and might even love you. If you take anything from what I say here today, please hear this, He is not your ex! He wants nothing but the best for and from you. He has a good heart, but he is just as afraid of getting hurt as you are chica. Both of you are going to have to work together to overcome those fears as a team if you really want this to work. But if you keep hiding and comparing him to a past, that no longer exists or serves you, then you will lose him. It's time for you to turn the page and start writing a new chapter in your life. One that you get to create, not one that someone else creates for you." We sat on the wall and cried for a while. As much fun as I had in Cali, it was time for me to head back to Atlanta the next day.

She told me before I left, "you know, you would make an awesome Life Coach. You have helped me change my life in so many ways, that you are not even aware of and if you can do it for me, there are so many other people on this planet who need you to help them to do the same". I had been thinking about that for a while, but she poured a lot of water on those seeds that day! That was the first real serious conscious thought I had about becoming a life coach.

When November rolled around, I had just finished my second Spartan Beast and was one race away from completing my double trifecta. Before running my final race, I had my first ever public speaking event scheduled at a women's empowerment summit. At this public speaking event, I was sharing my entire life story for the first time publicly. I had shared parts of my story here and there about my depression and about the childhood sexual abuse, but I had never shared my story as a whole to anyone, much less a room full of strangers.

I had been doing Facebook lives almost every week now for roughly a year. I loved being able to share my heart and inspire so many people in that way. I was getting a lot of positive feedback from people about how those live videos were truly helpful and inspiring to them. This gave me quite a bit of confidence that the public speaking would be my next step and it would be an easy thing to transition into. Ultimately, it was just more water on the seeds of a future that I had never imagined could be mine.

Sharing my whole entire story in front of a room full of women, I'd never met, was as exciting on the outside as it was terrifying on the inside! I had a 30-minute slot to share what I believed would help them grow and to help expand their beliefs the most about who they could become if they chose to do so. I wrote out my speech way in advance and went over it several times to make sure I had timed it perfectly. I mean, it was my story, I knew what happened, but I wanted to share it in a way that would empower them to believe they could overcome whatever part of their past may have been holding them back. I was on the phone with Teresa several times a week reading it to her, timing it, making sure all the pieces were there. Making sure I didn't have a "Ummm" at every other word. I also wanted to make sure I wasn't talking 500 mph! Which I tend to do a lot when I am nervous, as I am sure so many other brand-new speakers do as well. I just knew I wanted it to be perfect! In my mind, I saw so much coming from this one event. I honestly believed with all my heart this would be the first of many events that would be in my near future. I wasn't sure how or where they would come from, but in my heart, I just knew this was the beginning of a new chapter in my life.

That day came. It was finally here! November 12, 2016! I had to be there by 10am, and it was an hour away, so of course, I was there at like 9:30 am to make sure I wasn't late! Oh, and to be sure that if I had to throw up because I was so nervous, I would have time to do that and be presentable before my time to go since I was first one speaking at the event.

Every hair was in place, my makeup was perfect, and my outfit was phenomenal if I do say so myself! I had rehearsed it 100's of times, so I knew every word, every pause and every thought behind it. I prayed every morning when I got up, but this morning was extra special. I thanked God for giving me this opportunity, and I hoped I would make him proud of me by the end of the event. I asked him to let my words flow effortlessly and help me to touch at least one heart in the room to make their world a better place. I was about halfway through my drive there and my stomach was in knots. I really thought I might be sick. I tried calling Teresa but got her voicemail. I mean it was only 6:15 am on a Saturday morning, she should have been up waiting on my call for my big day! That was a real thought in my head as ridiculous as it sounds coming out of my mouth now lol. So, I started running through the people I knew, I thought would be up that early and it would be ok for me to call. I needed someone who could talk me down off the cliff I was standing on in my mind. Who can I call, who's up? Debra Hand!!! Yes! She is always up early! She has known me for 25+ years and I knew she could help calm me down!

Debra: "Hey girlie! Are you ready for today?"

Me: "I am as ready as I'm gonna get right now! I am a nervous wreck! My stomach is in knots, and I feel like I might actually throw up if I don't calm down before I get there!"

Debra: "Why are you nervous? You got this! You know you were born to do this! You spoke this into existence, remember. You have been practicing, and I know you have got it all down pat. What's the matter, baby?"

Me: "I know everything I'm going to say. I only know one person in the whole entire room. I know this is what I am meant to do. I know it's a part of my purpose. What if I let God down? What if I mess it up?" Tears welled up in my eyes, and my voice cracked a little.

Debra: "Baby, you can't let God down! He loves you so much for doing this. Where are you right now?"

Me: "I'm about halfway there."

Debra: "Well the only way you could let him down was if you didn't show up! If you let your fear win and you gave up and went home! Are you going to turn around and go home? I can answer that for you. I know that you're not because you don't know how to quit! It's not in your DNA. You also don't let fear run your life anymore! This is just some nervous jitters. You are going to be amazing, and I can't wait to hear all about it when you get done!"

Me: "No, I'm not going to turn around. No, I'm not going to quit. Hell, I'm trying not to cry right now because my makeup looks perfect!" We both laughed at that. "Thank you so much, Debra. I know its early, I just needed someone to help me calm down! I love you so much! I promise to call you as soon as I am done!"

I hung up, and then my phone rang again, this time it was Teresa.

Teresa: Hey girl, you okay? Are you on the way to your event?

Me: "Yes. I'm nervous as hell and feel like I am gonna throw up, but I'm on the way. I just got off the phone with Debra. When you didn't answer, I figured you were still asleep, and I needed someone to talk me off this cliff."

Teresa: "Yeah, I heard the phone, I saw it was you, so I went and got a cup of coffee and went to the bathroom so I could talk to you until you got there. I was pretty sure you would call me this morning. How are you feeling now?

Me: "I'm still nervous, but a little better. I told Debra I was just afraid of disappointing God and I didn't want to mess up this awesome opportunity he has given me to help more people."

Teresa: "Aren't you on the way to the event now?"

Me: "Well yeah, don't you hear me in the car? Debra asked me the same damn question."

Teresa: "Well, we both know you can't disappoint God unless you quit and you don't know how to do that, so problem solved chica. Girl, you know you got this! You spoke this into existence just a little over four months ago. You are going to be an awesome Life Coach and a public speaker. This is what you came to this earth to do. It's who you are. I know you're gonna knock it out of the park."

Me: "Don't make me cry and mess up my makeup! This is why I love you and Debra so much! You guys are so awesome, and I just want to say thank you for all your help in getting me ready for this event. I so appreciate all of the time you spent helping me put it all together and timing me to get it laid out perfectly. I don't know what I would have done without you."

Teresa: "Well, you never have to worry about that! I'm always going to be here for you! You can count on that!"

I have the best friends ever!

The Power to Exhale

I was sitting outside waiting for the library to open and everyone to get there. There wasn't any traffic, so I arrived way earlier than I had anticipated. I had my notebook so I could journal if I needed to calm down any more and go over my speech to add a little more confidence in my heart. I took a minute and sent up another prayer. "God, thank you! Thank you again for all you do. You got me to this place, and I know everything is going to work out exactly as its planned. I know I am here for a reason and a purpose and you brought me to it so you will bring me through it! Please help my words flow and see to it that I don't throw up right there in front of everyone, please and thank you! Today is going to be a good day because you took the time to wake me up. That is all I need to know right now. Please help me to touch whoever it is that needs to hear my words this morning. I am so thankful for everything you have and are doing for me. In Jesus name, I pray, Amen."

I saw other cars starting to pull up. I didn't want my nerves to show, so I talked to myself one last time before I went in, "Breathe in. Breathe out. You got this Tammy. This is your journey. This is your story. This is the new beginning of a life you never imagined could be your reality. You are strong, powerful and beautiful! Now go in there and do what you do best…be you and everything will work out perfectly!"

Despite the cool weather and the awesome pep talk to myself, I felt the sweat running down my back. My nerves were still going strong, but I was determined to make it through this event. I was determined to be strong, and my intention was to do my best not to cry while I was sharing my story. I got my stuff, took a deep breath and walked inside. I went straight to the bathroom to freshen up and check my makeup. I sent up one last prayer, took a deep breath in and then blew it out. I felt a rush of peace come over me. I knew everything was going to be okay. I looked up and said, "I know that was you, God. Thank you".

I walked into the room where the ladies who had organized the event were setting everything up. They were anticipating 20-25 people, but I think there were only about 18 ladies who attended. Silently, I was kind of thankful for the smaller crowd. I introduced myself to everyone as I walked in. Everyone at the venue was so nice from the minute I walked in the door. I got lots of compliments on my outfit which boosted my confidence about speaking to the group. As they were setting everything up, I had the thought to turn this event into a Facebook Live! Since I did those all the time and I am comfortable in front of the camera, it was an easy way for me to ease my nerves about doing the event. This was going to be perfect. I just needed someone to hold my phone. I planned to ask Leila, who was the one who invited me to come speak and introduced me to Bonnie, the event coordinator, to get it all set up. Doing the Live would also mean I would have my first ever speaking event recorded! That was WIN in my book if I could pull it off!

When Leila got there, she gave me a huge hug and said she was so happy to see me. We had only met one time at the auto shop where we got our oil changed. Here is a little something about God's divine timing, and I can tell you I do not believe in coincidences at all. We were both at that little shop getting our oil changed, the same day at the same time, for a reason. The reason was this right here! This event. My first stepping stone to the next part of my life journey. I asked her about holding my phone for the Facebook Live, and she was happy to do that for me. I was the first person up to speak. That in and of itself would make anyone nervous. I would set the tone for the rest of the event and everyone who followed along behind me.

Another sweet lady introduced me to kick off the event, and as I walked up to the front of the room, I handed Leila my phone, and it was game time! I started off talking kind of fast. I told a little joke about how grandkids are the reward we get for not killing our kids when they were teenagers, we get to spoil them and hand them back. All the ladies in the room were mothers, and we had several grandmothers in the room as well, and they all laughed with me. In my mind I said "Here We Go!" then, I settled in and went into the rest of my story. I walked back and forth across the front of the room as I spoke. I believe it was more nerves than anything else, but it looked really natural when I got to watch the replay. I started off a little fast, as I kind of expected I would, but when I caught my flow, it felt perfect!

A couple of times I got close to crying, but I made it through with just a few minor cracks in my voice. The emotion that was coming from me was raw and genuine. The women in the room were all drawn in and were hanging on my every word as they listened to my story. I asked questions throughout my speech and learned that most there had been through some sort of sexual abuse and/or depression or knew someone who had. I finished up my speech with the story Steve Harvey told at the end of one of his Family Feud shows titled "You have to Jump." Basically, what he said was, we all have two choices in life, we can sit on the sidelines and let life pass us by. Or, we can choose to jump toward our dreams and off the cliff, knowing our parachute will open on the way down. My wish for all of them was that when they Jumped, they would soar with the Eagles as they saw all their hopes and dreams come true.

I got a standing ovation and lots of hugs! One woman met up with me as I walked to the back of the room. She told me how I touched her heart, and she shared she almost had to walk out because it hurt her to know all the pain I had endured in my life. Something made her stay, and she was glad she did as I helped her to see we all can become whoever we choose to be. She was inspired that I was not only able to forgive my mom but also others who had hurt me and she shared how amazing she thought that was. What touched her so deeply was how I was able to actually have a relationship with my mom after all that had happened. She said it was something she truly admired me for. I hugged her neck with eyes full of tears and thanked her for sharing that with me. I told her I learned from my experiences and healing process that we have to separate the person from the act. At the end of the day, she was still the woman who gave birth to me and most of all; she was my Mom. She had her own demons that she was never able to beat and I had learned a lot from her in spite of all the hard times we had over the years. I told her I am who I am today because she was my mom and for that, I will always be thankful and love her for it.

When I left the meeting, I had the most awesome feeling. I did it! I knew I not only touched just one person in that room but ALL of those women. I don't know the butterfly effects that may have come out of that day, but what I do know is, I did it! I also learned I have a passion for being in front of a room sharing, talking, teaching and giving back. I didn't know the how, but I knew deep down inside of me this would not be the last time I would be in front of a room. I was going to be on many stages. That was a reality stamped on my heart at that moment!

RACE DAY IS HERE!!

Race day was finally here! This was all so surreal to me at this moment. I was still reeling after my speaking event the previous weekend and the response I received from the event planner, the women who were there, and not to mention the amazing responses from all of my Facebook friends/fans. I was really just in awe of it all. I had to find a way to focus on what was in front of me at this moment, race day! Now was not the time to be focusing on all the awesomeness that had just happened the weekend before. It was time to dig in and finish this race strong.

At the beginning of the year, I had decided I was going for my first ever Spartan double trifecta. For those of you who are not familiar with what a Spartan Race is all about, it's an obstacle course mud race. I fell in love with doing the races the year before when I completed my first trifecta. It was in Arizona and the venue was beautiful. The scenery was absolutely breathtaking! Michelle competed with me in our first ever Spartan race in February of 2015. She was afraid of heights, which I had forgotten until we got into the starting gate. I saw the color wash out of her face. She had a "what the hell did I just get myself into" look lol. It was then I realized, this race was no longer about me; it was about helping her to overcome her fear and finish the race no matter what. As we went through the race, I helped her with any obstacle she struggled with. I was so stinking proud of her for finishing that race and attempting every obstacle there! I think we ended up doing something like 130 damn burpees'! We had tears in our eyes as we crossed the finish line and hugged like 2 high school girls who had just won a pageant or something. It was so empowering to complete all of the obstacles for the first time ever at an event like this. I finished the trifecta that year with my friends Jennifer and Allie! The 3 of us went on to do the Super in Atlanta and the Beast in Dallas. We even made Jennifer's school newspaper with our Epic Jump over the fire to finish the race, in Dallas! It was definitely an Epic Finish to my first year of Spartan races!

I was so excited about the previous year's races. I even appreciated the days it took to recover from them. When March rolled around, I took nine of my clients from the gym to run their first ever Spartan Race. I was scheduled to run back to back days. This would be the first time I had put myself through that kind of physical challenge. Saturday I ran by myself and Sunday I ran with my team. During the race, I not only helped my teammates with motivation and encouragement to complete the obstacles, but there were several places I stopped to help other people who were not even on my team.

There was one girl in particular who got stuck at the top of the vertical cargo net. She was afraid of heights and was frozen there in fear, with a death grip on the net. I got Tal, Pia's husband who was on my team, to stand underneath her as I climbed up on the front side of the net where she was frozen. I coached her on how to take her leg over and know that she was safe. We had people under her who were there to support her on her way down. She just had to trust herself and believe she was strong enough to do it. She finally threw her leg over, took a deep breath and let go with one hand, quickly to grab on the other side. Then she made her way down on her own to the bottom of the obstacle. She hugged my neck after she made it down and thanked me for helping her.

It was after that race that my clients told me I should become a Spartan Coach and they started a GoFundMe account to raise the money for the trip and sent me to Dallas to do just that, get my Spartan Coach Certification! What a humbling experience it was, to have my clients believe in me so much that they helped put all the pieces in place to get me certified.
In April it was the military race at Fort Benning I ran with Shaun and Vince, the stadium race in Dallas while I was there for my Spartan certification class. Followed up by the Super in Asheville, NC the first weekend in August. Which, by the way, was one of the hardest races I had ever done. My teammates for that race were Becky, Shaun, Vince, Kai, Joey and myself. The terrain there was ridiculous, to say the least. Then add in a temp of 102 degrees plus the humidity on race day. The elevation started at 2200 feet scaling all the way up to 3402' at its highest point. Afterward, I went to So Cal in September to run the first beast of the year with Teresa on her birthday, as I've already mentioned. That was the closest I have ever come to thinking about quitting a race. It was 102 degrees in the desert, not a cloud in the sky and I didn't have all of the race day supplements I typically ran a race with. It was that day I truly learned to appreciate Advocare and their O2Gold. The breathing capacity with it versus without it is enough to make it a staple for any type of

cardio workout or race I would compete in, from that day forward. After So Cal, I only had two more races to go, first stop was my second beast in Dallas on October 28th with Becky. This is where she completed her first ever trifecta and I was so stinking proud of her! There was a drought that year, and the terrain was as hard as cement. And it was over 17 miles to reach the finish line. Her husband Brad was a trouper following us all over the course. Our joints hurt for days afterward, but it was worth it to see her finish and get her first ever trifecta!

November 18th had finally arrived, and I was in Mobile, Alabama to complete in my first ever double trifecta! I was stoked. I was still way more sore than what I had expected from the previous two races. I was nursing an IT band injury, but I didn't care! I was finishing this race if I had to crawl across the damn finish line. My only goal was to finish! I had brought all of my other medals from the previous races, seven in total, so I could take my picture at the end with all of them on! Including the one solid medal which said, Trifecta X2! All the pain, travel, sweat and tears had all come down to this one race! I chose here because it was flat! I wanted little or no hills so it would be easy on my knees. The Dallas race had been just three weeks earlier and was 17 miles of rock-hard ground that beat my poor joints to pieces. They were in the middle of a drought, like the rest of the country, and it hurt walking/running to complete the race. Thank God for the Cryotherapy appointments afterward to help reduce all the inflammation in my joints!

I got there early, as usual, to walk around so I could ask some of the other racers what to look out for during the race and to learn what was the hardest part. I also wanted to know if there was anything, in particular, I needed to avoid if I could. This is my typical race day M.O. I started the race with Kai and Joey, but it wasn't far into the race when I told them to go ahead without me. They were runners, and there was just no way I could keep up their pace with the pain I was having in my knees, plus it was swampy. My only goal was to finish the race that day, not to break my record time. I finished in just over 3 hours! I was stoked! I collected all my medals full of tears as I took my pictures and even did a Facebook Live to celebrate! I was even interviewed by an OCR YouTube channel! I was so freaking stoked!!

It was a truly amazing experience from beginning to end! I had just turned 49 and had had an amazing year! I finished eight races, to complete my first ever double trifecta. I passed my Spartan SGX and Obstacle Specialist certifications and nailed my first ever public speaking engagement. Wow! I really just wanted to soak it all in. I realized I had just completed one of the most epic years of my life. I did it man! I planned, orchestrated and completed every event of the entire epic year. If anyone would have told me ten years prior, this is how I would finish my 49th year on this earth, and I would have laughed hysterically in their face and asked them to pass me another shot of Tequila!

I was hard for me to comprehend the reality of what I accomplished. I was truly amazed I had gone from having no dreams or goals, ever in my life, to not only learning how to dream but also planning all of my goals in advance! I'd also become strong enough to follow through in not only taking the steps toward them but also completing them in the time frame I had laid out for them. I think this was the first time in my life that I really truly consciously believed my life was different because I made the choice to make it different. And with it came the realization that what was in front of me was going to be even bigger.

7 MY BESTLIFE STARTS NOW

After 2017 ended up being such a tremendous year with so many achievements under my belt, I finally felt happy, accomplished, excited and maybe even a little relieved. I had a lot on my plate, and silently I wondered if I could really do it all. There were times I had a lot of self-doubts that tried to creep in with whispering thoughts in the back of my mind, but I quickly dismissed them, so they could not gain any momentum. I refused to let any negative thoughts, beliefs or doubts, take root and derail any of the plans I had laid out. If there is one thing that is just not a part of my DNA, it's quitting anything. I have never been good at quitting or losing for that matter. I guess it's the athlete in me.

Given the way my life started off, I sometimes wondered how I was able to have so much determination and a will to succeed at something once I made the decision to do it. I attribute the majority of that to playing team sports. We were taught from day one on the field, that you never give up. You never quit unless you just physically can't go on anymore. I carried that "You never quit" attitude into all the other areas of my life I guess. I believe it was Steve Jobs who once said "You can't connect the dots looking forward. You can only connect them looking back." I would have to be 100% in agreement with that statement. When we look forward to the things we want to do, we call it a dream or a goal. Some "Hope" they can make it happen. Some of us "Know" we will make it happen, even if there is a "Someday" attached to it.

Then there are times, even though we think we know the "How" it will happen when it finally comes about, the path we took to get there looked absolutely nothing like what we thought it would when we began the journey toward that goal. It's not until we look back to when we first laid out the plans, where we can see clearly, the path we chose, what we could have done better or even what we didn't do so well. All of those things become lessons in what to do or not, with the next set of goals we set out to accomplish.

As I said in an earlier chapter, becoming a certified life coach was my next big step. I had been coaching friends, unofficially, for about three years. At the time, I didn't know that's what I was doing. I just knew I had a gift for helping people, so I did. I started doing searches for life coaching companies to see what all was going to be involved in the process and the financial investment it would take to accomplish it. I actually checked into the Tony Robins course first because he was someone I admired in the field. This was in 2012 when I was living in my apartment in Smyrna. It was close to $5000 or maybe even a little more if my memory serves me correctly. I could barely pay my bills, my rent was past due, and there was no way me taking his course was even a slight possibility. So I just dismissed the idea altogether, believing it was probably just a pipe dream that would never happen anyway..... until now.

There were so many life coaching companies out there. I know I spent several days, maybe even weeks, just to get some ideas about which way I wanted to go. The last week of December 2017, I was checking my email and came across an email from a company called BestLife Creation Society offering a Level 1 coaching certification! I opened it up, and read the email from Sue Adams. She was running an end of year special for $99, regularly $495. I was like SOLD! I sent her an email immediately to verify what the email said was correct. She sent me a PayPal invoice, and it was a done deal! Starting January 16, 2017, I was embarking on my journey to become a Certified Life Coach! Woot Woot! To be perfectly honest, I had no idea, whatsoever, how Sue or BestLife ended up in my inbox. I just assumed they were one of the many company's I ran across during my searches. I didn't have anything else from them in any of the information I had saved even though I looked trying to figure it all out. But at that moment, I didn't care how they made their way into my inbox, and I was just super excited they did! When I share this part of my story, me and Jen (the owner/CEO of BestLife) laugh and say we don't care how it happened, we just believe it was divine guidance, and we are both so thankful it happened the way it did!

My friends, family, co-workers, and clients were all super excited for me as well. They all agreed with Teresa. This was a perfect path for me. It went hand in hand with what I was already doing, and they could see the potential with that in my toolbox to be able to help more people. The 16th of January came up quickly. I had ordered the books that were required for the course and was super excited to get started! I wasn't really sure what to expect. The entire class was done via teleconference calls, which was a new way for me to take classes. There were people from all over the world on the call. We had the United States, Canada, Amsterdam, Holland, and Norway there! I was super impressed right away!

I got on the call early, partly out of excitement and partly because I didn't want to be late. Sue, the instructor, was already on the call waiting for her new students to jump on. I enjoyed getting to chat with her for a few minutes before everyone else joined in. She gave us a quick run-down of how the class would work and then paired us up with peer partners. We each had two people who were coaching us and two different people we would be coaching. I really loved the hands-on experience I got throughout taking the course. Sue was absolutely amazing at reading people and helping us to look at situations from different perspectives. She was, and is, a truly gifted instructor.

We learned how to muscle test and how to do this really cool breathing technique called the Freedom Release Method. I didn't realize this right away, but this was and is an amazing tool that would change my life quickly and dramatically. There was so much info to take in, but she made us feel like we could do anything. As we were going through the various coaching assignments with our partners, I was receiving lots of great feedback from both those who were coaching me and those who I coached. They had asked me how long I had been a life coach before choosing to get certified? When I said I wasn't certified, they were shocked. I explained about my personal training background and how it really incorporates a good bit life coaching, to a certain degree, because you have to help people push through their mental/emotional blocks to help them reach their health and fitness goals.

After finishing the course, we were required to do a certain number of practice coaching sessions and turn in all our information to get our official certification. I think one of the biggest confirmations that I was on the right track was when I did a session with the GM at my gym, Dionna. She was so sweet, and I loved her so very much. She was young but passionate about helping people. She was excited for me, even though she really wasn't sure what life coaching was. I convinced her to be one of my practice sessions and took her to lunch to do a dream building exercise. She said, "I don't know what that is, but you said lunch at Grub Burger, so I'm in."

Grub Burger on Briarcliff Road in Atlanta is one of the most awesome places to eat and was my favorite. We went to lunch, sat at the bar so we could get full service, and I started explaining what we were about to do. The look on her face let me know she still wasn't sure what this was all about, but she was willing to do it to help me get my certification. The first thing we did was a Wheel of Life exercise. This is to see what the areas were that would be her biggest priority. As we went through the exercise, I saw she was completely unaware of how unbalanced her life had become. I knew she really wasn't happy at the gym anymore and I wasn't sure I could help her, but I knew I could at least open her eyes and give her a better view of where she was in order to help her make better-informed choices from that point forward about where she wanted to go.

After we finished that exercise, we went on to dream building. I took out another sheet of paper and had her write at the top of it, "If money were no object, and you knew you couldn't fail… what would I want, be, do or have?" I had her number her paper from 1 to 20. I let her take about 5 minutes to think and write down a minimum of 10 to 20 items she would like to get, things she would do and/or places she would go, if money were no object and she knew she couldn't fail. I saw she was having a really hard time and almost looked distressed that nothing was coming to mind.

As Dionna was trying to think of things, she was drawing blanks. So I started prompting her to help her get started. "What about a new car, I know your last car just died? Is there anywhere you want to travel? Would you want to do something special for your family?" That is when she started thinking outside the box. I just had to remind her "Money is No Object and You can't fail… What do you want?" She sat there for a minute looking at the paper. I said to her gently, "You've forgotten how to dream baby girl. Open up your mind and your heart and see where it leads you?" When we finished the exercise, she hugged my neck and thanked me for helping her to open her eyes.

Less than three weeks later she pulled me to the side and told me she was leaving. She had turned in her notice and was excited about what had happened. She said "I want to thank you for helping me to see I had quit dreaming. I got a job at Brain Balance helping children with Autism and other learning disabilities. Plus, I have another part-time job at a Pediatric office. It's always been my dream to work in occupational therapy and to help children. Until you did those exercises with me, I didn't see a way I could make it happen. Thank you so much! Please don't stop doing what you're doing! People need you in their life!"

I hugged her neck with tears in my eyes and laughingly said "There is no crying in the gym! I am so excited for you! I know you are going to be awesome! Thank you for giving me the opportunity to work with you and the confirmation that I made the right decision in becoming a life coach".

It was then I knew, deep inside, my life was about to change.... Again. I didn't know the how or the when I just knew things were going to be different and better than I could have ever imagined.

I want to step away from the story for just a minute to dig into this dream building exercise with you and give you some reasons I believe the majority of us, as humans, have given up on our dreams. If you have never done anything like this before, I would encourage you to take a few minutes and do this for yourself. Grab a blue pen and white piece of paper and follow the instructions as I laid them out with Dionna. It may take you a few minutes to come up with just a couple of things on your list, and that's okay. Take a breath and really let your mind wander. It could be a new car, a new house, pay off all your debt, take your family on a cruise, pay off your parent's house, pay off school loans, start a non-profit, travel to exotic locations just to name a few.

The reason this feels so uncomfortable or maybe even hard for you is because your dreams were stifled as a child, while you were still in school. Think about the reality of that for just a minute. When we were in elementary school, our teachers always encouraged our dreams. They would have us write about what we wanted to be when we grow up. Then we get to middle school where all the brainwashing begins. Teachers began to tell us, "Now it's time to be realistic"; "No more pipe dreams, you have to get a real job so you can pay the bills and take care of your family when you have one." High School gets here, and they are pushing a career or job field on us, based on "their opinion" of what they think we should become. They base it off of our grades and label us successful or no hope of being successful.

We can tell exactly what they think when the full court press comes from them to either go to college, go to a trade school or they push us toward a local store in town. Then they even get our parents on board with their "Opinion" of who they think we can be.

Sometimes it starts with the parents who push us towards certain careers or jobs. In their minds, they want us to turn out better than they did, so they think they know what is best for us. Again, they don't ask us "What makes you happy? What do you want to do when you get out of school?" Does any of that sound familiar? They mean well and I believe they have the best intentions when they do this, not realizing they are limiting our possibilities of doing great things with our lives because they have now taken away any belief we may have had in ourselves to make our dreams a reality. All because we see them as an authority figure and we trust them. If they "Say" this is what we Should do, well then that's as good as it gets and our Dreams Die in that Moment!

I'M A LIFE COACH Y'ALL

I did It! I completed all of the requirements and was now, officially, a Certified Life Coach with BestLife Creation Society!! At the time I finished, I had not yet made the decision to become a member. I wasn't sure if I wanted to join the company or not. They explained how they were a personal development company with a focus on life coaching. The classes were held daily, so I could continue my training to help me grow personally and as a life coach. They would also teach me how to build and grow my life coaching business. That was what got my attention, learning more about the business and how to build it. I knew I was good already, but I did not have a clue how to market myself, where or how to find my clients, or how or what to charge for my services. After I went over all of the questions swimming around in my head, it just made sense to join the company for those reasons alone. If I got anything else out of the company then, it would be an added bonus as far as I was concerned. I knew it was way more affordable than any of the other companies I had looked into and for the value, I would be getting in return, it was a win in my books!

I joined on March 5th, 2017. All of the classes were just like the level one class, as in they were all on a teleconference line. I really liked the interaction with the other people on the call and being able to ask questions in whatever class I was in. I was a sponge for everything they were teaching, and I was taking every class I could possibly be on. Plus, I was still running my full-time personal training business at the gym. I knew what I wanted. I wanted to be a full-time Life Coach at some point, so I took notes, asked questions, read book after book, picked up pro-bono clients to hone in on my skills and to see where my niche was going to be.

I was excelling quickly and was getting recognized in the company regularly for my wins. At the time, we had a class called the City Leader Program. I didn't know what it meant, but it had the word leader in it, so I was on the call! It's now what we call the Ambassador Program. This is where members of the company held small groups to introduce BestLife to new people. I saw it as an opportunity to one, work on my public speaking skills and two, an avenue to get new clients. Then a couple of days later when the class schedule came out for that day, there was a class listed as Leadership Call. I quickly sent a text to Jen, the owner/CEO of BestLife, and asked her for the call-in number to the leadership call. She texts me back "Oh, I'm sorry, it's by invitation only." Before I could reply, I got a second text "wait, you would be perfect for our leadership team! Here is the number. See you at 1pm"! Boom! I was in! I had no idea what it meant, I just saw the word Leader, and I knew I had to be on that call! Period. (Jen and I laugh all the time about how I finagled my way onto the leadership team lol)

It was around this time, Sue (the level one instructor) had another class coming out called "Releasing Past Traumas." I wasn't sure what I was in for when I signed up for the class, but I knew my past traumas still needed some work. As much as I tried to put up a front like I had healed from all of that, I knew deep down inside there was still something hiding I needed and wanted to get rid of forever! I wanted to finally step into who I was meant to be. So, I put on my big girl panties and showed up ready to be shaken to my core. I had missed the first class because I had to work, so Sue sent me the recording so I could listen to the class and do the homework prior to the next class.

When I tell you my heart and soul was put in a blender, that is the biggest understatement of the year! We had to list all of the traumas of our life. No matter how big or small we thought, they were. Then write down the emotions we felt at the time the trauma happened, as well as, how we felt about them at that moment in time. Then we were instructed to muscle test each trauma and the feelings we had written down, past and present. Anything that tested as weak, we were to use the Freedom Release Method to release what we found. I jumped on the next call early, as usual. I wanted to chat with Sue before everyone got on. I told her what I had found and what I had trouble with from the previous class. She said we would address it in class when we went over the homework and she would work with me then. There were a couple of things that came up which were easier to release than what I thought they should have been. I told her what they were, and we changed the wording and Boom! There it was, singing loud and clear. The second week was clearing traumas around pets we had lost throughout our life.

I want to share this part of my story because this was one of the biggest breakthroughs I had at the beginning of my career as a life coach and how it helped me, number one, to be a better me as a person and to heal more completely. Number two, how it has helped me to become the best coach I can be to help the people I am blessed with the honor to coach.

The structure was the same, list the pets with events, plus the then and now emotions/feelings about those events. Then go through the releases, and this is where I realized I had so much more healing to go through. I recalled being 15 or 16 years old, and I had just gotten a new puppy named Ziggy. He was a beautiful little snowball Eskimo Spits. I went to school, as usual, that morning, after I fed and played with him for a few minutes while waiting for the bus. That afternoon, when I got off the bus, mom's car was gone. I saw Ziggy lying down over by the tree where mom always parked her car. I called out to him, but he didn't move, which was super unusual. Normally he always ran up to me as soon as he heard the bus pull up to the house. I walked over to pet him and he still didn't move. reached down to pick him up and he was stiff as a board. That is when I realized he was dead. It looked like he had been run over by a car. He was probably asleep under the car or something, and she didn't see him when she left. She came home, and I was sitting under the tree, in the driveway, holding him and crying. She got out of the car and asked me what was wrong. I was so hurt and angry. I just screamed at her "You killed my dog! You ran over him with the car and killed him!" She just looked at me in disbelief. Then she said "It's just a damn dog Tammy for God's sake! You will be okay! You didn't need it anyway!" Then she went into the house and slammed the door.

While we were doing the pet exercise, I wrote the word "nothing," for my now emotion because, honestly, I didn't feel anything at all about that event now. There was nothing I could do to change it, and I had not even thought about it in years. So, to me, there was really not any point in focusing on it any further. When I tried to clear it though, I went through the releases four or five times, and it was still weak. Sue said "It has something to do with your mom. We can talk about it after class if you have time" I replied "I have a whole laundry list of things about my mom, we could be on the phone all night if you get started in on her" and I tried to laugh it off. In my mind (and my heart) I knew I was going to take whatever time Sue would give me because I wanted it to go away.

After the class was over, Sue turned off the recording, waited until everyone else hung up, and then asked "Can you tell me more about what was going on with you and your mom? I'm not trying to be nosey, but I need a little more information so I can help you finish releasing this trauma?" I told her how it all happened, as well as the childhood sexual abuse with my mom and my biological father. Sue thanked me for being so open and asked if I was willing to do a couple of releases with her? She said she believed we could get to the bottom of it and it would probably even help me sleep better at night. I was all in!

The first things she cleared was "You should have protected me." That one brought on instant tears. It was followed by, "Why didn't you protect me," "You should have protected my dog" plus a couple of other ones I don't really remember, but they were along the same lines. When we were done, she asked me how I was feeling and, although I had tears streaming down my face, I felt lighter than I had felt in a really long time! She finished the call by giving me a couple of follow up steps to do. She was right. I did sleep better that night. Better than I had slept in a really long time. Sue is truly amazing. I have taken this class two more times. Each time is like a layer of an onion, and I always feel like a brand-new person when I'm through!

I had been involved in personal development since 2012 after I became a personal trainer, but this was very different for me. The energy from being on the live calls was phenomenal! I was learning so much, at such a high rate of speed and I felt absolutely amazing. The more of my underlying negative thoughts, feelings, and beliefs I released and replaced with positive, forward-thinking beliefs, the stronger I got emotionally, mentally and spiritually. I knew this company was the place I was supposed to be. Every class I could fit into my schedule, I was taking it. I didn't care that my free time was minimal, all I knew was I was learning all I could learn and it would make me a better life coach and a better me. That's where it all started for me as a life coach.

MANIFESTING NORWAY

As we were heading into June and summer season at the gym, graduations and vacation time all made the gym a little slower than usual. I went on an amazing trip to Florida with my Advocare team which also served as a much-needed vacation. While I was there, I got to teach my first ever class with BestLife on "What is Edification."

I drove down to the beach and checked into the condo. I was the first one there, so it was nice and quiet, which was perfect for teaching the class. I was very nervous, but I was able to calm my nerves and lean into the information. There were a lot of people who jumped on the class that Friday afternoon, and it turned out amazing! I really felt like I knocked it out of the park! The owner, Jen, sent me rapid-fire texts with emoji's and hearts and love about how awesome it was. I knew if Jen liked it, then I would definitely get the opportunity to be able to teach again!

As the amazing weekend in Florida was coming to an end, I got up early to catch the sunrise on the beach and to get some meditation and writing in my journal before heading back home. I was taking the time to look back at my amazing life and all the lessons that turned into blessings. I thought about those things that tried to crush me but only made me stronger. I felt something shift so strongly in my spirit. I wasn't quite sure what it was, but I knew something brand new was headed my way, and it was something big. I didn't focus on it too much because I knew God only gives me the information when I'm ready for it, but he was definitely nudging me to let me know there was a path being laid for me to travel soon. As I was driving back home, I was flying high on life! I had the windows down, radio up, and sang at the top of my lungs!

I was taking it all in and just enjoying life as it came every day. It was a good place to be for me after spending so many years dreading the upcoming day. I never took the time to enjoy the little moment's life gives us each day. J'son had recently, in February, moved to Puerto Rico. We had a lot of phone calls and texts as of late. I thought about how anytime I have been on the road, and he has always been very present during my trip, which has always made me feel safe. Growing up, feeling safe was never a part of the equation. So to have that now meant a lot and gave me a new perspective on my life. Where I was and where I was creating the opportunity to go.

A couple of weeks after my trip, I was on the BestLife leadership team call and heard them announce the next retreat was going to be in Norway! They wanted all of the leaders to be there if they could, so they were announcing it so early so everyone would have an opportunity to schedule off work and get the money together to make it happen. I was excited on the outside, but logically in my heart, I honestly didn't think I would be able to make this trip happen. I had my passport, but financially, without even looking at anything, I knew I wouldn't be able to go. Then, I felt a little nudge again, like what is that? I looked up and found myself asking, 'What are you trying to tell me'?

I had made a lot of friends in BestLife. It has always been such a warm, open, loving environment, which made it easy for me to participate regularly. I was talking to one of the members, Vana, pretty regularly. She was quickly becoming a best friend because she was so warm and always giving of her time and help when I needed it. I just loved talking to her any chance I got the opportunity to do so. She called me a few days after the announcement about the Norway leadership retreat asking if I planned on attending. I confided that although the hotel seemed reasonable, the flight was just out of my budget. She reminded me some of the members were having great luck with a particular website in finding better flight prices. Together we decided to go to the site right then and see what was there as she hadn't booked her tickets either.

Then I had a thought that maybe buying one-way tickets to break up the flights would be more affordable than one round trip ticket. We spent nearly three hours on the phone looking at flights, hotels, different sites, and everything. After we spent some time digging and finding the routes the airlines always took out of Atlanta to go to Europe, I found super cheap flights going from Atlanta to Boston; Boston to Iceland where I would do an overnight and share a room with Vana and Doug to save costs. From there we would fly to Oslo, Norway, rent a car and drive the rest of the way to Loen where the retreat was being held. When I totaled up just the flights alone, I could do all the flights, there and back, for a total of $567 plus bag fees! That was when I really started believing there might be a real possibility I could make the trip happen! The hotel was around $500

US dollars, so I was looking at probably $1500-2000 total round trip for everything. This was the beginning of June, and I had until the second week in August to have everything booked. The only other additional expense was a Spartan race coming up in July right before the trip.

I had listened to some audio's and watched some video sessions about the law of attraction and how it worked. It seemed fairly straight forward and simple. I had started working with it a little bit before mom passed, but not enough to really say I knew what it was or how it worked. It was time to see if it was real or fake, because my belief that I could really get all the money together during the summer season at the gym and no paying life coaching clients, was super slim. When I looked at how my life was working, I realized any time I really wanted something; I was always able to get it or do it. The money always seemed to show up right on time. So, that's what I was going to focus on, NORWAY!! I really wanted to go on that trip, so I was going to give this my best effort and try to make it happen.

In my mind, there really was no trying, there was only do or do not, according to Yoda! There was a lot I didn't understand, but the one thing I knew was the intensity of emotion, coupled with desire, was a powerful engine to get what I wanted from the universe. I had the intensity of emotion just waking up and breathing every day! Now it was time to put some laser focus on the trip to Norway and let's see what happens.

I started telling everyone I was going to Norway. I didn't know how I was going to make it happen. I just knew there was no way in hell I was going to miss out on the opportunity to go on this trip! It would be my first time out of the country and during my birthday month too! I was turning 50, and I couldn't think of a better birthday gift to give myself! A trip to Norway with a stop in Iceland to go to the Blue Lagoon!

I started hustling harder at the gym and picked up a couple more clients. Then, I got my first paying life coaching client! That in itself was amazing, and I was so stoked! Then one of my other clients, Evan, during our morning workout handed me $700 to go toward my trip! My eyes welled up with tears, and I hugged his neck and thanked him. I couldn't believe his generosity! I thanked and hugged him again. He told me I deserved it and hoped I had a great time. People never cease to amaze me, and Evan's generous gift covered the cost of my flights! I was going to Norway!! All I had left to do was get the money for the room, spending money and my life was about to be even more off the chain!

REMEMBER YOUR PROMISE

I had originally planned to go to Costa Rica for my 50th birthday, but I felt like Norway was a once in a lifetime opportunity! It was a leadership retreat, a tax deduction, I got to go out of the country for the first time ever, and I even got an overnight in Iceland with a visit to the Blue Lagoon! I can tell you I am not a fan of cold weather or snow, so Iceland was never on my bucket list. But about four or five months prior, I had seen some videos of the Blue Lagoon, which quickly moved it to my bucket list! At the time I saw those videos, I didn't even look to see where in the world it was located, I just knew I wanted to go there someday.

I was talking to Teresa after I had booked my flights and told her all about the Blue Lagoon. She said, "You, Tammy Loftis, the one who hates the cold and snow, are going to Iceland? Really? Where is my friend and what did you do with her? Lol". It wasn't until that conversation when I remembered the blue lagoon videos and the light bulb went off! I told her "I manifested this trip! The stop in Iceland to the Blue Lagoon! I did all of that!" I was practically screaming in the phone. She was totally taken off guard. I had to slow down and backtrack to explain what I was so excited about.

It was the first, real tangible proof I had been manifesting without knowing that was what I was doing. My next thought was, how do I make this more intentional? How do I do it quicker? What is the key I am missing? My brain was in a spin and I had to know more. I was doing more releases to make sure I had no blocks, and I was reading more, watching more videos, taking notes, meditating, affirmations, all of it! I knew I was still manifesting some things but it wasn't consistent, and I wanted to start making happen.

In July I started having these weird feelings, super emotional for no reason at all and waking up in the middle of the night with no explanation. I couldn't figure it out. I had been in a good mood all morning, but as soon as I walked through my door, I was instantly angry, like almost in a rage it was so intense! I was like WTF just happened!? I called Teresa, and she couldn't talk. I called Vana and told her what was going on, and I didn't know what was causing it. I went into the bedroom to get the phone charger before my phone died and all of the sudden it felt like I hit this wall of anger and the word MOM flashed in my head in big red letters! It was the first time I had ever experienced that type of negative energy in such a vivid way while I was wide awake.

I told Vana what had just happened. I knew mom's remains were in my closet. They had been there since I moved into the apartment. There was no reason for me to get them out because I wasn't going to do anything with them any time soon, if ever, so I just left them safely put away in there. Outside on my patio, there was a storage closet. If my mom's energy was angry and she was the cause of my sleepless nights and my mood swings, she was going outside to get out of my living space. I wasn't having it. I wasn't sure if any of this was even possible if she could really do that or not, but the message was very loud and very clear! It was MOM, she was angry, and it was directed at me! I was not okay with any of this. I don't know how to fight with an angry spirit or energy or what the hell ever this was, so I did the next best thing.

I took the box she was in, I put it in a plastic bag to protect it, took her outside and in the closet she went. I shut and locked the door, went back inside, sat down, took a deep breath and just sat there for a minute. I still had Vana on the phone. She was patiently waiting for me to settle down when she asked if I was ok and how did the energy in my apartment feel now? I sat there quietly with my eyes closed and let my mind clear for a few seconds to see how I felt now that mom was not in my living space anymore. I felt at peace and somewhat calm again — no more anger or rage which was a win in my book. My heart rate had slowed back down to normal, and I was breathing freely again.

Me: "That was the weirdest shit I have ever experienced while I was wide awake! Is that even possible? Did that really just happen?"

Vana: "Well evidently it is because it did. Why would she be angry at you? Why so much anger and rage now? What do you think it could be about?"

Me: "Honestly, I have no idea. But she can stay her ass out there in the damn closet until she gets a better attitude because she is not going to disturb my peace man! I will take her ass to the nearest lake and dump her in it and not think twice about it!"

Vana: "No you will not! You know you would be so upset after you did that. You have worked so hard on healing and moving forward. She just has you agitated right now. Wait until you calm down and then you will be able to think more rationally about it. Okay?"

Me: "I know. It's just she has always bullied us as kids, and now she is dead, and she is still trying to push me around. Like seriously Vana! What the actual Fuck is she doing?! I am not okay with this Bullshit! Sorry, I am just angry right now because I can't figure this out."

Vana "It's okay. Just go get something to eat. If you have time to take a nap, do that too. If you want to do an RTT session either later today or tomorrow, we can do that, and maybe we can figure it out then."

Me: "Okay, sounds good! Thank you for being so awesome as usual!"

We finished up with some small talk and got off the phone. I got something to eat and jumped on a class call. Those always made me feel better. It wasn't long after class when Teresa called me back. I filled her in on what had happened, and I didn't know why she was giving me problems right now. I was just working, getting ready for the trip to Norway...

Me: "Oh my God! I know what the problem is now. I had forgotten about it."

Teresa: "What are you talking about, forgot about what? What problem?"

Me: "Remember when I went to Birmingham the night mom was dying? We took her off of life support the next morning?"

Teresa: "Yeah, what has that got to do with this? I am lost Chica, what's going on?

Me: "Don't you remember, we took mom off of the life support and were basically waiting for her to pass away. I walked up, held her hand and whispered in her ear when I started traveling the world that I would scatter her ashes in the first place I traveled too. Girl, I am going to Norway in less than six weeks! She is mad because I haven't said anything about taking her and setting her free."

Teresa: "Oh snap! I forgot about that! Can you take her overseas to do that? How are you going to make it happen? Are you going to make it happen? It would definitely explain why she was pissed off at you!"

Me: "I don't see why I couldn't. I will look up the rules about flying with her and see what I need to do. I will check both countries and see what needs to be done to see if it's even possible. I may have to do it on the low, but I am pretty sure mom will be going with me on this leadership retreat. It's time to set her free. Set us all free."

Teresa: "You okay Chica?"

Me: "Yeah. I am actually really okay. I have no idea how easy or difficult this is actually going to be, but I know when it's over, the whole family will be finally free! So, whatever has got to happen to make this a reality, will happen."

Teresa: "I am so proud of you right now! You never cease to amaze me."

We got off the phone, and a tear rolled down my cheek. I whispered to the room, "It's time to set you, free mom, I love you."

The day was finally here! I was packed up and ready to go! I had all of my ticket information ready, my I.D., Passport, and money. Most importantly, I had mom packed away in a book bag to carry on the first leg of my flight. After that, she could be put in my checked suitcase for the rest of the trip. Consciously, I was happy. I made the decision to do this. I also knew when the day actually came, it was going to be very emotional, and I had no idea how hard it would be or if I would be able to go through with it for that matter. I pushed all those thoughts and feelings to the back of my mind. I didn't want to think about it right then. I wanted to enjoy the journey and all the experiences that came along with it. I didn't want to miss anything. I had no idea what this trip had in store for me, or if I would ever go back. I wanted to be present in every moment from beginning to end.

That was the only goal as I was waiting on Uber to show up to take me to the airport.

I remember feeling my heart race and my stomach feeling a little off as I got into the Uber to head to the airport. Mom was finally going to be set free. I had reached out to all of my brothers to let them know my plans. My oldest brother, Billy, probably the most detached from mom, thought it was cool and told me to have fun. Scott, my middle brother who had lived with mom, was really happy about the decision to do this. I was so proud of him. He had really worked hard on his recovery. He was finally drug-free, working full time at a printing company and was doing well. I know that made mom happy to see he was going to make it after all.

When I told him of my plans, he said "That would make mom really happy. She always talked about traveling someday, and she wanted to go somewhere that was cold because she hated being hot. Thank you for taking care of her like that Tammy". I told him I was happy to do it. Mom had lived her whole life in a box, and it was time to be set free from her own self-imposed prison. I asked him if he wanted any of the ashes before I left. He declined and said to set her free. Next, I talked to Daniel, my baby brother, who has been in prison since he was 18. He was surprisingly happy about the decision as well. He didn't get to say his goodbye to mom like the rest of us did so I wasn't really expecting a happy response from him when I gave him the news. I am very glad I was wrong. He also declined to keep any of mom's ashes.

I got to the airport and was going through security. I put the book bag on the conveyor belt along with everything else. I felt my heart start racing again. I knew they were going to pull it when it went through the X-ray machine and I was right. When I got all of my other belongings, I walked over to where the nice lady held my bag. She asked me what was in there as she was undoing the plastic bag I had put the box in. I nonchalantly told her it was my mom's ashes and I was taking her to Norway to finally set her free. That poor lady got visibly shaken by my statement. All the color drained out of her face as she took the swab to wipe the outside of the box to make sure there were no explosive materials on it. I then asked if she wanted me to open the box or show her the paperwork? You would have thought a cat jumped out of nowhere at her because she was so frightened. She said, "No! No, Ma'am! I just need to swab the outside of the box for explosive materials. I'm sorry for your loss. Have a safe trip." Then, she abruptly handed me my bookbag with mom all tucked away safely inside. I still laugh, even today, about her reaction when I told her what was in the box.

The rest of the trip was uneventful, and I successfully met up with Vana and Doug in Iceland and traveled with them for the rest of the trip. Iceland was absolutely beautiful. The Blue Lagoon is definitely a place that needs to be on everyone's bucket list. I want to go back to see more of the island and hopefully see the Aurora Lights. We left Iceland early the next morning and went to Oslo, Norway where we spent the night. We drove into Loen, and I will tell you it is one of the most beautiful places on earth! The countryside was breathtaking. The Fjord was so beautiful and was a bluish green or maybe even a teal color all the way through, including the rapids.

We saw so many waterfalls on the drive to and from the hotel. We were there during the beginning of Norway's fall season and got to see the dramatic color changes of the trees. If I am not mistaken, I believe I took 1400 plus pictures on that trip. That was just on the camera and didn't include the ones I took with my phone. Snowcapped mountains at every turn, cascaded down into the Fjords. When the water was still, it looked as though you were looking into a mirror. You could see the reflection of the mountains, clouds and sky in the smooth as glass, pristine water. Their tap water was so clean it tasted better than the bottled water we drink back home in the states.

It was so awesome getting to put faces with the voices I had been hearing and speaking with for the last six months of being a part of BestLife, and I felt like a rock star! Everyone was running up to me and so excited to see me face to face. To be honest, I was really eating up all of the attention. My silent thoughts were, in just a couple of days, I would be on top of the mountain 3500 feet in the air and saying goodbye to the woman who gave birth to me one last time. I wasn't sure if Leslie, who lived in Atlanta and had just lost her mom a few weeks prior to the leadership retreat, would join me for this event, but my hope was she would, and it would somehow give her some inner peace by sharing my moment with me.

The food at The Hotel Alexandra was amazing! All of the food on the buffet was so fresh. It had all kinds of fish, steak, cheese, vegetables, desserts, coffee, wine, etc. You name it, and they had it. The conference was great. We all had a ten-minute Ted Talk-style presentation that we were to give the first day of our event. I was the first one up, just like my first public speaking event. We all got to speak on whatever topic we felt fit us best. I chose leadership since that's the reason we were there. I knocked it out of the park again. It was obvious I had made an impact when the other people would reference something in my speech during theirs. Just more validation for me, I was on the right track. Public speaking was going to be a big part of my future. I didn't know how or when I just knew it was happening.

The rest of the event went off without a hitch, and then Sunday arrived. It was time to say my final goodbye to mom. It was time to set her free.

FLY HIGH AND BE FREE MOM

Early Sunday morning, I roll over, and the clock staring back at me says 3:36am. My eyes are wide open. I quietly get up to not disturb my roommate Alee, I walk over to the window and looked out toward the Fjord. I'm staring mindlessly. My heart was pounding in my chest, and it felt like I had a boulder sitting in the pit of my stomach. I heard no thoughts running through my head. There was complete silence in my mind. Which if I am completely honest, I was really happy there were no thoughts or voices up running out of control that early. I quietly go to the bathroom, shut the door before I turned on the light. There was no need to wake up Alee because I couldn't sleep.

I got a drink of water and then a hot washcloth and put it on my face. I was just standing there looking at myself in the mirror. I have no idea how long I was standing there. It felt like I was numb. I shook it off and tiptoed back to bed, only to toss and turn for another 3 hours before I finally just got up. I got ready for breakfast. I looked at the bookbag sitting by the window, took a deep breath and left the room. I went down to the buffet, where the entire team met every morning before our events started for the day. It was going to be a tough day, so I just put on a smile and acted like everything was okay.

I must have been a little quieter than my usual jovial self during breakfast. Han came over to sit beside me and asked if I slept well. He was one of the people who coached me during my Life Coaching certification class. I told him I had slept pretty good, but I had woke up earlier than I had intended and I was still a little sleepy. That let me know my mask was down. I got up to get another cup of coffee and put the smile back on my face. The thoughts started running through my head. I couldn't let them see the doubt pounding in my heart, the fear welling up in my throat or the tears I fought back with every blink of my eyes. I started talking to myself, "I am Strong! I am Powerful! I am Beautiful! I can Do this! Now is not the time to be acting like a weak ass baby Tammy! Suck it up!"

There was Wifi at the hotel, and I was chatting with J'son on Facebook. I knew he would help me stay grounded. He knew what was happening later that day and kept asking me if I was okay. I just said: "I'll be fine, aren't I always?" He replied "you better be. You would tell me if you weren't right?" I think he knew the answer to the question, but this was different. I had made him a promise a long time ago after he found out about me almost taking the sleeping pills, if I ever felt trapped by the dark places again, I would call him right then.

I was far removed from those days, and my healing was as complete as I believed it could be. The last piece was scattering mom's ashes. Neither of us had an idea about how I was going to handle it emotionally. I think that's what bothered him the most. He had seen all of my positive changes and me being unsure of anything was not something he had seen from me in a very long time.

We had our morning meeting, and then when we broke, it was time to go get ready for lunch on top of the mountain. I got up to the room before Alee and pulled mom out of the bookbag and sat her in my lap. I said a prayer as the tears trickled down my cheeks. I freshened up, put mom back in the bookbag, packed my camera and went down to meet everyone out front so we could walk over to the Sky Bucket. Vana came and found me as soon as we met out front. She saw the look on my face, and she didn't say a word, she just hugged me. She whispered in my ear, "I'm so proud of you, and you are going to do just fine." That meant a lot to me. I'm not sure if she knows how much I loved her at that moment and even more today.

We arrived at the restaurant and found our table, and it was right in front of the window. The view was breathtaking! Soooooooo many pictures. As we were looking out the window, right before lunch was served, three people walked in front of the building outside in squirrel suits and had GoPro's strapped to their helmets. They were going to cliff dive right then and there! OMG!! I got the Wi-fi password and recorded it on Facebook Live! It was so freaking awesome to watch, especially since I had just experienced skydiving for the first time in July, and it had been one of the most exhilarating experiences I have ever had. My friends on Facebook were asking me when I was going to do it. I was really clear when I said I am not sure my balls are big enough to jump off a cliff like that willingly! It sure was exciting to watch from that vantage point though. They just dove right off, went all the way down the cliff like an eagle soaring across the sky, then pulled the chute and landed over in the fields at the bottom of the mountain.

As we were eating lunch, it got harder and harder for me to breathe normally. Another BestLife member, Cynthia, was sitting beside me and I think she must've seen the panic move across my face as she started asking me about my story. She told me about herself and let me know everything was going to be okay. Scott, Jen's husband, came over when he saw I was crying. He sat beside me and reassured me they were all going to be right there beside me and it was all going to be okay. He then did some releases with me right there on the spot, and it really helped me start to breathe a little easier. Everyone finished eating and it was time to head out. I paid my tab, grabbed the bookbag with mom in it, and asked who all wanted to go with me. Everyone got up, and they were all going to go with me! My heart was just overflowing with love. More tears started flowing. As we walked up to the trail, I began snapping pictures to keep my mind distracted.

Brit, who lived right there in Loen, already had a special place picked for me and it was off the trail, which was one of the requirements to scatter ashes. We walked way down so there would be no chance of anyone walking on her ashes after we left. The view from there was breathtaking and overlooked the Fjord, with nothing but snowcapped mountains in every direction. Everyone walked out there with me. Cynthia videoed the event for me so I would have it as a keepsake and something to share with my brothers.

I took a deep breath, turned to everyone and thanked them for coming to share this moment with me. My voice was cracking, and the tears were flowing more freely now, there was no stopping them at this point. Then I walked down to the rocks where I was going to stand. I pulled mom out of the box, and before I set her free, I shared these last words...

> *"It's time to set you free ma. God knows I love you so much. I made this promise to you four years ago. You've lived in a box your whole life, and it's time to set you free. I picked this perfect spot where you can be close to heaven and have this beautiful view for the rest of eternity. I love you."*

It had been cloudy all morning with the sun peeking out occasionally. As I spoke those words, the clouds started moving and opening up. I opened up the bag, turned toward the Fjord, held the bottom corners and shook her up toward the sky. A big wind came from behind me and her ashes went up into the air. It swept her away as if it was perfectly orchestrated by God himself. The sun came out just as she was carried away to her final resting place. I imagined that her spirit was finally carried off into the lights of heaven at that moment. I stood there, face in my hands, tears streaming uncontrollably down my cheeks. I turned and walked back up the hill, where I was engulfed in one big group hug. All of us were in tears, but they were not tears of sadness, they were tears of freedom. Tears of forgiveness. Tears of pure love and peace. #RIPMom

Leslie was up there with us, and she had recently lost her mom as well. I was so glad she decided to join us. She told me she wanted to be there as it was a way for her to say goodbye to her mom too. We formed a bond, there in Norway, that will never be broken. There were several people who were there and had lost a parent or loved one in recent years. It wasn't just me who was set free on that mountain that day. We all were. There was also a bond that was forged between all of us as we stood on the mountainside, that few will ever know or understand, as I said goodbye to the woman who gave birth to me, one last time. People who were complete strangers to me just six months ago, whom I had never met in person until just three days prior, are now forever engraved on my heart. Strangers …..to friends …..to family. Bonded forever.

THE VISION COMES ALIVE

We walked back down to the hotel, and some of us went to the pool, while others were getting ready to check out because they were leaving that night. After getting back to the hotel, I headed for the hot tub with a glass of wine. As I relaxed back in the water, I went over everything that had happened throughout the day. All I could think about was mom was finally free. We were all free! I'm not sure anyone could really understand the significance of what I had experienced on the top of that beautiful mountain.

I felt like there had been a choke hold on my family for generations. I had no idea how many, but I knew I had broken those chains and set us all free. I knew all of the abuse, and everything went along with it, was finally gone forever. My grandchildren and future generations would never have to experience any of the things I did as a child. That would have been enough of a win for me, but to know the generational curses on my family were now broken, meant my legacy was going to be dramatically different from this moment forward and for generations to come.

The drive back to Oslo, in the rain, was so beautiful and we got to experience the full and amazing vibrant colors of fall, the Norway way. Everywhere I looked there was purple, red, orange, yellow and green and it all created such vibrant, bright and stunning eye candy.

They were installing snow sticks on the sides of the road as we were driving through each of the little towns along the way. They were over 8-feet-tall, I couldn't even begin to imagine living anywhere that required such tall markers to know where the road was under the snow, and I knew I would only be visiting during the warmer months!

We spent the night in Oslo, and we all flew out the next day. My flight didn't leave until almost 5pm, so I spent most of the day wandering around the airport. I was Still trying to take it all in. I was really in a different country, enjoying another culture, seeing how a different part of the world goes about its day to day life. Reindeer is a regular menu item along with moose stew. I would have never imagined how phenomenally good reindeer would taste without getting to experience going on this trip.

The airports were spotless and beautiful. All of them looked like a high-end mall inside. When I finally arrived in Boston, I had missed my connecting flight to Atlanta, which was the last leg of my trip. The next available flight wasn't until 6am the next morning. There was no point in being upset about something I couldn't control. So I found a comfortable couch and was able to catch a few hours of sleep before I had to check in for my flight at 4:30am when security opened up. As awesome as this trip was, I was Tired! I was ready to be home in my bed. I was feeling this overwhelming feeling like there was something more. Like God was trying to tell me something and there was just too much static in my head for me hear it clearly.

A couple of weeks after being home, I went to go visit my kids, and we went to church together. After service, I asked Bradley if he would pray with me. I told him I felt like God was trying to tell me something, but there was a block somewhere. It's really awesome to have my kids are on the prayer team at Church of the Highlands. A family that prays together stays together.

The best explanation of how I felt was a little like when I was pregnant and waiting for my kids to be born. Lots of excitement filled with anticipation and a lot of being uncomfortable for what felt like no reason at all. In my heart, I felt like there was a big move coming. My life coaching was picking up, and my gym clients had started asking how much longer I would be training at the gym. They could feel my shift too. Looking at my current circumstances, I was planning on being there one more year at the most. That was in the summer of 2017. Little did I know God had other plans.

One thing we did a lot of, in class at BestLife, was dream building exercises. It really opened up my creativity and helped me figure out what it was I truly wanted in life. It also helped me to narrow down a sweet spot goal to work toward, to allow me some momentum before working on the bigger dreams and goals. I knew after my first public speaking event that I wanted to do more events of that nature. I knew that was a large part of my purpose, and I just didn't know the how or the when. Experiencing the Ted Talk in Norway really solidified the desire for me. I wanted to speak at big events, run workshops, help people change their lives like I had changed mine. I started researching public speakers who were doing what I wanted to do. It was hard to find well known female speakers outside of the Christian realm who were on the same level as Tony Robins, Les Miles, Eric Thomas, John Maxwell, etc. Something inside me whispered, "that's you!" I caught myself looking up and said: "I know that was you!"

Between the trip to Norway and going to Birmingham to see the kids right after, I was still more than a little tired from all of the traveling. It felt like I just needed to sleep for a week. I had a conversation with Teresa, telling her about the feelings I was having, and I couldn't shake it. She said she felt it too.

I want to step away from the story for just a minute to give you a little back story on my conversations with God. I am a very matter of fact person, and I generally do not sugar coat things when speaking to people. Whether you're a friend, family member or a client, it's all the same. I always come from a loving place and I give it straight from the hip. My conversations with God are no different. There have been many mornings he has woke me up at 3am when my alarm was set 4am anyway. I would say out loud like he was standing in the room next to me "Can we please have this conversation when my alarm goes off? I have one more hour to sleep. Please, and thank you." Needless to say, that doesn't generally work like I want it to lol, but he made me this way so our conversations can be pretty hilarious at times, just like conversations I have with anyone else. Now let's get back to the story.

A few nights later, as I was meditating in the shower, I started talking to God, "I know you are trying to tell me something. I feel like I am in labor and I didn't like either of the first two times it happened. So, I am staying in this damn shower until I am a prune if I have to, but I am not getting out until you tell me what it is you are trying to tell me already." I no sooner got those words out of my mouth and then I had a vision. It was like an out of body experience like no other I have ever had. Wow! Did that really just happen? Was that real? When I got out of the shower, I started getting all of these downloads, or steps, on what to do next. I guess it was real! I decided to keep it all under wraps for a couple of weeks before I made any announcements. If this was really happening, it would be fast, and it was going to be a shock for quite a few people.

As the days progressed, I was just going through the motions at the gym, training my clients, and working with my life coaching clients, all the while the vision I had received from God, kept running through the back of my mind. I am very grounded and spiritually centered, so I didn't doubt this was something God showed me, I was clearing the doubt I had about myself, out of the way, to be in alignment with what he had shown me. At the core of my being, I was excited beyond belief, but my conscious mind was looking at my current reality and circumstances which was attempting to cloud my judgment.

I had not told anyone about what this vision was about. Actually I had not told anyone I had a vision at all. There were only a few people, who were aware I had the gift of visions which were my children and all 3 of my best friends, Michelle, Teresa, and LaTaunya. They all have experienced them and knew the power they held. Why did I have any doubts at all? That is what was so baffling to me. My visions have never been wrong. They all have been very specifically pointed at a purpose and/or relaying a message to someone. Every single time, they were spot on, and I knew nothing about what those visions meant to each person until I shared with them what was shown to me.

I think my confusion and/or doubts were attempting to creep in because this vision was about me. It wasn't a message to someone else, and it wasn't about helping someone else. It was about ME! A message for me! It had been a very specific message for me to move and I had to make a decision now. It involved nobody but me and my faith in my purpose and my dream. I had to decide if I was willing and ready to jump off the cliff of faith and trust my parachute would open before I crashed at the bottom of the ravine of life. My answer was a great big resounding YAAAAAASSSSSSSS! I closed my eyes and said out loud, "okay. God, I trust you, so let's do this!" I took a deep breath and let it out. Then I allowed the download of plans to come freely and as frequently as he wanted to share them with me.

8 I CHANGED MY STARS

In my heart, I was torn between fear and worry over two major hurricanes hitting Puerto Rico back to back. Hurricane Irma on September 6th and then Maria, the worst of the two, was going to make direct landfall through the center of the island on Sept 20th. J'son was still there and had chosen to stay and weather it out. With eight years of Air Force survival training, I was not in fear of him surviving the storm itself. What I knew about him was he would give up his life to save someone else's. That's just who he is and how he's hard-wired. He has always been the epitome of protect and serve from the day I met him. He has always stood for justice and the freedoms, we as human beings deserve. With that knowledge, I knew there was a chance I may never get to speak to or see him again after Maria hit the island. My heart was in my throat the minute he signed off all communication to conserve power and get ready for the impact of this category 5 hurricane. My faith stood strong on the facts that He was a Survivor, and he was going to come out of this just fine. I prayed for him every day and filled his inbox with messages letting him know I was there and sending him prayers, love, and protection. I waited and hoped every day I would hear the notification go off on my phone and it was him.

My 50th birthday was in a few days, and there was the excitement from my vision. I just might burst from inside out if I didn't let it out soon. Or at least I believed it was excitement. I knew there was a little bit of underlying doubt and fear there, but I refused to give any attention to it. What you focus on grows, so I chose the Excitement! I needed no fear or doubt in my mind or heart about anything that was going on! I needed strength! With Hurricane Maria beating down on Puerto Rico, not knowing if J'son was okay or not, it was hard for me to share my excitement of what I knew was to come for me.

Teresa, checked in on me every day. She knew I was trying to hold it together because of the hurricane. She did all she could to keep me distracted.

I had everyone praying for Puerto Rico and J'son. I finally couldn't take it anymore. I knew there was nothing I could do but wait the storm out. I had no magic wand to just magically push the hurricane away from the island and save everyone on it. I had to put my focus on something I could control, and that was me. I knew focusing on J'son and the hurricane would throw a roadblock in the plans being made.

I texted Teresa and told her when she had a few minutes to talk to give me a call. I needed to talk to her about something just so I could get it out. Her being the awesome friend she has always been, took her break and called me right then. She only had 15 minutes to talk, and I really needed more time, but that's what we had so I went with it.

Teresa: "What's up Chica? Are you okay?"
Me: "Yeah, I'm good. I just needed to get this out, so I don't explode inside."
Teresa: "Did you hear from J'son? Is he okay? Or is it something else?"
Me: "No word from him yet and from what I can tell, nobody has heard from him yet. Still praying and sending him all the good vibes and protection I can. That is not what I wanted to talk to you about though."
Teresa: "Well will you please just tell me what it is, because I only have 15 minutes on break woman."
Me: "Yes I am going to tell you, chill out woman! Anyway, remember how I have been saying for months there was something big coming? And I knew God was trying to tell me something and I felt blocked?
Teresa: "Yeah, did you finally get unblocked? Did you figure it out?"
Me: "I was in the shower and basically told God I was not getting out until he told me whatever it was he was trying to tell me. I didn't like being in labor either of the first two times, and I was ready to hear whatever it was he had to tell me."
Teresa: (she laughed) "And how did that work out for you?"
Me: "Well, it was really weird. More like an out of body experience, I guess you'd say. I no sooner got it out of my mouth than I got a vision!"
Teresa: "Really? Well, are you going to tell me or just keep me in suspense?

Me: "I am moving. I saw me loading up my car, actually an SUV, which was odd since I don't have one of those. But anyway, then I saw a sign that said San Diego and I pulled up into a driveway, you and Jeremiah were standing there waiting for me. I then heard a whisper "Get there, and I will show you further.""

Teresa: (A loud scream on the other end of the phone) "Are you serious right now? Are you really moving to San Diego? When? Are you sure?"

Me: "Well, my lease is up at the end of the year. There is no reason to sign another lease and move twice. I have gotten all of these downloads about what to do next, where my clients are going and the numbers 2018. So I just have to pick my final day at the gym, start selling everything and whatever will fit in my car will be what goes with me across the country. I am going home for Christmas so whatever date I leave to go home will be the last day I am at the gym. I haven't told anyone yet, not even the kids. I have to keep it quiet until I am ready to make moves."

Teresa: "So you expect me to keep it quiet that my best friend is moving to Cali where I am going to be in at the first of the year? Really? Okay, this is going to be a challenge!"

Me: "It won't be for long, I just got to get some more pieces of the puzzle figured out. I want to tell the kids before I make it public knowledge. I am not sure how they are going to respond, and I want to get that taken care of before anyone else finds out. I know my energy has changed because my clients keep asking me how much longer I am going to be there. They feel it, so I have to be careful about who I tell what at the moment, but you needed to know what was going on since it had you in the vision. I don't know if you will be there when I get there or not, but I know you will eventually be there one way or the other so there you go. Now go back to work and have fun!"

Teresa: "You just made my day! Even though I can't say shit about it to anyone! Love you later! I will call you when I get off!"

I took a deep breath and let it out nice and slow. I saw the sign for San Diego again flash through my thoughts with the backdrop of the ocean splashing on the rocks. That was my destination. I didn't know all the details or the how I was just trusting the process, and I knew it was all going to work out exactly as it is meant to. It always does and usually better than my mind could even visualize, which is always a good thought to remember.

I started looking at apartments in San Diego and looking at the distance to get from Atlanta to there. I mapped out how long it would take me, where I wanted to stop, and how long I wanted the trip itself to last. I had friends in Louisiana, Texas, Colorado and Utah. I tried not to put too much weight into where I was stopping as I still had time to figure it all out. There was a lot going on at home, at the gym, and in Puerto Rico. I tried to stay off the news because it made my heart sick. I stayed focused on the best outcome possible. J'son was going to be okay and I would hear from him soon.

PLANNING THE ROAD AHEAD

My 50th birthday came and I enjoyed a nice dinner with a glass of wine out by myself. That weekend I hung out with Blake, one of my clients at the gym. Marguerite, one of my other clients, was supposed to join us but got lost and just ended up going home. Me and Blake had a great time though. We had a few drinks, and laughed… A Lot! Blake was the first of my clients I told I was moving to San Diego at the first of the year. He was upset at first, and then I told him it was a God Inspired move, he was totally supportive. We sat upstairs outside on the rooftop talking about God and our beliefs. (I just want to say again, we were at the Bar and talking about God and our Dreams.) The things we wanted to accomplish in our lives and how we wanted to grow spiritually by the end of the year. He is a really great kid. I say kid because he is younger than my kids, even though he is Grown! I saw great things coming into his life. He still had a lot of healing to do, but he was well on his way. I am so thankful for him, and the time he spent as my client and my friend. I know there was a purpose in him walking into Snap Fitness that day, looking to train for a Spartan Race. It ended up being more than just about a race to both of us. We both served a purpose in each other's lives. This night was a great way to spend my birthday weekend, and I wouldn't have had it any other way.

The days kept rolling by, Puerto Rico was still getting hammered by Maria. There was no power on the island and the videos coming in were heart-wrenching. Still no word from J'son, but something told me that he was safe and he was ok. I just knew if there was something wrong, I would feel it. Much of the next week was a blur with planning, working, coaching, all in an attempt to stay busy, so my thoughts and emotions wouldn't spin out of control. There was too much at stake and in my mind, failure wasn't an option. I was especially focused on a plan of how to tell my kids. I didn't want to tell them over the phone and them finding out on Facebook was definitely not an option.

There was one more leadership event coming up at the end of October. It was something I knew I needed to attend, despite the financial restraints. One day I was listening to a Tony Robbins CD where he was sharing his story about when he first got started on his journey to becoming a life coach. He shared he could barely pay his rent or have food on the table, but he chose to go to a seminar with his rent money. The way he rationalized it was if he didn't do something different, he was always going to be struggling for his rent. I put myself in that place and made the decision to go even though it was going to put a financial strain on me. I knew going would be worth it so I made plans to stay with a friend to save on hotel costs and I found a cheap roundtrip flight.

September 29th, shortly after waking, I got a text from J'son! "Hey, you" was all it said. I was so excited! It was before I went to work, so I had a little time to talk to him. He had no power but had food and water. I had tears streaming down my face, and my heart was about to beat out of my chest! I was so thankful that he was okay. He was trying to get a flight out, but with the weather still so unstable it was difficult and the airlines were gouging the people trying to get out as the tickets were close to $2000. All I wanted was him off the island and to give my best friend a hug! All would be well in the world then.

I knew the time would be coming soon that I would have to tell him I was moving to California to chase my dreams. He had always pushed me to be the best me I could possibly be and encouraged me to get out and see the world! Go do awesome shit he would tell me!

In fact, it seemed to be one of his favorite sayings. With the trauma of living through two hurricanes, I wasn't sure how he would respond to the news. So, I chose to wait until he was back in Atlanta and had some time to decompress before saying anything. I knew once things settled down, he would be able to help me plan. He had moved across the country before and just recently from Atlanta to Puerto Rico. I trusted him to make sure my trip was a safe one and to be sure I was properly prepared the whole way.

My middle granddaughter, Janeice, was getting baptized in October so I planned to share the news about my move across the country with the family then. My hope was they were going to be supportive. The plans were already in motion, and I knew I had to do this for me. When I moved to Atlanta to get out of Alabama, it was one of the best decisions I ever made in my life up to that point. I had pushed myself way out of my comfort zone to make that move and had been rewarded by my life leveling up at least 10X! Atlanta was only a short three-hour drive from home, so there was a small safety net if things didn't go as I had hoped after I moved. This time, there was no proverbial safety net! I didn't know anyone there, have a job yet or a place to live. I didn't have the answers to the questions I knew were coming.

The one thing I held fast to was that my kids knew I was very God-centered and grounded by my faith. I hoped when I told them about the vision, and it was a God-inspired move, it would quiet down any objections they had. I was trusting the man upstairs to light my path and take care of me as he promised. My faith was strong in that. I just wanted my kids to understand and support me too. Deep down I knew they would, but my subconscious mind was attempting to cloud my judgment. I had spent so many years in the negativity that those voices, although mostly silent these days, sometimes started to get loud at the slightest bit of doubt or fear. I was very intentional about feeding my faith during this time. I knew it was the only way for me to keep the path clear in front of me for this journey. It was time to jump and build my wings on the way down.

The weekend was here! I told my daughter, Brittnie, and the first thing she said was "That's awesome Mom! I am so proud of you!

And you know we are coming to visit right?" Whew! She was the one I was worried about freaking out the most. She loves her mommy being close enough to visit at any time. This was going to be a big change for all of us. Bradley and Paige were next. Paige wanted to know how much the flights were so they could come visit. Anything near a beach was a good thing where she was concerned. Bradley, my numbers and statistics child, asked "Have you looked at the cost of living out there mom? Have you seen how expensive it is? Have you got a job and looked at apartments yet?"

I assured him I was going to be okay. I said "No Brad, I haven't looked at any numbers, to be honest. I looked at apartments and they are roughly the same price as what I pay in Atlanta now. It depends on what part, just like Atlanta. I can get a job at any gym out there, so that's a non-issue. I will make more money at gyms out there than I do in Atlanta." I could see the concern in his face as I waited for more questions. He said "Are you sure about this mom? That's a really long way from home. It's not a three-hour drive anymore. It's a plane flight!"

There were the questions I'd been waiting for. I took a deep breath, not wanting to get in a battle of wills with my son, knowing we are so much alike and it would be a long night if we stood there debating the issue. I looked at him and said "I had a vision, Bradley. This is a God-inspired move. He said to get there, and I will show you further. I don't know all the answers. I don't know how it's all going to work out. I just know he said GO! So, I am going to obey. I am going to let him lead my steps, and I have faith that it's all going to work out better than if I had planned it out myself." He stood there looking at me for a minute and then said, "Okay. If you had a vision, then I guess you know what you're doing. It's obvious you've made up your mind so we will all pray for you and support you." He gave me a big hug and told me he loved me.

We chose not to say anything to the kids just then. It would have been too stressful on them and me. We would wait until it was closer to time and I knew more details about dates and how long I was going to be home for Christmas. I felt so much lighter telling them and having their support. I love my kids so very much. They are the reason this is so important to me. The legacy I am building will be for them and for generations to come. I know that even though they don't know all the details behind what I am doing or why they do understand I am purpose driven. They have seen me accomplish everything I have set out to do. They had faith in the fact that I don't know how to quit. Add to that, the faith we all have in the man upstairs, and it's a win all the way around.

Sunday came, and after church, we delighted in watching Janeice get baptized. She was growing up so quickly. I was full of tears and so happy for her. There is always a big crowd at Church of the Highlands on first Sunday to be baptized. The pastor asked her all the questions to make sure she knew what the decision was she was making. She acknowledged, held her nose, he dunked her, and when she came up, she was ALL smiles! What an awesome way to end my weekend there and back to Atalanta I went.

J'son finally made it off the island a few days later. It was so good to hug him when I picked him up at the airport and know he was safe! Although, I could tell the hurricanes had affected him. He lived through two of them in less than a month. I can't even imagine what he must have gone through or experienced during that time. I could only relate it to when all of the tornadoes were dropping down all around me like flies, and I got caught in Walmart. I remembered being so afraid I wouldn't make it through the night. I can't imagine going through days of not knowing if I was going to make it out alive or not. I tried to get him to open up about what happened, but he just wouldn't. I could tell with what little he did share that it was hard for him. Showing emotion is hard for him as it is and I honestly didn't want to put any added pressure on him. I was just so thankful he was alive and safe off of the island. I knew he didn't want to be here in Atlanta, but there was nowhere else for him to go. Atlanta was safe for him, and that's what he needed at that time.

Just seeing some of the pictures he took and hearing the stories he told about having to fight the lines for water and bare necessities. There were so many people they couldn't even get to. Puerto Rico was his home now, and although the island was pretty much destroyed, his home survived with minor damage. There were so many others who lived there who were not so lucky. Mother nature is fierce when she rears her angry head. She is merciless. There is no prejudice if you are in her path or get caught in her wake. The mental and emotional destruction is far worse than the physical things that can be replaced.

When I got back from the Colorado leadership training, he seemed to be handling the adjustments of being back in Atlanta a little better, although still very quiet for him when we were together. We were hanging out, and I told him I had something to tell him.

J'son: "What's wrong."
Me: "I'm moving at the first of the year. I wanted to tell you so we could hang out as much as possible before I go. I know you haven't been home long, but this was planned before all this happened. I just wanted to make sure everything was solidified before I told you I was moving."
J'son: "Cool, what part of town are you moving to?"
Me: "I'm not staying in Georgia, J'son."
J'son: "You are not moving back to Alabama are you?"
Me: "No. I am moving to California."
J'son: "What? Really? That's my girl! I am so proud of you."
Me: "Thanks! That means a lot coming from you!"
J'son: "Who's out in Cali?"
Me: "Nobody. I am moving out there for me J. I have a purpose and a dream, and that's where it's taking me. My purpose here in Atlanta is over. I have been feeling a move coming for a while. I just didn't know where it was going to be until right after I got back from Norway. I have kept it quiet because I am not ready for everyone to know just yet."
J'son: "Do you have a job out there yet? You found an apartment? Have you got enough money to take care of you for 3-6 months when you get there?"
Me: "I will have everything in order J. Don't worry about me. I am not the same person I was when you met me a long time ago. I am not even the same person I was when you left here in February to go to Puerto Rico. I got this. I just need you to trust me and believe in me to do this. Okay J? Please?"

J'son: "If you say you got it, then you got it. You have grown a lot, Tammy. I just want to make sure you're safe, and you are ok. You have never made a move like this before, and there is a lot more to it than you have probably thought about."

Me: "Which is why I'm telling you now! I need your help in planning the drive across the country. The farthest I have ever driven by myself is to New Orleans, from here, to see you. You drive all the time. It's what you do. I trust you to plan out my route, where to stay and what to look out for. You have always kept me safe, and I know this time will not be any different."

J'son: "You know I got you. When it gets closer to time, let me know the dates you are leaving. I know you will be going to see the kids in Birmingham, so I will help you plan out your route while you're at home with them. Okay?"

Me: "Deal!"

I gave him a big hug, and he kissed me on the forehead. I breathed a deep sigh of relief, and I knew everything was going to be okay. Now it was time to start planning the details for the move like when to tell my boss at the gym, to pass off my clients to other trainers, sell all of my stuff, look for a job and God only knows what else would need to be done. I had less than 60 days to get this all taken care of, and I was off to see the wizard on the yellow brick road to my destiny of dreams.

THE CLOCK IS TICKING

Ok, it was time to tell Greg, the owner of the gym, before he found out from everyone else. In my excitement, I had told a couple of my clients, and they let it slip to the GM when he was asking them about renewing their membership. He pulled me to the side and asked if I was leaving? I knew I should have kept my mouth shut, I whispered under my breath. I then asked Greg to meet me for lunch that week. I thanked him for the previous six years of amazing opportunity and support from him and everyone. It was time for me to move on and chase a bigger dream. He already knew. The GM had called, as soon as he heard, thinking he had been left out of the loop of things. He told me he knew I wasn't a lifer and I was too smart to stay there. He had seen my posts and knew the day was coming that I was leaving. He thanked me for all of my hard work and dedication to the gym, gave me his blessing, and offered any assistance to help me get a job in Cali when I got there.

I can honestly say I am truly blessed to have had the time in Atlanta I've had. I literally transformed my entire life from 2011 through the end of 2017. From overcoming my depression, getting away from dancing (which I hated) to becoming a personal trainer (which I Loved) and walking away from a dark world of drugs, alcohol, abuse, low self-worth, and self-esteem. Then growing into a life coach and public speaker with a heart to help as many people as I could along the way. The life I had built there was amazing, but it was coming to an end only to start a new chapter in my life. I didn't know what I was getting myself into by moving across the country, but I knew it was the right thing for me to do. The purpose I started with, in Atlanta, had grown and it was time for me to grow into the new purpose God had planted in my heart. My clients said they were sad to see me go, but they saw the growth and knew I had outgrown the little gym I had called home for so very long. It was definitely a bittersweet moment. The excitement of the new journey coupled with the sadness of leaving all of the people I had grown to love behind.

I went to go see my hairdresser right before Thanksgiving. We always talked about my life coaching and how awesome the Freedom Release Method was for me and the results I was getting with my clients. He asked me if I had ever heard of the Emotion Code? I had not and was very much interested in other modalities to be able to help my clients progress. He sent me a link from YouTube for the audiobook and I started listening to it right away. I had no idea what a trapped emotion was, but from what I was listening to, I was quite sure I probably had a Lot of them. It was almost a seven-hour recording, and I listened to the whole thing in less than two days. I downloaded the app from Google Play and immediately started using it on myself. The way he had explained it in the book, this was going to be a simple process. I wanted to see how it worked and how I could use it in conjunction with the Freedom Release Method.

The first night I started just releasing whatever came up. I was amazed at the accuracy of some of the emotions I found. The program presented information on trapped emotions which included a timeline and the years were spot on! What was an even bigger surprise was what I then learned about inherited trapped emotions and how they went back generations! When I read the definitions of those emotions and the explanation of what they would cause, generationally, it all made so much sense! I had done so much work on myself that I was exhausted and fell asleep on the couch while watching a marketing video. It was about midnight when I woke up, like what the hell am I doing out here? I took my foggy headed self to bed and slept it off for the rest of the night.

A few days later my daughter called me and said she needed my help with Janeice. I still remember this like it was yesterday. She was in her room reading her Bible after doing her homework then she went into Brittnie's room, and this is how the conversation went:

Janeice: "Mommy can we talk for a minute?"
Brittnie: "Yes baby, what's wrong"?
Janeice burst into uncontrollable sobbing and said "Mommy I miss my baby brother! I didn't get to see him or hold him or spend any time with him."
Brittnie: "What baby brother, you are an only child remember? What are you talking about baby?"
Janeice: "My baby brother that my daddy had that I didn't get to see."
Brittnie: "Do you want to talk to GG and see if she can help you."
Janeice: "Yes ma'am" ... she was still crying uncontrollably
Brittnie called me: "Mom, I need your help with Janeice. She is crying, and I don't know what to do to help her make it stop" And then she shared with me what had been said. Janeice never met her half-brother and, to our knowledge, never even knew about him. He died from a rare disease when he was just five months old.
Me: "I will see what I can do. I have a new technique I have been using, and I think it will work better than the breathing technique I used with you last time. Let me talk to her"
Brittnie: "Okay mom, just help my baby to stop crying please."
Janeice: "Hey GG" (still crying)

Me: "Hey baby, what's the matter? Tell GG what's going on and let me see if I can help you okay?'

Janeice: "I miss my baby brother. I never got to see him or hold him, and I miss him."

Me: "Okay baby, can GG connect to you and see if I can find a Trapped Emotion we can get rid of? I think that will make you feel better."

Janeice: "Yes ma'am"

Me: "Okay baby, take a deep breath for me and focus on GG okay. Pretend you are here with me and you're giving me a hug okay?"

Janeice: "Yes Ma'am" (Brittnie has this all on speaker phone, so she can hear what is going on at the same time.) I used the same steps as I'd been doing on myself. I found the trapped emotion of longing and released it.

Janeice: (no longer crying) "I feel better GG, thank you! I love you!" she handed the phone back to her mom and left the room her little happy self like nothing had happened.

Brittnie: "Mom, what did you just do? She went from crying to nothing in like 45 seconds. Like nothing was ever wrong with her? She wasn't doing that breathing thing you had me do before. How did you just do that?"

Me: "I told you it's a new technique I just learned a few days ago. I have been using on myself and have been feeling great. I have only done it a few times with a couple of my clients who were willing to be test subjects, and they loved it too. I am just glad it worked for her too. That's all that matters to me."

Brittnie: "Can you do that to me next time instead of the breathing thing?"

Me: (laughing) "Yes baby. Are you guys good now? It's getting late here, and I am still packing and getting stuff ready for the move."

Brittnie: "Yes mom. Thank you so much for making her feel better. I don't know how she knew about the baby. She never met him, as far as I know, she didn't know anything about him. She was just reading her Bible, and then all of a sudden had a meltdown on me."

Me: "Well God wanted to show her something evidently. Maybe it was a way to test what I was working on with the emotion code to show me it really does work and it's going to be a part of my practice when I get out to Cali."

Brittnie: "Well whatever it is, it's awesome, and I want some of that next time."

Me: "Okay. I love you. Talk to you tomorrow."

We hung up, and I was truly amazed at what just happened. I shared it on one of our BestLife calls. I was super excited to see where this could lead so we could help more people.

I started putting things up for sale right before Thanksgiving. I wanted to sell as much as I could before I left, so I would have extra income for the trip. Plus my car was small, and I wanted to keep it as light as possible on this long trip across the country. My bed was practically brand new, along with all of the furniture in my apartment. All of It was in excellent condition so I felt sure it would sell quickly. Obviously, I was not as smart as I thought I was. J'son had told me I needed to start sooner because it was going to take longer if people started shopping for the holidays. I made up some lame excuse I didn't want to be without my bed if it sold quickly. Needless to say, he was right, I should have started sooner! I hated admitting it to him though. In the end, I sold what I could and donated the rest to a disabled veteran's organization.

I started teaching a new class in November for BestLife what I called "Life Awakening." I had talked to Jen and came up with a plan. I was going to teach the principles out of the "Mastering the Seven Decisions" book by Andy Andrews. That book changed my life back in 2012, and I knew with all the new tools I had as a life coach, this class was going to be even more incredible. I knew I could really help people understand the principles on a deeper level, add in the Freedom Release Method and some on the spot life coaching and this class was going to change lives! We had made the decision to start this class, right after the Norway Leadership Retreat, before I decided to move to Cali. I had so much planning to do for the class, but I was going to make it work. I loved teaching, and I loved that book, and it was really a perfect time for me to showcase how much I had grown since I joined the company in March. I had 7-8 people who joined the class. Scott, Jen's husband, was on all the calls with me. He was really impressed with the way I taught the class. That meant a lot to me. Jen had to be on another class call, so she missed the first month of classes.

The clock was beginning to tick Really Loud in the background of my mind. I wanted to make sure I got to spend as much time with as many of my friends as I could before I left, especially J'son. In my heart of hearts, I had the feeling this would be the last time I would ever see him again as I knew as soon as the power was back on in Puerto Rico, he was going home, and I was now going to be on the other side of the country. I knew he would still be a part of my life, just from a distance, but this was of little comfort to the pounding of my heart beating in rhythm with the sound of the ticking clock in the back my mind. I made him promise not to be mad at me about being selfish and wanting to spend as much time as I could with him until the day I left. He worked a lot, and I had a lot on my plate getting ready for the move as well. So, it was a little difficult at times for us to get our schedules to match up, but we managed to make the most of any time we were able to get. My friends threw me a going away party at my favorite sports bar where I had watched my Alabama football games every year since moving to Atlanta; Smith's Olde Bar. We had a great time laughing and sharing stories of our time together. As we laughed, there were also a few tears as the realization hit us all, that in just a few short days Atlanta and Snap Fitness would no longer be my home.

My last day in Atlanta was scheduled for Friday, December 22nd. Things were moving so fast now. Since I had limited time, my clients were not renewing big packages as they had done in the past. Money was way tighter than I had anticipated and it left me feeling more than a little stressed. I had learned a lot about the law of attraction over the last couple of years, but especially since I had joined BestLife. With my understanding of how it worked, I knew my thoughts would manifest whatever I was focused on with the emotion being the driving force and the intensity behind it would determine the speed in which I would receive it.

I knew being in fear of not having enough money was not an option right now, because I would manifest exactly that; not having enough money. I would call Jen, and she would do releases with me around the move and around money, to help me get rid of the negativity and the emotional charge attached to it. Her and Super Dave were great at helping me stay mentally and emotionally clear so I could focus on the move with as few distractions as possible. I was using the Emotion Code almost every day now, and it was really helping too. It was taking the edge off in a way that I couldn't explain. I didn't care to try and figure it out right then, and I was just happy to be feeling better about the move.

My first "Life Awakening" class finished with huge successes from the students. Twana was my best student. She showed up every week, homework complete, with wins in hand to show the work she was putting in was paying off in her real-life circumstances. I have a big soft spot for Twana. I met her during a workshop I was running for BestLife back in August. After her first workshop, she never missed another one of mine. The fact she was getting such awesome results from the classes warmed my heart because I wanted to see her win more than anything. It also planted the seed that I could develop this class into something even more after I moved. I just knew with the tools I had learned as a Life Coach, and the experience from using this exact same system to change my life more than 5 years prior, I could really develop something life-changing for the people who were ready to change their current circumstances.

The second class in the series of eight would finish up on the day of my move, December 22nd. I planned it that way so I could finish the class before the holidays and then I would be completely moved prior to starting class number three in January. The first week of the second class I had 14 people show up! Wow! Twana was the first one on the line that day as usual, and this was Jen's first live class as well. I was excited to have her join so she could feel the energy being generated with the material I was teaching. This month, we were learning to Seek Wisdom in our everyday life and also, how to recognize it. The ah ha's people were having during the class was absolutely amazing.

When you realize you have control over what goes into your brain, you also have the conscious awareness that you have control of your circumstances and not someone else. Coming from the dark places of my mind, where I lived for so very long, I can tell you from my own personal experience, I felt as though I had no control over my life at all. It felt as though life was just beating me up and I was left all alone at the hands of life itself to determine when my circumstances would change. Learning I had control over my life, good or bad; I had control over what I allowed to come into, not only my head but my heart, was life-changing in ways I never imagined at the time I was originally going through this program myself.

Now I had the honor of helping others change their lives in ways they couldn't even dream about from the mindset they held when the class began. I saw their changes come so fast and it genuinely warmed my heart and truly excited me to see their transformations happening right before my eyes. Teaching this class while I was getting ready for the biggest move of my life, was more than a pleasant distraction from the stress attempting to take over my conscious thoughts. I was able to focus on the happiness I felt from helping others which kept my emotions in a place of positive focus and manifesting positive momentum toward the move. In my mind, that was a win and mission accomplished!

ITS BEEN FUN ATL

Wow! My last week at Snap Fitness arrived. It's really happening! I had all my clients scheduled for their last workouts that week and had a box of tissues in my drawer and ready. I knew I was going to be a big ass cry baby ALL week! Boy was that the understatement of the year!

One by one my clients came in. They brought cards, wine, tequila, gift cards, care packages, and cash. Every person who came in hugged me so tight it was hard for us both to breathe. Each of them thanked me for all I had done for them and for helping them change their life. Whether it was giving them the passion for spartan races, losing weight, making them stronger or in some cases, just helping them to realize they were worth it while helping them build their self-esteem! I knew that week would be hard, but damnit man, I'd barely get done crying, and someone else would come in and there I'd go again. It was such a blessing to know that I touched so many people in this little bitty corner gym.

Wednesday night was the last night of my Lift Like a Girl Class. I had developed the class a couple of years after starting there to help teach women how not to be afraid of lifting weights and show them they wouldn't look like a man if they did. I wanted them to know that being strong was empowering, not to mention they would look fabulous with muscles. I had the same core group of women who started the class with me and watched it grow into a co-ed class over the years, which was really amazing to me. The guys who came into the class didn't care about the name. They said it was one of the best conditioning classes they had ever taken. I had built a community of people in that gym who loved to lift. They all became friends who really enjoyed working out together and all the soreness that came with it. It was a built-in accountability system for them each week. They looked forward to seeing everyone and planning on how to make the workouts harder than what was written on the board. They knew they were making themselves better by pushing their own limits and each other. They might complain during class but they grew to love the challenges I gave them, and they always came back for more.

Becky was not only my Spartan sister but my friend. We had grown really close and spent a lot of time together over the last couple of years. She gave me a card after class that said "I suck at goodbyes, so I'm just going to hug you now and tell you I love you! I'm going to miss you so much. Be careful and keep in touch" Then she ran out the door full of tears. I knew how much I helped change her life. The 40lbs she had lost and the strength she had gained led to confidence to do anything she put her mind to. I opened the card and read the beautiful note in it and some cash for the road. Even more tears! The rest of the girls all gave me a group hug, and now we were all crying. Becky came back on Friday morning before she went to work because she didn't want me to leave without me knowing how much I helped change her life, how much I meant to her and she was going to miss me so much. Her last words were, "This is not Goodbye, this is, see you later!"

Meghan was the other one who had my eyes full of tears and my heart all in knots about leaving. She was my first client at that location. I wouldn't let her leave the gym the day she signed up until she scheduled her assessment with me. She showed up for her assessment and became my client on the spot. We worked so hard together to help her get stronger and lose weight. She started out as my client and moved into becoming my friend and workout partner. Me, her and Becky worked out on Monday nights as a team, especially when Becky and I were getting ready for the Spartan races. We worked hard and almost every day was Leg Day because it was our favorite workout! Meghan came in with a gift bag for me the day before I left, with a Starbucks gift card and a big mug that said "Shine Bright." Her card made me cry, just like Becky's and a hug full of love and tears, with plans for her to visit Cali as soon as I got settled in!

I could go on and on about each one of my clients and the goodbye's I received. That would be a book in itself. This was the hard part about goodbyes. My fear was after I left, without me there to keep encouraging them and giving them a reason to Show Up, the next coach/trainer wouldn't take the time to make the connection as I did with them, my class and most of my clients, would no longer be at the gym despite my best efforts to pair everyone up as best as I could before I left.

Before leaving, I took the car in for an oil change and had it checked. I had just had a part replaced a couple of weeks before and there was this weird oil smell that had never been there before. I wanted them to make sure everything was okay before I hit the road to drive this 2500-mile trip across the country on my epic new life journey. Ms. Shirley, at Signature Auto over off Lawrenceville Highway in North Decatur, was the only shop that had ever worked on my car. I had always trusted them with it completely. They had saved me a lot of money and had always taken care of me like I was family. It was at their shop where I met Ms. Leila who invited me to speak at my first public speaking event. It just goes to show you there are no coincidences in this world. Everything happens for a reason. I told Ms. Shirley about the smell and I wanted my last oil change from them before I left for Birmingham on Friday. We chatted about all the times I had been there and all the things that had happened over the years while my car was being serviced.

It was taking them longer than usual to do just an oil change. She went to the back to see what was taking so long. When she walked into the room, I knew the look was not good news. She told me I had a rear main seal leak and that's where the oil smell was coming from. I asked her how much it was going to cost to get fixed and if it could be done today depending on the price. It was going to cost me $679 to get it done. I didn't have much more than that in my bank account, so there was no way it was going to work. I asked her if the car would make it on the trip and she said she thought it would. They changed the oil, using the thickest oil they had to slow down the leaking and gave me some for the road. She told me I needed to check the oil every morning and/or every time I got gas to make sure the levels stayed good. She also said as soon as I got to Cali, I would need to get it addressed relatively quickly. I said "Cool, I can definitely do that! If she's gonna make it, let's get this party started!" I asked Ms. Shirley how much I owed her for the oil change and extra oil for the trip. She handed me the invoice with a balance of zero and Have a safe trip written on it! She refused to let me pay her. That was a thank you for all the years of being a good customer of theirs and sending them business. I hugged her neck, cried some more and drove away. I didn't know what a rear main seal was, but I was quite sure if oil was leaking, it was not a good thing. She had put it on the receipt, so when I got to where I was going, they would know what the issue was and could just fix it.

Christmas was the next week. My schedule was packed and father time did not seem to be my friend. My daughter, Brittnie, had always done the packing when we moved. She was a rockstar at it! But, she was in Birmingham, so I had to do this one on my own. My girl Twana, who I met through one of the workshops I did for BestLife and was taking my Life Awakening class, had quickly become one of my best friends. I had watched her start transforming right before my eyes in a short period of time. She came over several nights and helped me pack and clean up that last week. I was so very thankful for her and her generous heart to help me get it all done. If it had not been for all her help, I wouldn't have gotten it all done in time, and I quite possibly would have had a meltdown before I left! She was definitely a God sent blessing! I honestly don't think I would have made it without her help.

My last day J'son told me he wasn't going to get to see me because he was working and on the other side of town. I was heartbroken! I just let the tears flow. I had no choice but to accept it and told myself I could only control what I could control, which was me. As I was cleaning the bathroom, he walked in and scared the hell out of me!! I screamed so loud, pushed him, then hugged him full of tears! I was so thankful and excited he made it there before I left. I realized then he had lied on purpose because he wanted to surprise me. We talked as I was continuing to clean stuff up and I told him about the car. He tried to hide the look on his face about how serious the problem was. He told me just to drive normal and not to push her too hard and to keep extra oil where I could get to it and do exactly as Ms. Shirley had said. I trusted him since cars were his thing. He said he would send me my travel schedule next week before I headed to Louisiana. He gave me the biggest hug ever as he was leaving and I cried even more. As he was pulling away, he wiped a tear from my cheek and told me to relax. Everything was going to be okay, this wasn't goodbye, and we would definitely see each other again. He said how proud he was of me for following my dreams. J'son had seen me during my worst times and all the trials I had been through over the last nine years. If anyone could honestly say they were proud of me, it was him. He told me he was going to miss me, he loved me, and we were going to be okay. Forever Friends.

What a journey! I knew it was only the beginning and a new uncharted water was being entered into. The sails were set, I saw the lighthouse in the distance, and the course was being charted. In my mind, I heard it again…. "get there, and I will show you farther." It was on constant replay day in and day out in the back of my mind. The song by Shawn Mendez "There's Nothing Holding Me Back" was my anthem, but not for the relationship undertones of the song, just the title I had a decided heart. I would persist without exception. I would face every obstacle and rise above it with an inner strength that, through the years, I had learned I could always count on. I knew no matter what storm tried to come against me, the journey was going to be one hell of a ride and way outweigh anything that tried to get in my way.

So, with those thoughts in mind, I took whatever wouldn't fit in my car over to the Goodwill and took one last look around. I stood in each room remembering friends, family, mom, J'son and all the growth I had accomplished in that little 524 sq ft apartment. Tears trickled down my cheeks as I closed the blinds one last time and whispered, "Off to see the wizard." It was finally time to go. It was time to follow the yellow brick road, the road that leads to California. I went to turn in my keys to the apartment manager and thanked him for all his help.

As I walked back to my car, I took time to really look at all the colors of winter around me as it had snowed the week before and I realized I wouldn't be seeing that again any time soon. It was an overcast day, crisp and cold. The cold was definitely not something I was going to miss. I inhaled deeply and realized this was the last time I would take this walk. A smile came across my face as my inner warrior said "You got this! Its time to go conquer the world!". I sent a text to the kids, Teresa and J'son to let them know I was stopping to get gas then I was on the road to Birmingham. I checked all the tires, got in the car, seat belt on, radio on, on your mark... get set.... Gooooooo!

ON THE ROAD TO A NEW BEGINNING

There has been a scared, timid little girl who's been hidden deep inside me for my entire life. It was time to bring her forward into the now. To join her with the new and improved me. The one who is beautifully strong and powerful! Sharing her motivation and inspiration to help others step into their own power and find their inner superhero to save themselves as they finally defeat the victim that has held them captive for God only knows how long.

It was time to go! Gas? Check! Water? Check! Snacks? Check! Gut Check...hmmmmm! Did I really just sell everything I owned and give away what wouldn't fit in my little '97 Mitsubishi Eclipse? Was I really loaded up and driving away from a city I had called home for the last 6 years? Was I really leaving the place I ran to when I was desperately trying to save myself!

So many thoughts were running through my head about the move to Atlanta, which now seemed so long ago. Was I running away from a past I no longer wanted to be a part of anymore? Or was I searching for a light, looking for something to run toward? I know I wanted something better than what I had, even though I had no idea what something better looked like. I had known only one person when I moved here, and he was the only one I needed to know. If he was there, then I knew I would be safe. After surviving the storm of tornadoes that destroyed a lot of Alabama on April 27, 2011, it was time to see if leaving a state, that had only shown me heartache and grief, was going to change my current circumstances. I didn't know if it was the right thing to do or not, but it didn't feel wrong, and that was good enough for me. I already had a job at a strip club, and it would do for now. I was going to figure out some way to pass that personal trainer certification….. "Someday." Those were the words I told myself on that long drive from Huntsville, Al. Through all the destruction and devastation the tornadoes had left behind, on my way to a town I knew nothing about. Something inside me just told me to go and don't look back.

I had accomplished everything I set out to do and so much more while here in Atlanta! I had walked away from the dark world of dancing, with all the drugs, alcohol and money, to start a new life I was still so unsure about. To be perfectly honest, I wasn't even sure if I could make a living as a personal trainer. The one thing I knew was that I would finally be able to sleep with peace in my soul at night. For the first time in two years, I would be able to tell people my real name again, instead of the fake names I danced under. I didn't want them to see past the mask I tried to hide behind every day. I knew that life was not me and I wasn't going to let anyone attach that life to my soul.

They couldn't see the "Real Me." I had been hiding for so long, and I wasn't even sure who the real me was anymore. But you know what? I did It! I had finally shed all the layers of shame, hurt, depression, grief and despair and the humiliation, anger, bitterness, and frustration that had become a part of my normal everyday life for so many years. I became this whole new person. I looked in the mirror with my eyes wide open for the first time in my life, and I honestly loved the person I saw staring back at me without any judgment or shame and without any condemnation or hatred. I looked back with total unconditional love and forgiveness. It was so unlike anything I have ever known before. I did that for me! I had become my own hero. I saved myself, from myself and from the generations of hurt and abuse that had been passed down for God only knows how long. I not only learned to love myself, but I learned how to let someone else love me too and how to let them in, even if it meant I might get hurt again. I had learned that taking a chance on falling in love was worth it all! I did all of that while I was here in Atlanta, not once but two times. Even though those relationships didn't work out the way I had hoped, expected or even planned, each of them taught me so much about myself.

I learned how to love myself and another person completely. I learned that I had to become the person I wanted to have in my life. I learned there's no one person at fault for any relationship. It has to be all-in from both sides. I learned that how we think and our perception can cloud our judgment, which can change our circumstances, whether in a positive or a negative way. I learned the things I liked and disliked in each of my relationships. I learned what traits I wanted to have in myself, for myself, for my mate and in my mate, as well as the things I didn't. I learned what I was willing to accept or not. I learned that if I didn't have expectations for my relationship, there could be no forward progress in it. I learned that what I chose to allow I gave permission to exist. I learned that I didn't want to just exist on this planet man! I wanted to leave my footprint on it! I learned that I didn't want to spend my next 50 years living scared and trapped inside a damn box! I wanted to travel the world and help as many people as I could along the way. I learned I am worthy of unconditional love, not only from my partner but from myself! I learned I am worthy and deserving of not only a relationship but a partnership with someone who wants to grow with me and make this world a better place. I am worthy of someone who is not afraid to hold me accountable to my goals and dreams! I learned I deserve ALL the things and experiences this big beautiful world has to offer and then some! I learned the power of "I AM"! I AM beautiful! I AM powerful! I AM bold! I AM strong! I AM a leader! I AM a Woman of grace and forgiveness! I AM a woman of faith! I AM enough! And, I AM unstoppable because I choose to be!

All of these thoughts were running through my head as I traveled west on I-20, headed to Birmingham, AL. The first stop on my trip across this big beautiful country, a trip I knew would change my life forever... Again! At least that was the belief in my heart. I had driven that road hundreds of times over the previous six years, but this time was different. It would probably be my last trip down this stretch of highway. I didn't know what the future held, other than a big basket full of hopes and dreams at the end of the yellow brick road. I was willing to risk it all in hopes that I was right. It was then I noticed a tear running down my cheek, as I stared down the road in front of me. I glanced up in the rear-view mirror, only to see a life I have now left behind, fading away in the distance....

I made it home to Birmingham to spend six days with the kids and my grands before starting my trek across the rest of the country. I wanted to be in San Diego by the weekend of the 4th, that was my goal anyway. I stayed at Brittnie's house when I first got there through Christmas morning. I am not sure Janeice left my side the entire time I was there. I have a special bond with each of my kids and my grands. They all have something we share that is "Theirs."

I was in the delivery room when Janeice was born. The umbilical cord was wrapped around her neck, and every time Brittnie had a contraction, they would lose the baby's heartbeat. The doctor told Britt to see if she could calm the baby down so she would stop moving. We were so close to delivery, and we didn't want to have an emergency C-Section if we could avoid it. Brittnie looked at me in a panic and said "Mom get her to be still she will listen to you" I looked at the doctor who had this weird look on her face. I walked over to the bed, put my head on her belly, and started gently rubbing it with my hand. I said "Janeice baby, this is GG. Me and mommy need you to be really still right now okay. We know you are excited to get out here with us, but we keep losing your heartbeat and its scaring mommy and the doctor. So, I want you to be really still for GG right now, and I will see you in just a few minutes okay? Touch GG's hand if you understand?" You saw a little knot poke out of her belly and there was no more movement. The doctor looked at me and said "how did you do that? I have never seen anyone, but the mother be able to calm an unborn child down before. And never seen one follow commands like that." Brittnie told her, "They have had that bond ever since I found out I was pregnant. She always does what my mom asks her to do."

She was 9 years old and was so excited about life. She had been making straight A's in school and looking forward to waking up Christmas morning with her GG there! I think the funniest event that happened was we all had Christmas dinner together, including my ex-husbands and his girlfriend at her house! Bryan and I have a good relationship now. Michelle, his new girlfriend, was so sweet. He told her when we first met, I was the "Good ex-wife," although we had a rough time when we were younger. We didn't know what we were doing back then. We just did the best we could do with what we knew. Now that we are all grown up, we appreciate each other and the beautiful children we raised who have blessed us with some pretty amazing grandchildren as well.

We had a great time laughing playing with the kids and watching the football bowl games, which was always a family favorite during the holidays. As gifts were being handed out, I got one from Bryan and Michelle! Wow! That was totally unexpected and off my radar. As I sat there watching everyone open their gifts and taking in the scene in front of me, I had the thought, "how did I cross over into this amazing life?" Like wow! I am really friends with my kids' father (and his girlfriend). I remember a time when we couldn't even be in the same room together and hated even to hear the others one's name. Through the years we somehow found peace and forgiveness and had cultivated a friendship. I am very thankful for still today. We are a Family now. Or should I say still? I had this overwhelming love well up in my heart as I thought to myself, "You really have this amazing life, Tammy. You did it! And you're just getting started!"

As we were sitting there talking over dinner, the subject of moving to California came up. It was difficult for everyone to believe I was moving all the way across the country. The cost of living always came up, and then the politics of the state was usually not far behind. They all got the same answer, "It's a God-inspired move. He gave me a vision. He gave me a dream and a purpose. He said 'Get there, and I will show you further.' I am following the yellow brick road he has laid out before me. I don't need to know anything else other than that"

I am not sure how much anyone, other than my kids, actually know how in alignment and grounded I am with God. I take inspired action when the thoughts/feelings come to me. I generally don't ask a lot of questions. I just follow the impulse to wherever it leads me. It hasn't been wrong yet. If it's a huge step like this move across the country, I may ask "did that really just happen," and I always get a quick download of impulses of things to do or whatever to let me know its real and its happening. I truly believe that's why my life has changed so dramatically from where I was in my darkest times back in 2009. I asked, and he answered.

Brittnie woke me up like super early on Christmas morning and already had coffee going. She was ready to start cooking breakfast because we all had a long, busy day ahead of us with extended family and friends. If I didn't know any better, I would have thought Brittnie was 9 and not Janeice! Christmas has always been her favorite time of year. Janeice had made me some gifts to take with me. I just love that kid man! When I had to leave later in the morning to go to Bradley's house, it was so emotional for all of us. Janeice was crying, Brittnie was crying, and I was crying. It was the first realization I was going to be too far away to come home for a weekend whenever I wanted. It was a plane flight or a four-day drive now. I told myself as I walked down those stairs at the apartment, "Your purpose is bigger than these tears right now. You know the legacy you are building for all of you, will have all of you back together soon and then you can travel the world together. So just breathe Tammy! Don't sweat this part right now. You can do this!" I wasn't sure I believed the words coming out of my mouth, but I kept saying it until the tears quit falling.

Off to spend the second half of Christmas with Bradley, Paige, and the kids. We always go up to Missy and Jimmy's (Paige's parent's house) on Christmas day, and I help Missy cook. Then we open presents, play with the kids, watch Brantlee ride Marley (her horse if you hear her tell it), and always play some kind of card games throughout the day. Oh, let's not forget somewhere in there is always wine! My son did a good job when he picked Paige to be his wife. She is an amazing mom to Brantlee and Cruce. She is God-centered, an awesome sister, daughter, friend and probably the most awesome daughter-in-Law a mom could ever ask for. Her family has adopted me in as one of their own. When I am home for the holidays, they always include me. It feels like home there and it's a family full of love! As the day progressed, I was waiting for the question to come up about Cali. There was no way Jimmy was not going to ask. It's one of the things I love about him most; he always speaks his mind and is not afraid to ask questions when he wants to know something. My son is a lot like that as well. You always knew exactly where he stood on any subject.

I recall one time when we were all out on the front porch, one summer afternoon when he asked me right out of the blue "Tammy, I just want to know, why do you date black men?". You could have heard a pin drop right then. I remember ALL eyes were on me waiting for my response. Bradley just put his head down, because he had no clue what was going to come out of my mouth. I just smiled and said "Honestly, I am just not attracted to white guys. I haven't been in a really long time. I had my first black boyfriend in the 6th grade when we first moved to Alabama." I saw the sigh of relief on my son's face. I think Paige actually held back a snicker. He really just didn't understand my attraction and that was okay. I wasn't upset because he asked and nobody was angry about my response. I think it was the first time I really experienced someone granting me my beingness and me granting them theirs. There was no judgment, just an acknowledgment we had a difference of opinion, and that was it. How the world, as we know it, could change if everyone did the same as we did that day.

Jimmy was slicing some ham for his plate while the rest of us were getting out drinks and finding our places to sit at the table when he asked.

Jimmy: "What's this I hear about you moving to California? Don't you know people are running to get out of that state?"
Me: I just laughed as I said: "Well if they are all leaving then that leaves more room at the beach for me!" I don't think he thought that was as funny as I did!
Jimmy: "Those people are weird over there. How you gonna handle that"?
Me: "There are weird people everywhere, Jimmy. If I run from weird people all the time, then I would never go outside!"
Jimmy: "Have you looked at the cost of living out there? It's too damn expensive."

I glanced over at my son because I know this was a conversation he must have had with Jimmy already, but he wasn't reacting.

Me: "The apartment prices are the same or at least comparable to what I was paying in Atlanta. I will be making more money there anyway, so it won't be a problem. I'm good Jimmy. This is a God-inspired move, and everything will work out better than I could have ever planned on my own"
Jimmy: "Well I hope you know what you're doing. The kids are going to miss you."
Me: "I am good. I know the kids will miss me. I am going to miss them too. But this is something I have to do for me. There is a bigger picture here and a legacy for them I am building. That is all I am focused on, and there is nothing that is going to stop me from making it happen."
Jimmy: "Alright then Cali girl. That's what I'm gonna start calling you from now on, 'Cali.'"

I just laughed and thought it was appropriate. He held to his word and called me Cali the rest of the day. I love holidays like this when we all love each other, pray together, for each other and over one another. Everyone was close, and it was such a blessing to have all of this in my life as an adult. I remembered Christmas as a child. We would open presents, eat and then go to our room and play. It wasn't about family and loving on each other. We did get lots of love and attention when we were at my grandparents' house though. I believe these are many of the reasons my journey has turned out the way it has. Without going through the things I didn't want or didn't like, would I have truly appreciated the good things and times as much as I did that Christmas? I honestly don't think so. I think they would just be "Things" without the gratitude and appreciation. Having the ability to look back and connect the dots from my journey, I get to experience all the blessings this life has to offer.

We had one more Christmas event on the calendar with my brother Billy and his family. We have Thanksgiving and Christmas at his house while I am in town now that mom is gone. It's another one of those moments when I realized sometimes you have to go through hard times to get to the good times. Me and Billy had a rough childhood. But we made it out. We got in a fight as adults, and we missed a lot of each other's lives because of it. We managed to stay in touch, but we weren't close.

 When we go over there to visit with my brother, his wife Heather, my nephews, Brody, Seth and Devin, we always have the best time. There's lots of laughter, football, fun and most of all, love! All the kids get together to play and it's like a fun house at the carnival. There is always so much food, more wine, and we all laugh until our faces hurt. This is what holidays are for…. family, fun, food, laughter and love! Oh….and Wine! While visiting, the same conversation about California came up, and I gave him the same responses. When the night came to an end, they all gave me a big hug. Billy was the last one and gave me a big bear hug, kissed me on the top of the head and said: "I love you Sis, be careful on the road okay?" I told him I loved him too and I would, and with that, we left.

When we got back to Brad's place, we started playing cards. This was a family tradition I remember from when I was a kid playing with my Grandpa. Rummy was generally the game of choice. They all wanted to beat mom since I don't lose very often. Even the kids know, when GG picks up a bunch of cards, I am going to run out soon and win the game. Never a dull moment when I am here! I had made some spiced rum bread pudding which was to die for! That would last about a day if we were lucky. They always love it when GG is home because she cooks. It doesn't matter what meal it is. I always cook at least one meal a day while I am there. I missed cooking for the kids now that they are all grown up and have their own lives. So whenever I get the opportunity, I cook their favorite meals and dishes to spoil them just a little bit.

Before I left, my daughter had a going away party for me at Bumpers Billiards in Hoover. My best friend, Michelle, and her husband, Scott, along with a host of other people I had not seen in years were all there! It turned out to be another one of those bittersweet moments when nostalgia hit the heart and came out of my eyes as tears. We played pool, laughed, cut up and had a really good time. There was one person I was so happy to see, my brother Scott! I ran up gave him a hug and burst into tears! He was over 200lbs!!! He was clean, working a real job and got his life together! He had made It! He broke free from the cloud of addiction that had haunted him for so long! I was so happy to see him and have that knowing in my heart that he was really going to be okay. As the night came to an end, everyone was hugging me and here came all the tears all over again.

Birmingham, where my kids and so many friends were, would always be what I called home, but my feet would soon be planted on the other side of the country, in a new place that I hoped someday, I would call my "home." I've had so many thoughts running through my head over these last 24 hours as the time winds down for me to head west. This time when I left though, I wasn't running away from something, I was running toward something. Something that was bigger than myself. A vision and purpose had been stamped on my soul that would not be denied. It was time to follow the yellow brick road on a journey that not many have the guts to do alone. I was a single female who had just turned 50 years old. I chose to sell everything I owned, load up and drive across this country all by myself to a new place called San Diego. I didn't have a place to live, nor a job, and I had less than $700 in my bank account, and some gift cards and cash given to me by clients, friends and family. I made decent money with my life coaching, but it had not yet become a consistent source of income to call it a "JOB" at this point. Then there was the rear main seal leak in my car. I had plenty of oil for the trip, although it was still a little concern in the back of my mind, I was determined just to take my time and not push her too hard. I had faith and a deep seeded belief everything was going to be okay, and I would make it safe and sound to Cali without anything getting in my way.

9 PURPOSE DRIVEN
CALI HERE I COME!

The day had finally come. It was my last day in Birmingham before I set out on this epic journey across the country with just me, myself and I! I spent the day with the kids, laughing, playing and talking with Brad and Paige. Brad wanted to be sure I was going to make it when I got out there. As I said, he is my analytical child. He needs numbers and details so he can weigh everything out before he makes a decision, which I admire a lot about him. He is a great provider for his family. They get to do awesome things and travel because he is the way he is. We never did any traveling past Florida when the kids were small. I assume the desire he has to travel is partly due to that. The other is because his wife loves the beach and that's her happy place! You know the saying, 'Happy wife, happy life!'

He was sitting at the kitchen table. When he just asked;

Brad: "Mom, how are you going to make money out there? You don't have a job yet, and you don't seem real concerned about getting one."
Me: "I am a personal trainer with six years of experience Brad. I can walk in any gym in that state at the beginning of what we call Feeding Season, and get a job. So, you would be right; I am not super concerned. While I am in Louisiana, I will start looking up clubs in the town I want to work and see what's available. I will put in my applications online and have an interview set up before I get there."
Brad: "How are you going to market your life coaching?"
Me: "I have been doing stuff on Facebook with ads. They haven't generated a lot of interest, so I need to become more familiar with how they work and the marketing tactics it uses to show the ads to people. Other than that it's been word of mouth and getting a lot from my life coaching company when people call looking for a coach."
Brad: "I can show you how to figure out your target market and how to run Facebook ads. I don't want you to have to come back here because you couldn't make it work. I would rather you come back to visit because you're successful or because you decided this is really going to be your home. Also, if you come back, you're not living with

me. You would have to live with my sister, and that should be enough motivation to make sure you don't fail when you get out there!" He snickered like he always did making fun of his sister.
Me: "Stop being mean! I am not coming back here to live and I am not going to fail. If you can help me figure out the ad thing, that would be great. From there I am giving the reins to God and let him guide my steps. I know my book will be finished not long after I get there and I am getting more life coaching clients each month. Everything is going to be okay. I promise! I love you! Thank you!"
Brad: "I love you too. I just don't want you to go all the way out there and it not be what you thought it was.
Me: "Have a little more faith in my purpose and my faith in everything will work out … okay… please?"
Brad: "Okay mom."

I unpacked and repacked the car at least three times as I was getting ready to head out. I was able to leave some stuff at Brad's house, and I would send for later or pick it up when I came back to visit. My goal was for the window to be clear so I could see while I was driving and to be able to put my car under the least amount of stress possible during the trip. My friend Leslie, who is also a part of BestLife, had given me a whole bunch of Tony Robbins CD's and I was super stoked to play them on the way across the country. Typically, I'm a note taker, but I would have to put that desire aside and just take mental notes while driving. It was a seven-hour drive to where I was going, and I didn't want to be out on the road any later than I needed to be, so it really was time to go.

My heart began pounding a little harder. This was really happening! I went inside to tell the kids how much I loved and appreciated them for all they have done for me. I gave the grands the biggest hugs and kisses ever. I told them I would be back in the summer or sooner. Brantlee teared up telling me she didn't want me to go. I told her she could talk to me on facetime any time she wanted too. I hugged Paige and told her how much I loved her. Then I gave my son a great big bear hug! He is a big reason I am the person I am today. He fed into my spirit to help me grow in my relationship with God and because of that, I truly trust my inner being and can walk out on faith to take inspired action when the opportunity arises. All of this is possible because he loved me enough to want to help me to become a better person, a better mom, and a better GG for my grands when I asked for his help so many years ago. I hope when he reads this, he knows just how much I appreciate what he did back then. I'm not sure he realized then, exactly what his actions of love would create for me, but also within me. I just want to say Thank You Brad, and I Love you!

It was time to go, and I didn't want them to see me cry. It would make it even harder on the kids (or more so, me, because I am a big ass baby when it comes to them!) and that is not what I wanted. I knew it was going to be a challenge being so far away from them and knowing I couldn't just jump in the car and go see them on a whim anymore. They were (and still are) my world. I reminded myself that my purpose was bigger than the pain my heart felt at that moment as I got in the car to drive so very far away. The legacy that I will leave them, the places we will travel, the world we will change to make it a better place for them will be worth this discomfort and the short time we will be away from each other. At least that is what I kept telling myself. Somehow, I know this is going to work out! I walked down the stairs, and I heard the door close behind me…and then the tears, out of the corner of my eye, slowly trickling down my cheek. My heart beating faster as the feeling of excitement, anticipation and even a little fear was trying to creep in as I reached the bottom of the stairs. As I sat down in the car, I took a deep breath. and whispered to myself "Purpose-driven, you got this Tammy. It's time."

With that, I put the car in reverse, pulled out of the driveway and up the hill I went. The tears kept coming, but my breathing was getting easier. I knew it was going to be different this time. It felt almost like a weight had been lifted off of me. As the suns bright rays started shining through, the dark cloud this town once held over me for so very long was fading away. It's hold over me has finally been broken….Forever!

I was headed down I-65 South toward downtown where I would hit I-20 West. I had to keep telling myself to stay in the right lane, "we are not going back to Atlanta anymore Toto, we are off to see the Wizard." I turned the radio up and started cruising along. The sunset that first night of the trip was amazing. It was the first time that I could actually say I was riding off into the sunset! I took a picture to memorialize that moment of my epic journey. I am not sure there has been any other sunset that had so much meaning to me, all woven into the bright colors of orange and red blending into the clouds. I'm just getting comfortable on my drive, and my mind is just quiet. I am waiting for it to start racing with all the thoughts or reasons I should turn around and just go back. To change my mind. That this isn't going to work or what if you fail BS that has been trying to overtake my thoughts for the last few weeks. But I heard nothing. Wow, actual silence ringing loudly from the recesses of my mind. I laugh at myself because it's a rare occurrence when my mind is silent about anything. Just then my anthem came on the radio "There's Nothing Holding Me Back!" and I turned it up even louder then proceeded to sing at the top of my lungs like I was on my way to the beach! Wait, I was on my way to the Beach! The West Coast Beach that is! I cracked the windows to let in a little fresh, crisp, cold air.

A new life awaited me. I was ready to see what this big, beautiful world had in store for me now. I had made the decision that No more will I ever be boxed in like a scared little animal afraid to wander and roam. The lid is off, and the walls are down, the road is open and free, Just Like Me!

ARE WE THERE YET?

I spent a couple of nights in Louisiana and visited with friends. J'son text me early in the morning as I was packing up to leave. He was planning out my route and needed my exact location so he could make sure I wasn't driving on the road longer than need be. He wanted to be sure the places he had me doing the overnights were going to be the safest for me to stop. He told me to go ahead and reserve hotels for my overnights in so I wouldn't get stuck without somewhere to stay. Of course, I didn't listen, what would an adventure be if you followed instructions all the time, right? Ha! I didn't know there was a way to share my location from google maps so others could follow the journey, so he walked me through how to do that, allowing him to know exactly where I was at all times. I shared it with Teresa and the kids too, so they could watch my journey and know. Mom was safe.

I felt so much better knowing all he had to do was click a button to see where I was at any time. Kinda like my own little guardian angel. He was my "Safe Space." He told me repeatedly, "Do Not try to drive past Midland, TX today. I already have you driving 7 hours. Once you pass here, it's nothing but flatlands and oil fields. There were long distances between gas stations and not a lot of hotels either. If you're in Midland, you will be safe. And make sure you unpack your car and put everything in the hotel, so nobody breaks into it". "Yes Sir, Captain Sir!" as I saluted him as if he was standing in front of me. I thought to myself, he might can see where I am located on the map, but he can't see my face or what I am doing, so there! I knew he was only trying to keep me safe, but his military/combat/survival nature took over, and it was more like orders coming across. He didn't think my comment was too funny even though; I thought it was hilarious. I think it was my way of trying not to freak out because I was by myself and driving across the country. I was in a tug of war with myself. Part of me thought I knew what I was doing when in all reality, I had no clue what would happen when I reached my end destination. I was doing everything I could to lighten my mood. If that meant, making jokes about things that weren't funny to anyone else but me, then so be it. I knew I had to start taking him seriously though. I really needed to take the edge off of my nerves before they got the best of me. I am sure deep down, he knew why I was acting that way, even though he never said anything. He and I both knew I had Never in my life driven more than 7 hours away from my central location by myself. I was already way past that, and there was no turning back now.

It was so freaking cold that night that even with clothes and hoodie on, I was shivering when I got out of the car. The temperature was just 18 degrees. It made me happy I was going to Cali! I backed in everywhere I stayed, so it wasn't easy to access for anyone to get into the back of the car. I kept everything covered up with big blankets so you couldn't see what was in there. I had too much stuff to be taking it out every night like J'son told me to do. I took the most valuable stuff with me into the hotel room and I covered up the rest. If they wanted it that bad, they could have it. It could be replaced when I got to where I was going. The hotel in Midland, TX was terrible, but it was the last room available, and I just wanted to sleep, so I did.

It didn't take long for me to realize, J'son was not kidding when he said there was nothing once you left Midland! It was flat oil fields everywhere and signs that straight out said the next gas station was 50 miles, stop now! I had never seen signs warning a driver to stop for gas before!

When I looked at the schedule J'son had mapped out for me it showed two days were 7-7.5 hours of driving time. Me not being the person who makes trips like this regularly had not taken into account stops for gas, food, bathroom breaks, leg stretches or whatever. So, each of those days turned out to be more like 11+ hour days. As I was driving, the very real thought in my head was that El Paso was just words on a map. Driving turned into hour after hour of nothingness! There was nothing on the radio worth listening to if I could get a station to come in at all. Thank God for Leslie and the Tony Robbins CDs! What a life saver she was on this trip!

I called Jen and asked her to let me know when class calls were because I had zero concept of time zones or what times the classes were while driving. I looked forward to hearing real voices and having some human interaction. I needed to feel like I was not alone, even though at that moment, that's all I felt…. Alone. It turned out perfect as the kids, Teresa and J'son all called pretty regularly and with the class calls, my mind had plenty of things to focus on. I had a couple of moments where my emotions tried to get the best of me. My heart was racing, and tears would start trickling down my cheek. I didn't know if they were happy tears or if I was really doubting the decision I had made and letting fear creep in.

I wanted to believe in my heart that this was a good move. I had to find a way to be strong, so I told myself "I am not turning back now! I am not quitting! I have to do this for me! Everything is going to be okay!" Then, when I finally reached El Paso, I think I was actually on a class call when I said out loud, "Oh my God it is real! El Paso is not a mirage after all!" I was starving, my butt was hurting from sitting so long, and it was way past time to stop to get something to eat and stretch. My whole body was tight and just hurt! I sent a text to J'son to let him know where I was and how I was doing, forgetting he had me on the app and watching me as I traveled.

We chatted back and forth while I was eating when he told me "White Sands, NM was about 45 min off your route and since you are so close, you should go check it out. You will have plenty of time to do that and still make it to the hotel at a decent hour". He had sent me a video of him flying his drones there when he was in the Air Force. So, I took the "you only live once" attitude, and I went for it. We won't talk about the missed turn which added 3 hours to my trip that day lol. One of the coolest things I saw was a fighter jet do a barrel roll over the top of my car on my way into the park. I was trying to get my phone out so I could video it, but by the time I had it in hand, it was Gone! The view of the sunset over the white sand dunes was beautiful and totally worth the extra drive time to see all of it.

I spent the night in Wilcox, AZ, either the bed was like sleeping on clouds, or I was exhausted and passed out. I am quite sure it was a combination of the two. I got up the next morning, taking my time with breakfast as I was going over in my head all the things I had experienced in the journey so far. Then my mind wandered to what was to come on the road ahead. By the end of the night, I would be in Sunny San Diego. It was my last day of driving! I would be in California when I went to bed! As tired as I felt, emotionally and physically, the excitement of making it to California before I went to bed again made it all worth it!

When I left the hotel that morning, my head was in a better place than the night before. I was on the road about an hour when the landscape changed into this beautiful array of desert-colored mountains all around. Everywhere I looked there were deep reds, browns, yellows, and greens. I was blown away by the beauty of the amazing rock formations I was experiencing all around me. All of these emotions flooded through me and felt like a surge of energy as the thoughts came rushing in like a title wave. There is so much beauty to see right here in this big beautiful country. Why the hell would anyone not want to drive across the country just to see what's there? I grabbed my phone and did a Facebook Live while driving! (Yes I know, not smart and probably not legal either but I was living in the moment lol) I was so hyped on all this beautiful scenery I told everyone who was watching "I want you to get up off of your ass and Do Something Awesome with your life! Like, Quit making excuses for why you are choosing to live just a mundane Average Life!"

I had to stop to get gas and stretch my legs and I exited at probably the most Awesome spot on this whole road trip, Gila Bend, AZ! What an amazing place! They had hand-carved metal Raptors standing all over the place. There was pottery, pictures, collectibles and more! You name it, and they probably had it. I had exited the freeze zone of 18 degrees when I left Midland, TX and drove my way to a sunny summertime 82 degrees with not a cloud in the sky! It was HOT in all those layers of clothes I had on! I started stripping down, grabbed some summer clothes out of one of my bags, my flip flops and changed. I posted a picture on snapchat "Tank Tops, Flip Flops, and Tacos Every day!" It was still below freezing back home, and there were quite a few jealous replies afterward! It was great!

I was getting closer and closer to San Diego! The road trip across this big beautiful country was almost over. The new chapter of my journey in this thing called life was about to begin. I was so excited to be almost there. Since I had only flown to Cali one time in my life, the realization of how close I was to the Mexican border never entered my mind. I think there was a border patrol stop at about every 50-100 miles as I entered California. I hadn't considered this when I packed my '97 Mitsubishi Eclipse hatchback and loaded with suitcases, boxes, book bags, shoes, pictures, etc. with a big blanket covering everything up so it couldn't be seen when I wasn't in the car. All of that and Georgia state license plates. So, I got through the first two or three stops without incident. They asked me what I had in the car, and I told them everything I own, I'm moving to San Diego. They each waived me right on through without a second thought.

However, as I reached 5,000 feet on a huge mountain top on I-8 North, there is a line for the border patrol stop. It was dark, about 6 pm, and there were soldiers with M16s out and ready if needed. They were walking around checking cars and had dogs sniffing around too. I had never experienced anything like this before! I pulled up to the stopping point and said:

Me: "Hi, how are you tonight?"

Officer: "Fine. Where are you headed tonight?"

Me: "I drove all the way across the country from Atlanta. I am headed to San Diego."

Officer: "Ok you can go…. Wait what's under the blanket?" (I saw his grip tighten around his gun)

Me: "Everything I own sir. I can pull the blanket back for you to see if you like."

Officer: He quickly yelled, "No! Pull over there under the awning, and they will check your car over there."

Me: "Yes sir." I pulled over to the spot he had pointed out. I was quickly surrounded by several officers, two with dogs, and the rest with guns. I slowly pulled forward until they motioned for me to stop and then I released the hatchback lock so they could see inside.

Officer #2: "Where are you from ma'am?"

Me: "Atlanta, Ga. I am headed to San Diego."

Officer #2: "What do you have in the back of the car?"

Me: "I've already popped the hatch for you to look. I am moving to San Diego. I have been driving across the country for the last three days. Everything I own is back there."

Officer #2: "Why do you have it covered up with a blanket?"

Me: "So people won't see I have a bunch of stuff in my car and break into it."

Officer #3: "That's smart of you. So, you're from Georgia? I was stationed out there in the Marines. It's a beautiful place out there. Why would you come to San Diego? Do you have family out here or something?"

Me: "No sir. It's just me. I am chasing my dreams and this is where they start."

Officer #3: "Well don't end up homeless, we have too many of them around here already." With that, he shut the hatch, walked the dog around the car one more time and said "Have a safe rest of your trip. You don't have much farther to go before you get there. Maybe an hour at most."

Me: "Thank you! Oh, and thank you all for your service! I appreciate you and what you do to keep us all safe!"

I drove away and headed down the mountain. I talked to Teresa and J'son about the experience, and they both laughed at me and said welcome to Cali! Teresa gave me the address of her boyfriend's apartment as I would be staying there for a week or so while I looked for my own place. I plugged in the new destination and got super excited as I had about 90 minutes left of the journey. I was so tired and had to stop one last time for gas, stretching and to get something to boost my energy. I was out of Spark and needed something to get me through this last part of the road trip. I cringed as I grabbed an energy drink out of the cooler and jumped on the road. J'son text to see how I was holding up, knowing the stress that long trips like this put not only on your body but your mental and emotional strength gets tested as well. When I told him I was holding up ok but had to get an energy drink, I received rapid fire text back that said, "T, you don't drink those, what are you doing? There is going to be a big crash when it wears off. You need to pace how you drink it so that you're at your destination before that happens." I was happy for the reminder of the timing, as I had not taken that into consideration with the knowledge of the oncoming crash.

I was on I-15N headed toward Escondido, about fifteen minutes from my final destination when the tears started flowing like waterfalls. I looked at my sun visor where I had the words **"I Did It!"** Taped. I had made it all the way across this big beautiful country by myself. I knew I just changed my life in ways I couldn't even comprehend! I don't know if the tears were excitement, relief, exhaustion, joy, sadness or if I had just plain lost my damn mind. Whatever it was, I just let them flow and didn't try to fight it. Teresa called me to see how I was holding up, knowing I was so close to my destination. She heard me crying when I answered the phone and said, "What is wrong? Why are you crying? Are you ok?" All I could manage to say was **"I Did It Girl!** I really Did It!" More tears. She was now crying too! I just wanted to be in the moment, feeling all the emotions, cry all the tears, celebrate every minute on this road trip across the country.

As I drove those last few minutes, I was in almost a deep trance of thoughts. I really just drove 2500 miles across the country, by myself. I had no idea what I was going to do, where I was going to live or what all of these emotions I was feeling truly were. I didn't even want to try and sort it all out. I just wanted to be in the moment of **"I Did It!"** To feel the words that are stamped deep in my soul. Those are the words that inspire me into action when there is something I want to achieve. I am not sure I can accurately describe the feeling I get when I feel those words. I just know it's one of the best feelings ever when those words are screaming from my heart!

A few minutes later I pulled up to the apartments, and Teresa's boyfriend met me outside. He grabbed my bags and we went inside. We sat and talked for just a little bit before I finally had to call it a night. I had only met him a couple of other times when I came out here to see Teresa two years before, and I was so appreciative he had opened up his place for me to stay. I had no more mental capacity to take in any more thoughts outside of "I am in Cali!!!"

LIFE CHANGING IN PROGRESS... PLEASE STAND BY

I woke up the next morning, and the first thought I had was I had made it! January 4, 2018, was the day my life changed forever! I drove all the way across this big beautiful country, stepping out on faith. I left Atlanta with less than $700 in my bank account, no job, no place to live and really no plan other than the words from my vision, 'Get there, I will show you farther.' I was physically and mentally exhausted to be perfectly honest. There was really not a lot on my agenda that first day. I did have a couple of places to look at that had rooms for rent. Once I decided that I was going to zero in on which gym I wanted to work at. I was thankful for the place to stay, but I needed to make other arrangements sooner rather than later.

On my way across the country, I was blessed with three new life coaching clients! Which gave me the cushion I needed to get settled in. I had also taken the time to apply at about four different gyms in the greater San Diego area. On Sunday I received a call from Darren at 24hr fitness, one of the gyms I applied to. After introducing himself, he said: "Please tell me no other fitness managers have called you in for an interview yet?" If I was nervous about finding work, that definitely helped make me feel right at home. We set up the interview for the next day, and I was super excited to have gotten a call back so soon after arriving in Cali.

I woke up early and drove to the gym. I pulled up and saw they had an outdoor facility with an A-frame, basketball court and turf with several different sleds and a tire to flip! (sleds and tire flipping are my Fav!!!) I felt like a six-year-old at Christmas, and this was my gift under the tree! I walked in the front door, and the cardio area was almost as big as Sage hills whole gym! They had a Rig and a huge Group training room. I really hoped this interview went well and they offered me the job because I so loved what I saw! I went to the front desk and told them I had a meeting with the fitness manager. (In all honesty, I didn't remember his name at all because I was so excited just to have gotten the interview!)

Darren came out, introduced himself, and we went back to the office to chat. He asked how long I had been in town, what I was looking for and if I thought I would like the corporate gym style after coming from a small box. I told him I was good at what I did and I just wanted to train people. He took me on a tour around the gym and I fell in love with the place! Back at the office he showed me the compensation plan and said that with my experience he could offer me an elite trainer position if I was interested. He also said he would be able to opt me into the master trainer position within the next 30-60 days. I said YES! Now I just had to go through the formalities of a corporate gym hiring process of background checks etc.

It took me longer to find a place to live than I had anticipated. I went out to go get something to eat for dinner one night and realized my car was missing! At first, I thought it might have been stolen, but then started calling towing companies. They suggested calling the police department.

I forgot to move my car from the resident parking area and they towed it. There was no sense in being upset about it. I didn't move it, and that was the consequence of parking somewhere I was not supposed to. The blessing in it was that I had just picked up a new client from Holland which gave me just what I needed to get my car with a little left over. I also learned where not to park! Welcome to San Diego!

I moved into a hotel in Carlsbad the next day due to the limited time guests were allowed to stay with tenants. I continued looking for possible roommates, hoping not to have to stay in a hotel for long. I was less than 5 minutes from the beach, and that helped to keep me at peace. It was easy just to go sit on the rocks, watch the surfers and get lost in the sound of the waves crashing. This became my favorite place to meditate, quiet my mind and relieve stress during the roommate hunt that was weighing heavily on my mind. I had already spent over two weeks in hotels, and I needed somewhere I could call home and fast. Money was getting tight, and so were my nerves. Thoughts started creeping into my mind about if this was really the right decision.

I finally found a room to rent, just a few short days later, with a nice lady in San Marcos. I stayed there for the month of February. It was really an awesome house, and I really liked my housemate, but it really just wasn't a good fit and 21 miles one way was just too far to drive every day for work. I found this little place just a mile from the gym. When I met with the little Mexican lady, she seemed very sweet and excited for me to be there and I was excited to be so close to the gym. There were three of us in a two-bedroom, one bath condo. It turns out the place was really way too small for all of us, but at first, I thought since our hours were different, we would hardly see each other and it would be fine. It wasn't!

For the first time, I was really starting to feel homesick. I didn't feel comfortable in my living situation at all. For example in the morning on day three of living there, I was cooking oatmeal in the microwave. I didn't have to be at the gym until 9 am, so I was getting a little later start than usual. My roommate gets something out of the fridge and then slammed the door shut. She looked at me and said, "I need in there, so you need to move!" In my head, I thought, "Have you lost your damn mind lady?" I just left my oatmeal in the microwave and went upstairs to my room and shut the door. I got dressed as fast as I could and went into the bathroom to finish getting ready for work. I was just going to grab my breakfast and go. While I was in the bathroom, she came upstairs to her room and slammed the door. Then she slammed the door again, and again and again. Obviously, me being in the bathroom was now a problem. I just grabbed my stuff, left the bathroom, locked my bedroom door, grabbed my breakfast and out the door I went.

There was only one bathroom, and there was a basket on the back of the toilet for deodorant toothpaste, etc. So, I put my stuff in there too because there wasn't a lot of room for it anywhere else. She gathered it all up and set it outside my door and then took the basket out of the bathroom. Then, I put in the next roll of toilet paper in the bathroom because I used the end of the last one. When it was gone, they didn't replace it. So, I put in another one. When it was gone, they still didn't replace it, so neither did I. I really felt it was their turn. Then I saw the old woman walk in front of my door with her tissue in hand as she was leaving the bathroom. Imagine my surprise when I saw she carried her TP with her each trip! I knew then, just 6 days after moving in, it was time for me to go.

This was the point when I really started struggling with the thought of staying in Cali. I didn't want to go home during my break at the gym, because I didn't want to be in that house. I would sit out in the car and just cry. I was angry because they were so nasty to me and I didn't feel I deserved any of it. Then the whole corporate gym BS thing was about to drive me nuts. The hard push for sales, all the negative pressure and breathing down my neck was something I hadn't expected. I had never been pushed for sales or told what I had to accomplish with my business before. It was all up to me, in Atlanta, when it came to how hard I pushed myself. All of this corporate bureaucratic bullshit at the gym was definitely an adjustment for me. My living situation with my current roommates was so unstable that I felt like I was tied in a knot emotionally, and my breaking point was just around the corner.

I know it was taking me longer to build a business at the gym than what I had anticipated, but damnit man just fucking let me breathe! I felt like I was suffocating and being boxed in by the corporate way. My thoughts and emotions were starting to run rampant. I knew I had to figure this shit out! One day, I was on break and called into our BestLife leveraging call. Jen is always on the call with Tineke as the host. Jen asked how I was doing, and I broke down in tears and just lost it! I started ranting, "I don't know if I can do this! I didn't come here to be a damn personal trainer! I hate how they are always breathing down my neck! My roommates suck! They are mean to me, and I don't even feel comfortable being in the damn house! I don't want to be here anymore! This sucks! Why did I do this?!" Still crying, I took a deep breath, and as I let it out, I said "I know there is a purpose in all this. I know it will work out. I just have to stay focused on my goal. I can always get a new roommate, and I'm working on that now. I really love the gym and my clients. The people I work with are really nice too. It's just the corporate stuff is different. I am different. It's just an adjustment period. If I can drive across the country by myself, then I can do this. It's going to be okay." Jen replied, "Yes, yes it is! There you go. See you got this!" By the time I got off the call I was feeling much better.

What I realize now, looking back at this moment, was it's been so long since I have been in a lower emotional state that it really sent me off to a place that was no longer familiar ground to me. When I was in the dark places, before I started moving myself out of the depression and negative self-talk, these types of overwhelming emotions were my normal Every... Single.... Damn... Day! I had no vision, I had no dreams, and in my mind, I had nothing left to live for anymore. Everything in my soul felt so dark that I couldn't find any light shining inside me anywhere.

I had been out of that negative emotional state for 8+ years now. I knew I had let my current environment take me back to unfamiliar ground and way out of alignment with who I had become. I was in an internal struggle to get back to the new Tammy that I had worked so hard to achieve. The one I loved who was all positive and full of life. It felt like someone had sucker punched me and there was no longer any air left in my lungs. I honestly just didn't know how to handle those emotions anymore.

There is an emotional scale we all travel throughout any given day. The goal is always to be on the higher end where all of the positive emotions are, like joy, happiness, hope, love, etc. When one gets down around anger, frustration, sadness, hurt and similar emotions, it takes work to climb back up out of that. Can it be done? Yes! I have practiced it and learned to become pretty proficient at it. But at that moment, I was in a battle, and I knew it! I knew where those other emotions would lead if I stayed there in them. It was a battle I would win! Losing and quitting was not an option…. Ever!

J'son called after I sent him a message saying I didn't know if I was going to make it in Cali or not. I had a meltdown while I was on the phone with him too. He listened to me about what was going on with my current roommates and how I was feeling about my living quarters. Then I told him how one of the girls I worked with, Michelle, said she had a friend, Yogi, who had a room for rent.

I met Yogi at the gym the day before, and we set it up for me to move in by the end of the month. I was missing the kids, missing home, and I missed J'son, and I desperately needed a hug from him, and there was nothing I could do about any of it. He had told me before I left this day would come and I would have to suck it up and make a decision, either stay or go back to Atlanta? He said "Everybody thinks it's cool to move far away from home until they do it. Then they realize the shit ain't what they thought it was going to be." I wasn't going back without trying. I wasn't going to quit. He pushed my buttons because he knew that's all it would take to get me out of my own head.

By the end of our conversation, I felt much better. Before we hung up, he made me promise to call him if I started feeling surrounded by the dark places again. I don't typically cry or yell at him, and I did both of those things while we were on the phone, so he knew I was really struggling. He softened the conversation and really helped me. I knew I would still have to pay close attention to my emotions until I could get out of that house. I couldn't let them get out of control. Especially while I was still in this place, I disliked so much. The only thought in my head was "I'm not going back to the dark places! I don't belong there, and I'm Not Going Back!"

Back in 2009, when I was in what I call the "Dark Places," it was a very real depression that had taken over my life. To this day, 9 times out of 10, I will always refer to them as the Dark Places. Why? Because I refused to stamp a label on my forehead! Deep inside me, I knew that wasn't who I was, and I wasn't going to let that be attached to me by anyone else either. The headspace I was in during that time in my life, was a very all-consuming darkness. I fought tooth and nail for what felt like a million years when I was going through it. I finally found the light at the end of the tunnel. I never went to see a Psychiatrist, Psychologist or Counselor. I never took any anti-depressants. I healed myself through diet, exercise, personal development, prayer, and plain unrelenting determination to become a better person. I want to be clear when I say that there is nothing wrong with going to see someone about your depression and/or taking anti-depressants temporarily if they help move you forward to healing. It doesn't matter which path you take so long as you take one to help you heal and become the person you want to be.

I would like to say everything was super easy after that day and there were no more emotional outbursts. I would like to say it was all sunshine and rainbows, but it wasn't. It would be a lie if I even came close to saying that. There were days I sat outside in my car on break at the gym and cried. I would yell, "I didn't come here to be a damn personal trainer! I don't want to be here!" Then I would flip it to "I know there is a purpose in this, and this is temporary." To pull myself up, I began to list what I enjoyed! The people were nice, I loved my clients, I loved what I did, and I was good at it. There were going to be opportunities that came out of working at the gym through the people I met there. It was all going to work out better than I could have ever imagined. When I was done, I always felt better.

I joined the leveraging call almost every day. Everyone on the call focused on my dream with me, to be a full-time life coach, public speaker and to finish my book or even something much better. We all were intently focused imagining what it would look like for me for a total 68 seconds and then we would share what we felt and imagined.

During some of the more difficult moments, I would text Super Dave, the director of training at BestLife and one of the other master coaches in the company, and tell him I was about to have a meltdown and to please work with me to release the negativity. He would always call right away and get me through the process. I always felt better afterward. I knew the hard days were going to be over with soon and I had faith in that if nothing else. I had lived through things much worse than these emotions, and in the grand scheme of things, they were just uncomfortable. This was just a speed bump in my yellow brick road. It was all going to be okay!

I moved the end of March and the new place felt like home from day one! I moved in with an awesome family, and everyone was so nice. We ate together and laughed together and it just felt good to be there. It felt like "home." I started to feel more like myself again shortly after getting all moved in, and it was Easter. The first one I had missed with the kids in over five years. I watched Church of the Highlands online, and like usual I cried like a baby! I was so homesick and missing my family! Here come the feelings of homesickness again! Uhg! I was sitting outside at the patio table and said out loud, "I need this shit to go AWAY and Now! As crazy as it sounds, I really enjoyed doing Facebook Live videos, so I did an impromptu Facebook live to give some inspiration to others. I told everyone Happy Easter, and how much I appreciated their taking time out to come and hang out with me on Easter Sunday and like always, it seemed to inspire and uplift me after I was done.

When I finished the FB Live, I called the kids, and when Paige answered the phone, I just started crying. I told her how much I missed going to church with them today and the whole day had been a rollercoaster of emotions for me. She moved the call to facetime with me, and we visited for over an hour. Cruce and Brantlee really loved seeing my backyard with the basketball court and swimming pool. I was so appreciative of the time together and felt a lot better when we got off the phone.

As the days passed, I was starting to feel more like myself again, settled in and grounded for the first time, really, since I had arrived in San Diego. I had been going to the beach a lot to just sit out on the rocks to clear my head. I always made sure if I went, I was there for the sunset. I will say this, the sunsets here are Amazing! Absolutely Breathtakingly Beautiful. I knew it was time to start focusing on my purpose of being in Cali!

I really started working on mediation, feeling it would allow me to be more productive in my day to day activities. I was learning how to quiet my mind purposefully, but in the beginning, it was definitely a challenge. I think it was a couple of weeks later when I came out of one of my good meditations, and I knew It was time to finish my book. I had been writing since I arrived in Cali, but it was very random and sporadic without a lot of purpose behind it. I had a vision early on where the title came to me and I saw myself at a book signing. I knew what that meant, and it was time to get it done! I had met some really awesome people who were going to be key in helping me get to the next level of my journey. It was time to let the fun begin!

BELIEVING IN MY PURPOSE

I continued to work with my current life coaching clients and picked up a couple of new ones as well. I also began teaching classes with BestLife, including my Life Awakening class. Twana was still on every call. Darlene was back on and showing up more consistently, and her life was changing in a positive direction now, and quickly. I was so excited to see her winning too. There were different people showing up at each class, and I was always so excited about the classes and the awesome topics.

It was during this time of transition, and the idea came to me to turn the class into an actual course of my own. I wanted to be able to produce it and hold workshops to teach and sell it online. I talked to my friend, Cynthia, about it one day and she thought it was an amazing idea. So much so, she told Jen about it, and a whole new mastermind emerged on how to make this happen. I was so super excited about the ideas we created as a group. I still had a few months before I finished the first full set of classes, so I had plenty of time to work on the course after I finished my book. The book became my number one priority and focus.

I knew finishing my book wouldn't take long when I made the decision to do so. I had started writing a few years ago, but emotionally I wasn't ready to finish it. I would start writing, get to an emotional part and have to stop. It would be weeks before I would try to write again. It was taking me way too long to get and stay in the headspace I needed to finish. I decided then, to just put it to the side for a while until I was ready. I knew with all the growth I had been through, especially over the last 18 months, there was no doubt in my mind now was the time to start writing again. I knew I would finish this time!

I made time in my schedule to sit at Starbucks with my earbuds in and just write. When I first started writing, I was in a very different place, so I went back and read what I had written in the beginning. Everything I had written was still coming from a hurt, very dark, and angry place. It truly hurt my heart to read and feel the words I had written. I knew everything I had gone through served a purpose, but I had not completely healed from all of those hurts or from the things my mom had done. Although I claimed I had forgiven her, subconsciously, there was still a lot of hurt trapped inside me, and it was very apparent in my writing.

Every week I made it a priority to write something, but I wasn't consistent. I had noticed when I became more intentional about meditating at least 20 minutes a day, my impulses to take action were clearer and more precise. I woke up one morning, and I knew it was a day to be writing, so I started writing. I took a break to stretch and had the impulse to look up self-publishing through Amazon. I found a great blog post explaining all the ins and outs of how to go about it, which was so inspiring!

A few days later, instead of doing more writing, I found myself on a site called, Createspace.com. I felt my heart start racing, along with a rush of heat go through my body! My head also felt like it was floating in water. This is the feeling I get when I am in deep meditation, and I knew I was being led to take action to set up an account. I went through the sign-up process, and the next question was: "Do you want to assign your ISBN number now?".

I hadn't realized until that moment every book had its own number that attaches it to the author! I don't know how long I sat there and just stared at the screen, but I know when I checked the box and hit continue, I was instantly assigned an ISBN number for the title "Dear Victim, Its Time for Us to Break Up Now!" The immediate thought in my head was "The shit just got Real people! I am now an Author! A soon to be published Author! A soon to be a Best-Selling Author!" I took those thoughts, and I ran with it.

I took a screenshot of what I had just done, sent it to Jen and told her it was official. My book was now registered with an ISBN number! I sent the same message to Teresa, the kids and J'son. After that, every minute I wasn't at the gym, I was at my computer writing. Tammey Brown, who does all of the stuff with the BestLife website helped me get my new class set up. While we were working, I was telling her about the book, and I was going to need someone to help me edit it. She volunteered and told me that is actually one of her gifts! She is so sweet, and I love her, and her husband, Chris, so much and I was so thrilled to have her helping me edit my book. All of the pieces of the puzzle were finally starting to fill in.

I decided if I was going to have all this help, I better get moving so I set a goal date for me to be done by. It was challenging working at the gym when all I wanted to do was work on my book, so if I didn't have any clients scheduled, I blocked out time on my calendar as "Life Coaching and Book." It caused some riffs at first with management because I wasn't pursuing new clients as I had been when I first got there. I explained the book was my priority and I would take care of my responsibilities to my clients and classes to be sure everything got done. When it was done, then I would be more present, and I appreciated their understanding of how important this was to me.

I woke up one morning, and while my vision was still blurry, I heard the words "Body Code." I thought, well I guess I am getting the Body Code today! By the end of the afternoon, I had the system downloaded on my computer and was working with it. I was excited about the program way before I bought it, but after getting my hands on it, I realized it was way more than I had expected!

It didn't take me long to see this was a powerful tool and the results were often almost instant. Week after week, as I was working on clearing negative thought patterns and beliefs around money. I was tracking the results and realized they were showing up in less than 24 to 48 hours.

Now that I saw the great progress from limited use of the Body Code, I started incorporating it in with my family and friends. It was truly an amazing gift! I was (and still am) so thankful that Dr. Nelson followed his impulses from God to develop this program and to make it available to us all. This gave me even more motivation to move on with my book. I continued to use the system on myself. I wanted to be sure I didn't have any blocks about completing the book, and I wanted a clear path to finish and publish it! I knew getting this book out was just one of many stepping stones to where I wanted to go. When I checked, I had several blocks about success and allowing my creativity to bring me abundance and success. Once I cleared those, my writing really started to flow, and my belief level skyrocketed to new heights.

With all of this positive flow going on, I had even more inspired ideas coming in. That's what it means to be in alignment with your goals, dreams and God or Source or whatever it is you call your higher power. I typically keep a notebook or journal around me that way if I have an idea, I don't lose it because I am in the middle of something else. Another idea that came to me was to really sit down and develop my Life Awakening Class out and make it my own. I knew public speaking and workshops were going to be a big part of my journey, and I wanted to have a program with quantifiable results I could sell as a packaged program. So now the wheels are really in motion.

I knew right then I had to prioritize what I needed to do. If I attempted to do it all at one time, nothing would get done. The book was going to be the easiest and the quickest to finish. I knew I was going to need help from Tammey to get the Life Awakening class built out the right way as she was a teacher by trade and that was her area of expertise. I also knew we could really turn the course into something that could help so many people change their lives. I had experienced results myself when I used the program to turn my own life around starting back in 2012 when I started my personal growth journey.

Since I had developed the course as a Life Coach, the results were tremendous. Twana, one of my favorite students in the class, had changed her whole perspective on life after taking the course! It changed the way she talked to herself, her perspective on her life and how she looked at other people in her circle. She said she dreams and plans her goals differently after taking my class, and her self-esteem and belief that she has the power to create whatever it is she wants in her life are like night and day from where it was when I met her in August 2017 in her first workshop with me. A burning desire grew inside of me to experience more of that!

My priority list became book written and published and then start working on the Life Awakening Class. I wanted to create an audio and video version along with the online academy where my students could submit their homework. I was excited to develop the program to be customizable to suit each person who signed up. I had learned through my own experiences by putting myself through the course, as well as teaching the class, that some people learn better by going fast and others by going slow. I also knew some might only need certain sections since that was the area where they believed would give them the most growth to naturally improve the other areas of their life. I wanted it to be all about them and promoting their best experience.

ENJOY THE JOURNEY

They say every journey starts with the first step and our life is put together by the many single steps that follow. Some are moving forward, some are backward, some go up, and some go down. Some even move sideways because we don't know which way to go at all, so we linger around in familiar territory afraid to take a step in any direction at all. Sometimes we go really fast, other times we move at the pace of a turtle. Those steps can be physical, but many times, if not most of the time, they are mental and/or emotional steps. Those steps can be some of the hardest ones for most of us to take. I know that has truly been my experience just by going through the writing process of this book.

I love this saying, and I'm sure I've already shared it, but it's worth repeating! I think it was Steve Jobs who once said: "You can't connect the dots looking forward only looking backward." There is so much truth in that statement. There is nothing solidified in our vision of the future. When I'm looking forward, it is ever changing. For some of us, our wants and desires change with the direction of the wind. No lighthouse in sight, no pin dropped on the map to give us a direction to focus on, and we get tossed around by the waves of life as a result. Thoughts and visions can change, and some may grow into something so much bigger than we imagined while others will fade away because we decided they just were not what we truly wanted in the first place. Now, if I look back at key points in my life from the perspective of where I am now, I will see how and why I'm where I'm at today. Some of the roads I traveled I didn't really love, but they turned out to be the lessons I needed in order to help me grow into the person I needed to be. If it were not for those lessons, I wouldn't be the me I've become. Could I have taken a different path? Absolutely! Would it have turned out the same? I have not an idea, maybe, maybe not.

What I do know is that I am in love with the person I've become and all the growth I've experienced. When I think of all the things I've created and all I have yet to create, I have tears well up in my eyes with excitement! I had someone ask me how I was able to overcome so much adversity in my life, to be standing here the person I am today? I had to attribute a lot of it to the fact I have been an athlete my whole life where we were taught early on never to quit unless we physically just can't go on anymore.

Taking physical steps has always been a part of what I enjoy doing. It's a fairly easy thing for me to do, most of the time, as a result of that early training. Well, unless it's the day after leg day, then those steps are not so easy! Lol. I can look back now and see all the struggles I went through were because of my way of thinking and the lack of control I had over my own emotions. What I mean by that is I let my emotions control me and let my thoughts out think me. I was where I was because of how I thought! And right now, at this moment, I am where I am because of how I now think! Everything I do or don't do starts with the thoughts, so when I changed how I chose to think and respond to situations instead of reacting when I changed my perspective on situations and circumstances, my life changed for the better! Don't believe me? Go back and read my story again! It's all right here in black and white! I lived it and am living proof it works!

Have you ever had a thought come up, something that made you frustrated or angry? Then another one joins it, and another one, then it feels like you are on this endless rant that has the momentum of a runaway train. Then you notice the people around you are all on your rant too. All of you are on this merry-go-round of ranting hell. Then you end up going to bed angry and maybe even waking up angry. The whole world seems to be angry. Does any of that sound familiar? That was my daily life for so long. I truly believe that throughout my life, I was fed so much negativity and it had become my normal way of thinking. My mom never had anything positive to say about anything because fear ran her life all the way up to the day she died.

Without comparison in life, there is rarely conscious inspiration to want to make a change. The positive things I had in my life had to do with sports when I was a kid. I knew winning felt good and I was good at it. I knew I didn't want to struggle, to exist, like my mom had for her entire life, up to the day she died. Every decision I made when I was younger was a direct result of that thought. I made sure I went 180 degrees in the opposite direction because it had to be better than what I was living. If I liked a guy and she liked him, I wouldn't go out with him period. That's how deep seeded it was for me. I knew the kind of men she liked, and they were all abusive. They either were raging alcoholics and/or verbally, mentally and physically abusive. I knew I didn't want to have to spend my days numb with alcohol and drugs to escape from the pain of life. I knew there was no way in hell any of that was going to be a part of my life!

I didn't know what I was doing, but I knew my life was somehow going to be better than what I was living or I was going to die trying. When I was playing sports, I was enjoying all life had to offer. If I was at home, I hated life and everyone in it. There was no in between. I truly believe my desperate search to find love lead me down some very dark and empty paths. I didn't know how to love myself. No, that's not true. I honestly didn't know that I didn't love myself! I didn't know I needed to forgive myself or that I was harboring any unforgiveness toward myself at all. I had quit enjoying life. Hell, if I am being completely honest, I am not sure I ever enjoyed my life. Not until 2012 when I was taking the steps to become a better person from the inside out, did I intentionally start enjoying parts of my life.

For a very long time, I felt as though my soul was dark and I couldn't find the light switch. When I started coming out of all that, it was truly a journey down a long, hard, rocky road along the cliff's edge. One wrong step and I may not make it out alive. Those were very real thoughts. I listened to a lot of music to chase the shadows away when they got too close. Eminem had several songs out at the time that really resonated with me. When I really needed to get out of my own head and needed to get out of my own way the songs, "Lose Yourself" "Beautiful Pain" and "No Love" were on repeat. I would play them, sing at the top of my lungs, with tears streaming down my face. I knew every word by heart and sang it with all the hurt, anger and passion I was feeling in that moment. Music helped me to breathe when it was hard to find the air in my lungs.

Every day the first thing I do when I step outside is take a big deep breath and let it out nice and slow. Why is that significant enough to put in this book? Because there was a time in my life where waking up and breathing generally pissed me off and I didn't want to wake up and breathe ever again. Now, I can appreciate every single breath I take because I desperately want to live each and every day to the fullest! During the process of becoming a personal trainer and public speaker, I worked on myself and learned to Love, the person I saw staring back at me in the mirror. I even love the days that can sometimes be challenging. It's those days that help me to gain clarity about what I truly want. Without the contrast of things we don't like in life, we would never appreciate the good things we get to experience.

I had to learn to take responsibility for my life! I had to take responsibility for my actions and the results those actions caused whether good or bad. I had to take responsibility for my thoughts and emotions. Not doing those things in the past almost cost me my life.

The results I had been getting in life sucked! I knew if I wanted different results, then everything had to change. I had to change my surroundings and my circle of friends. To me, that meant moving and starting over. Finding and cultivating a new circle of friends who had lives I admired. Success leaves clues, and I can eat those breadcrumbs as fast as you can throw them at me. I was hungry for a new life! That hunger was the breeding ground for my new life!

My spiritual life kinda sucked for the majority of my life. (mainly because I had no spiritual life) I knew I had to cultivate a better spiritual relationship and build one with God. Who knew he wanted one with me too! I can tell you when I was feeling bad, angry, hurt or in some kind of discord, I was out of alignment with my inner being (AKA God, Source, Higher Power). It was evident by the way I was running my life that I was creating a financial situation where I struggled from paycheck to paycheck, eviction to eviction, and problem to problem. The only way to change my financial circumstances was to change the way I thought about money. I couldn't keep doing the same thing over and over again and expect a different result. That is the definition of insanity.

I've learned there are eight major areas of life that need tending to on a regular basis. Some of them may have more focus than the others at any given time, but they all need a plan to be improved upon in order to leave a legacy behind. John Maxwell asks the question "Do you have a plan for your personal growth?" to everyone. I took that question to heart and applied it to change my life.

I knew the areas of life to be cultivated are Spiritually, Emotionally, Professionally (Career/Job/Business), Money & Finances, Fun & Recreation, Health/Wellness, Personal Growth, Family & Friends, your physical environment and last but not least Romance/Spouse/Significant other. I filled out my own personal report card of where I felt I ranked in each of these areas. I listed them all out in my journal. Then, out beside each of them, I ranked each area from 1 to 10. 1 being absolutely terrible and 10 being absolutely phenomenal. I was raw and really honest with myself. I tried not to overthink it by writing the first number that came to mind in each of those areas.

I took a long hard look at each of them. None of them were a 10. I had several areas that were 5 or less, and a couple of areas were a 1! I was honest with myself and sat in those raw feelings for a few minutes? Was that easy? Hell No! I knew I was in control of those current numbers and whether or not they changed. Me, myself and I! No one else! I wanted to change my current reality, and it started right here!

In order to change my current reality, I had to take a long hard look at why I ranked those areas such low numbers. This required a level of vulnerability I wasn't really comfortable with. But I knew that's what it would take to create a different outcome for my life. I desperately wanted to change those numbers! I wanted a better life! I knew in order to do that, and I had to take control and change my circumstances and create my life by design from this point forward. I did it! It took time, planning, faith and focus but I made it happen! I created a dream journal, where I wrote out what my life would look like if each of those areas of life were a 10! That put an insurmountable amount of excitement into my heart! It helped me get through the days when life felt impossible. In going through this

entire process, I created a program that works for anyone who is ready to create positive change in their life. If I can do it…
You Can Do It too!

I want to encourage you to not sweat the small stuff. I want you to enjoy every single minute of every day. Be thankful for every second as it ticks off the clock because once it's gone, you can never get it back. You came to this planet to live an Awesome life! So stop sitting on the sidelines watching life pass you by! Reach for your extraordinary life and then Go Farther! There is so much out there for you to experience, and there is no lack of anything unless you choose to live a life of lack. The things that happen to you are just things, and if you can learn to change your perspective on how you look at them, you can change your circumstances and your life! Don't let anyone tell you that you or your dreams are crazy. That's their fear and their opinion of your dreams is none of your business! Just maybe, the bold actions you take to change your life will somehow inspire them to one day chase their dreams too!

Thank you for allowing me to share my life with you. I hope I helped you to open your heart and expand your mind to see the world in a brighter way. I hope, through my story, you can find belief in your own journey to have the courage to go out and break up with your inner victim so you can change your stars! You are awesome! You are strong! You are enough! And you are as unstoppable as you choose to be!

It is finished! She is now Me! The once scared, timid little girl, has now stepped into the fullness that is Powerful and Unapologetically Me!

With Love, Gratitude, and Appreciation,
Tammy

AUTHOR FINAL THOUGHTS

I can't believe I really just finished my first book! Just Wow! I know that if you have made it all the way to the end of my story, you have walked this journey of emotions with me and for that I thank you. I have been sitting here for a while now, staring at the screen, wondering to myself, what is one thing that I would want my readers to take away from my story? I want you to know that you are more powerful than you know! You are a gift to this world, and nothing that has happened to you diminishes your worth! It doesn't decrease your value, if anything, it increases it because you are now, wiser, stronger and more powerful than you have ever been in your life. The world needs you and your knowledge. The world needs you and your story, your flaws, your scars, your wins, your successes, your hopes, your dreams, and your passions.

I not only survived all of the traumatic things of my childhood and my past, but I also triumphed over them all! I am a better person today because of the experiences that I have lived through. With my story, I can help more people see that we may have been victimized at some point in our life, but being a "Victim" is always a choice! With all of the pieces of my heart, I want you to Break Up with your Inner Victim and Never Ever, Ever, Ever let it control your life again! Take the steps to learn how to love yourself from the inside out! Never dull your shine because someone forgot to bring their shades! Shine Bright my friend! Shine Bright! Remember that you are in control of where you go from here! You owe no one an explanation of your decisions, dreams, goals, and visions. Other peoples opinion of you is none of your business! Please escort them back to the nosebleed section of your life and carry on with your plans! You are worth it!

I have started my next book called *"**Don't Be a Glow Stick! Stop Letting People Break You and Shake You Before Your Light Comes On**!"* In this book, I will be walking you through the steps of taking your power back and creating your life by design. I will be coaching you through all of the stages of how to break up with your inner victim. From learning self-love and forgiveness, setting boundaries and learning how to say the word "No!" How to stop being a people pleaser, finding your passion, setting goals and creating a life you always dreamed of.

So until we meet again, raise your glass and lets toast to setting ourselves free! To breaking up with the inner victim, situations, circumstances, places, people, and things that no longer serve us! To being selfish when it comes to our self-care and loving ourselves more than we love the opinions of others! Let's toast to the New and Improved Humans We are Creating Each and Every Day! Salute!

ABOUT THE AUTHOR

Tammy is a Life Coach with a passion and a gift to helping women heal. She is a survivor of childhood sexual abuse, and teenage rape. She found her passion for helping people after she, herself, had to learn how to use the art of forgiveness to heal, and teach herself how to become a better woman, mother, grandmother and friend, after a bout with depression where she almost took her own life. She became a health and fitness coach which healed her body and in the process started healing her mind, spirit and soul. She mapped out those steps and now uses them to help others find their power to heal.

If you would like to book Tammy for your speaking event, 1:1 or group coaching go to her website at
www.TammyLoftis.com
email: Tammy@TammyLoftis.com

Want to follow Tammy on Social Media or listen to her podcast?
Podcast: **"Life Awakening … Let't Talk About It"**
Found on Apple podcast, spotify, Google Podcast or wherever podcasts can be heard
Facebook: www.facebook.com/TammyLoftisSuccessCoaching
Instagram: @tammy_loftis
Twitter: @lifeloftis

Made in the USA
San Bernardino, CA
16 June 2019